Cross-dressing in Turkish Cinema

Cross-dressing in Turkish Cinema

Politics, Gender and National Trauma

Burcu DABAK ÖZDEMİR

I.B.TAURIS
LONDON • NEW YORK • OXFORD • NEW DELHI • SYDNEY

I.B. TAURIS
Bloomsbury Publishing Plc
50 Bedford Square, London, WC1B 3DP, UK
1385 Broadway, New York, NY 10018, USA
29 Earlsfort Terrace, Dublin 2, Ireland

BLOOMSBURY, I.B. TAURIS and the I.B. Tauris logo are trademarks
of Bloomsbury Publishing Plc

First published in Great Britain 2021
This paperback edition published 2023

Copyright © Burcu DABAK ÖZDEMiR, 2021

Burcu DABAK ÖZDEMiR, has asserted her right under the Copyright, Designs
and Patents Act, 1988, to be identified as Author of this work.

For legal purposes the Acknowledgements on p. ix constitute
an extension of this copyright page.

Series design by Adriana Brioso

All rights reserved. No part of this publication may be reproduced or
transmitted in any form or by any means, electronic or mechanical, including
photocopying, recording, or any information storage or retrieval system,
without prior permission in writing from the publishers.

Bloomsbury Publishing Plc does not have any control over, or responsibility for,
any third-party websites referred to or in this book. All internet addresses given in
this book were correct at the time of going to press. The author and publisher
regret any inconvenience caused if addresses have changed or sites have
ceased to exist, but can accept no responsibility for any such changes.

A catalogue record for this book is available from the British Library.

A catalog record for this book is available from the Library of Congress.

ISBN: HB: 978-0-7556-3422-4
       PB: 978-0-7556-4252-6
       ePDF: 978-0-7556-3423-1
       eBook: 978-0-7556-3424-8

Typeset by Integra Software Servives Pvt. Ltd.

To find out more about our authors and books visit www.bloomsbury.com
and sign up for our newsletters.

Contents

List of Illustrations		vi
Acknowledgement		ix
Introduction		1
1	Framing Turkey and mapping cross-dressing films: Turkish modernization as cross-dressing performance	19
2	Choreographing theory	61
3	Ontological security: Meeting point between cross-dressing and national traumas	91
4	Fracturing language, voice and speech: Whose voice, whose language, who speaks? I cannot hear	103
5	Fracturing space and time: Where is my home? Where is my nation?	129
6	Fracturing masculinity and femininity: Why boys like that, girls like this?	161
Conclusion		177
Notes		179
References		187
Filmography		200
Index		201

List of Illustrations

Chapter 1

1.1	Ottoman women	22
1.2	Republican Women gathered around Mustafa Kemal at a ball	23
1.3	*Fosforlu Cevriye* film poster – 1959	30
1.4	*Gece Kuşu* film poster – 1960	31
1.5	*Aslan Yavrusu* film poster – 1960	33
1.6	Fatma Girik in *Belalı Torun*	34
1.7	Fatma Girik in *Belalı Torun*	34
1.8	Sadri Alışık in *Efkarlıyım Arkadaş* – 1966: Hulisi Kentman as Fatoş's grandfather tries to seduce Sadri Alışık as Gönlübol	36
1.9	Sadri Alışık and İzzet Günay in *Fıstık Gibi Maşallah* – 1964	37
1.10	Sezer Sezin in *Şoför Nebahat* – 1960	37
1.11	1980 Military Coup, Press Release, broadcast on Radio TRT	40
1.12	*Deliler Almanya'da* film poster – 1980	46
1.13	*Beddua* film poster – 1980	47
1.14	*Şabaniye* film poster – 1984	48
1.15	*Komiser Şekspir* film poster – 2008	55
1.16	*Plajda* film poster – 2001	56
1.17	*Şeytanın Pabucu* – 2008	57
1.18	Nehir Erdoğan in *Hababam Sınıfı* – 2007	57

Chapter 2

2.1	The front page of the *Hürriyet* newspaper (12 September 1980) announcing the military coup and its implications	63
2.2	News item in the *Hürriyet* about the new curfew regulation (1960)	64
2.3	The exaggerated body of Şabaniye in the poster for the film	75
2.4	Military coups in action: Archive photographs from the *Hürriyet* newspaper	79

2.5	Military coups in action: Archive photographs from the *Hürriyet* newspaper	80
2.6 (top)	Fikri-ye in the women's sleeping quarters in *Fıstık Gibi Maşallah*	82
2.7 (bottom)	Arzu in the male dormitory in *Hababam Sınıfı Merhaba*	82
2.8	Frames from *Fıstık Gibi Maşallah*	86

Chapter 4

4.1	A frame from *Hababam Sınıfı Merhaba*; Arzu in the male dormitory	107
4.2	A frame from *Şabaniye*; Şabaniye reacts to the workers' catcalls	108
4.3	Gülten tries to warm Fikriye up in bed	110
4.4	Aysel massaging Burhan's back in *Şeytanın Pabucu*	113
4.5	Aysel serves Burhan tea in *Şeytanın Pabucu*	115
4.6	Şabaniye and her boss fail to understand one another	116
4.7	Burhan's experience at a funeral in *Şeytanın Pabucu*	119
4.8	Nebahat with the other drivers	123
4.9	Nebahat leaving with her new clothes in *Şoför Nebahat*	123
4.10	Nebahat berates another driver, but her husband loves her for it: Two frames from *Şoför Nebahat*	124

Chapter 5

5.1	A screenshot from *Fıstık Gibi Maşallah*: Fikriye touches and kisses women while telling a love story	143
5.2	A screenshot from *Şabaniye*: Şabaniye tells a story about Şaban	144
5.3	The front page of the *Posta* newspaper (11 February 2018)	146
5.4 (left)	Arzu in the male dormitory in *Hababam Sınıfı Merhaba*	148
5.5 (right)	Naciye, Fikriye and Gülten in the hotel in *Fıstık Gibi Maşallah*	149
5.6	A screenshot from *Şeytanın Pabucu*: Burhan in Kaba	150
5.7	In *Şabaniye*: Şaban tells Nazlı's fortune using a Turkish coffee cup	155

| 5.8 | In *Fıstık Gibi Maşallah*: Naciye tells Gülten's fortune by reading her hand | 156 |

Chapter 6

6.1	A film poster for *Şabaniye* – 1984: Şabaniye shows off her jewellery	166
6.2	A frame from *Şeytanın Pabucu*: Fatih Ürek as a pilgrim	166
6.3	A frame from *Fıstık Gibi Maşallah*: Fikriye and Naciye wearing western-style outfits in a parody of being women	170
6.4	Filiz Akın is a European, urbanite and college girl of Turkish cinema	173
6.5	Türkan Şoray is the 'dark girl'	174
6.6	A frame from *Şabaniye*: Nazli is wearing a man's suit whereas Şaban is wearing women's clothes	175
6.7	Aysun Kayacı in *Şeytanın Pabucu*	175

Acknowledgement

This study would not have been possible without the help of numerous people and institutions.

Two important people have helped me and illuminated my pathway, which has at times been difficult, stressful, and full of anxiety. Professor Yvonne Tasker and Professor Atıl Eylem Atakav have not only been my supervisors but also my friends and my elders who motivated and encouraged me to complete my work successfully.

I wish to express my deepest gratitude to my mother İnci Dabak and father Seçkin Dabak. They always encouraged and supported me although there were miles between us. Without them, I could not have finished this work.

Finally, special thanks are due to my husband for his love, patience, and understanding support throughout my studies and my academic career. To my partner Asil Özdemir, I couldn't have done this without you. Thank you for everything you have done for me.

Most importantly, I would like to thank my daughter Ezo Pera who was born during the final stages of my work. The power which is caused by being a mom is incredible.

I dedicate my book to my daughter Ezo Pera Özdemir.

Introduction

On 15 July 2016, Turkey experienced very dark and interesting political chaos. One of the closest allies of the Justice and Development Party (AKP) government, the Fethullah Gülen Movement, attempted a coup against the government but the coup was forestalled by the civil forces. This was the beginning of a series of traumatic events. Everyone from ordinary citizens to the military, to the government and to public officials had many questions: What were the dynamics behind the coup attempt? How could this military coup attempt be explained? What would happen next? However, I had a very different question in my mind, one which no-one else would even have thought of: would any cross-dressing films appear in cinemas? This failed military coup attempt had a different meaning for me: it had the potential to help me make a convincing case for my study. I waited, and after six months, the first cross-dressing film appeared: *Olanlar Oldu* (January 2017, directed by Hakan Akgül). After this film, in May 2017, Şahan Gökbakar masqueraded as a woman for Halkbank television advertisements. These films showed me that my claim was correct: there are connections to be made between national trauma and cross-dressing films in Turkey. Indeed, if we look at the history of Turkish cinema, it can be easily recognized that cross-dressing films are repeated at particular times with similar narratives but different aesthetics and connotations. In the Turkish context, the production of cross-dressing films increased during times of national trauma such as military coups. In this book, I examine the reasons for this.

Discussing cross-dressing performance as fluid identity in Turkish cinema in relation to national traumas is a practical way to open the doors of the hidden and untold politic history of sexuality in Turkey. The Turkish language does not reveal gender. The third-person singular pronoun is simply 'o'. 'O' could be male, female, neutral or something else. Therefore, the written texts of Turkish culture can be said to be genderless. Furthermore, the modernization of the Turkish language in 1929 made it impossible to understand written texts from earlier periods. So translations of earlier written texts on Turkish culture and even more new written texts can be said to be genderless. The ambiguities in the written texts of Turkish culture make it essential to look at visual art and cinema to find types of language which are embedded in performances in order not only to understand the discourse of sexuality in Turkey but also to make connections between the discourse of sexuality and other discourses.

Furthermore, discussing cross-dressing performances in the cinema of Turkey gives an opportunity to transform and reconstitute western gender theories for eastern understanding. Turkey is regarded as a bridge between west and east. Therefore, its cinema can be used as a bridge for this transformation. The study of cross-dressing in Turkish cinema brings a new perspective on theories around cinema and gender. These new perspectives pull them away from the risk of being Orientalist. Moreover, this study can also be used for trauma studies. Trauma studies usually focus on narratives which are about identity, belonging, memory, recovering and similar issues. This study, however, has shown that the narratives which are usually interpreted negatively – in this case cross-dressing films which are usually accepted as escapist, misogynist, low-culture products – can be read as trauma narratives. This study gives a new perspective for trauma studies as well. Briefly, it can be said that, while this study brings eastern approach to cross-dressing that can affect all topics around gender studies and new perspective about trauma studies, at the same time, it starts new discussion in Turkish cinema studies.

The cinema of Turkey has previously been discussed in terms of both masculinity[1] and femininity.[2] However, cross-dressing films have been largely ignored and excluded from these discussions. The book not only analyses cross-dressing performance in Turkish cinema but also argues that there are parallels between the production of cross-dressing films in the Turkish popular cinema industry and times of military coups followed by political and social tensions. Cross-dressing provides its performer with mobility against the constraints imposed by a military coup, the ability to escape the panoptical social mechanism against the solid surveillance implications of a military coup, and experience of otherness without being other against the discrimination politics of a military coup. All these actions fracture time, space and language, which can also be accepted as institutions of power.

The importance and meaning of cross-dressing for Turkish culture

The act of crossing requires at least one binary opposition. These may be man/woman, upper class/working class, white/Black, traditional/modern or human/non-human: to put it in simple terms, the self and the other. There is a need for at least two stable and fixed notions. It can be claimed that cross-dressing is a rather western[3] idea. In other words, this idea belongs to western culture where the boundaries between notions are very strict, based on the Enlightenment system of measuring, classifying and categorizing a word in order to understand and regulate it. Furthermore, to understand cross-dressing in binary terms, a particular understanding of the differences and unequal relations between the binary terms, which are also the origins of the western philosophic tradition, is required.

This does not mean that cross-dressing performance cannot be seen in other cultures which did not experience the Enlightenment. Turkish and Ottoman cultures had their own cross-dressing performers – the *zenne*, the *köçek* and the *tavşan*: The *köçek* was a handsome young male dancer, cross-dressed in feminine attire. The *zenne* and the *tavşan* were also male dancers who pretended to be women, but their dress was different from that of a *köçek*. However, they were represented in a different way from western understanding. They were not located somewhere between binary genders. Being a *köçek* or a *zenne* was related to age and ethnicity. Only young boys and usually non-Muslims and non-Turkish speakers could be male-to-female cross-dresser dancers.[4] For example, having sex with one of them did not make a man a homosexual[5] because their sexual positions were completely different from western examples of cross-dressing. After the modernization/westernization process began in late Ottoman times, at the end of 1800s, their position in society changed and they were named cross-dressers by western travellers. Although their traditions were based on a different social organization and involved relationships between discourses of 'otherness' (age, religion, ethnicity, gender),[6] cross-dressing began to be discussed only between the elements of a gender binary which belonged to the western tradition of sexuality in the late Ottoman.

After late Ottoman, Kemalist modernization took its place in the history. With the Kemalist modernization of Turkey dressing gained another layer of meaning for Turkish culture during the early Turkish Republic in the 1920s. Dress and dressing are a kind of stage where the modernization history of the Turkish Republic can be seen. The distinction between two roots of identity in the Turkish citizen's formation – modernization and conservatism – has become visible around dress and dressing because no other symbol apart from veiling can express the differences between west and east so quickly and so efficiently. The modern face of the Turkish Republic was able to be determined from a citizen's clothes. Women were 'emancipated from' their veil by means of Kemalist modernization. The *fes* which was worn by Ottoman men as a hat was banned and a western style of hat was introduced and men were obligated to wear this instead of a *fes*. Anyone who did not want to wear a new-style hat was arrested. In other words, during the process of Turkish modernization, Turkish citizens can be considered as cross-dressers from tradition to modernity.

Dress is the symbol by which a person is identified as either modern or conservative in Turkey. In Turkey, women wearing a headscarf were banned from universities and the public sector between 1980 and 2011. However, the elected governments passed legislation to remove the ban on the headscarf in universities; even so, the ban could not be abandoned completely because of the strict opposition from secularist establishments, mainly the judiciary, and the military. In the last twenty years, the headscarf has transformed from being a religious symbol to being a threat to the principle of secularism. This is why dress became the symbol of anxiety about modernization. The headscarf is highly politically charged in the context of Turkey. It is not surprising that the AKP[7] uses this argument and embodies the anxiety about modernization under the name of 'türban'. After the AKP government, the meaning of dress and veiling became a hidden space of power relations between west and east which has shaped the politics of Islam in Turkey. Briefly, it can be said that dressing can be considered as a surveillance tool of its period and as a discursive and political practice in the Turkish case. So when discussing cross-dressing in Turkish cinema, the special meaning of dressing for Turkish politics and the cross-dressing tradition of Ottoman culture where the relationship between discourses of otherness can be seen, the new genderless Turkish language and Turkey's geographical and ideological position should all be borne in mind. The power of discussing cross-dressing in Turkish cinema and the opportunities which will be provided by this discussion are based on these arguments. These arguments make the discussions about cross-dressing performance unique and productive for the Turkish case.

Cross-dressing has been discussed in three different ways in Turkish academia: from the star persona of cross-dressing performers such as Bülent Ersoy, Zeki Müren and Huysuz Virgin; from an historical point of view such as discussion of the köçeks and zennes; and from trans-national cinema,[8] discussing the films of Ferzan Özpetek and Kutluğ Ataman, among others. In her essay 'The Stage: A Space for Queer Subjectification in Contemporary Turkey' (2012), Eser Selen focused on the relationship between stage and cross-dresser Turkish performers such as Zeki Müren, Bülent Ersoy and Seyfi Dursunoğlu. According to Selen, their presences on stage were based on the absence of queerness in their everyday lives. Başak Ertür and Alisa Lebow tried to read perceptions of transgender in terms of law using Bülent Ersoy's autobiography in their essay Şöhretin Sonu ('The End of Fame') in a book edited by Cüneyt Çakırlar and Serkan Delice in 2012 entitled *Cinsellik Muamması* ('The Enigma of Gender').

Barış Kılıçbay compared two recent Turkish-German films in *Lola + Bilidikid* (1999) and *Auslandstournee* (1999). Drawing on Butlerian theory of gender melancholy, he explored the close relationship between transvestism and cross-dressing, motherland and national identification in his essay 'Impossible Crossings: Gender Melancholy in Lola + Bilidikid and Auslandstournee' (2006). Tolga Yalur's essay Osmanlı'da Bir Cinsel Kimlik Olarak Köçek ('Köçek as a Gender Category in Ottoman Turkey') (2013) and Şeyma Ersoy Çak's essay Köçek ve Çengilerin Toplumsal Cinsiyeti ('The Gender of Köçeks and Çengi') (2009) discussed traditional performance art in terms of gender using queer theory. As stated above, none of these discussions focused on cross-dressing itself or on temporally cross-dressing performance in Turkish cinema. Neither did they focus on the relationship between politics and gender performance. They all ignored the special meanings of cross-dressing performance in the Turkish case.

In this study, cross-dressing is discussed as an act of crossing in order to release the term 'cross-dressing' both from the gender binary and from its western understanding. In order to discuss the term in relation to power and to establish a connection between the cross-dressing and the politics of the era, in this study, I argue that cross-dressing is not only about the gender binary or the clothes codes inherent in the binary, it is embedded in institutions of power such as time, space, language, memory and identity, which have been structured according to the historical position of a text. In other words, cross-dressing is not wearing the clothes of another sex but is wearing the tensions of a specific period which are embedded in time, space, language and memory in a gendered way. Therefore, in this study the discussion focuses on the question of what cross-dressing does in particular narratives rather than the question of what cross-dressing is.

I therefore discuss three principal effects of cross-dressing performance on its subject:

1. Cross-dressing gives mobility to its subject not only between gendered identities but also on the map where all relations between subjects and power are located. In films, cross-dressing characters not only change their gender but they also change other relations with power. That is why in films, cross-dressing characters change not only their gendered

identity but also their class, ethnicity, religion and whatever other characteristics they have, because we are connecting with the power relations map in many different forms. When one of these forms changes its position, all the other forms are affected by the change and the subject becomes mobile in this map. Briefly, they become a tourist on the map of power relations by means of cross-dressing, because cross-dressing is a kind of deterritorialization of identity in order to reterritorialize it. In this journey from deterritorialization to reterritorialization, the consistency of hegemonic discourse disperses and identity becomes mobile. In other words, identity moves away from 'being' and comes close to 'becoming' by means of cross-dressing. In this study, the act of crossing as a mobility effect of cross-dressing which is embedded in cross-dressing performance is explained by the idea of becoming. I claim that cross-dressing is a body of becoming and that therefore cross-dressing enables the process of becoming visible. Becomings are transformations – not of forms transforming into another or different form but of constantly transforming relations (Coleman 2008: 168). Briefly, it can be said that cross-dressing is a way of diverting and tricking the power which speaks through our bodies. The mobility of cross-dressing which is provided by the concept of becoming uses the body as a counter-weapon against power.

2. Cross-dressing can be accepted as a way of satisfying the desire to be visible and at the same time to escape from panoptic[9] social mechanisms. The narratives of cross-dressing films usually create a necessity for the character to change his/her appearance. A kind of panoptical society is created for the characters; they always know that they are being observed and are never sure, when they encounter their observer. The characters can escape this panoptical society of narrative only if they change their subject position on the map of power relations. They can escape from the panoptical social mechanism because, although they are still there, they are visible but not recognizable because their body has been emancipated from their determination. Because their bodies are in the process of becoming, they are the frame of undecidability. In order to discuss this effect, I use the theory of the grotesque body. A grotesque body transgresses the boundaries between bodies. Extenuated or escalated, the distortional and shapeless body of a grotesque challenges the stable and unchangeable body just as cross-dressing does. In this sense, a grotesque body is a

degradation of what is accepted as a normal body. It is exaggerated and unmeasurable. The cross-dressed body exaggerates the sexual orientation of the body in a very similar way to how the grotesque does. The sexual fragmentation of the body (breasts, buttocks, hair) is highlighted and caricatured. The elements of human anatomy can be seen to be in conflict. Cross-dressing might be perceived as a significant distortion of the known or recognized regulatory forms of the body. The grotesque can be seen not only in the form of the body but also in the performance of the body. By means of grotesque elements, the performance of the cross-dressed body becomes artificial and annihilated. That is why, even though their bodies are still there, they cannot be recognized and therefore they can escape surveillance.

3. Cross-dressing is a way of escaping the fear of being other and at the same time experiencing otherness. In order to discuss this effect, I use the term 'carnival'. Cross-dressing as a grotesque body usually creates a carnival atmosphere in films. According to Peter Ackroyd, 'cross-dressing is so deeply rooted in festive celebration and anarchic display that it survived centuries of persecution. It passed from the pagan rites of antiquity into medieval folk ceremonies and seasonal festivities' (1979: 51). The power of carnival to turn things upside down is facilitated by bringing it into a dialogic relation with official forms. Carnival enables open-ended, irregular bodies. The suspension of all hierarchical precedence during carnival time is of particular significance. Anti-authoritarian forces can be mobilized against the official culture. Carnival times are sharply distinct from the serious official, feudal, political cult forms and ceremonies. The joiner of the carnival can experience what s/he is not without any judgement. You can be what you want to be in carnival for a while. By means of the carnival in films which is created by a cross-dressing character, the character can experience otherness without any judgement.

All of these terms help to explain the subject's way of being mobile on the map of power relations by using cross-dressing. If a subject changes his/her position on the map of power relations by using cross-dressing, other forms of identity, forms of oppression and relationships between discourses and power relations are affected and then relocated by this change. The effects of cross-dressing performance fracture the place of power and the cross-dressed character becomes a tourist on the map of power relations, because s/he fractures power relations. Almost all cross-dressing characters in Turkish films can *escape* from the system and at the same time express themselves *within* the system. They can perform these two actions simultaneously because of their mobility, which is the tool for re-establishing power relations in their own way. On the other hand, performing both actions together fractures power relations and the order of the system. My aim is to follow these fractures in institutions of power – time, space, language and identity – in order to analyse the relationship between Turkish politics and cross-dressing films.

Turkish politics and cross-dressing films

In order to discover this relationship between cross-dressing films and military coups, it is essential to provide an overview of the cross-dressing films in the history of Turkish cinema. According to film historian Agah Özgüç (2006), the first cross-dressing film appeared in modern Turkey in 1923. It was entitled *Leblebici Horhor*, and the film is now lost. Özgüç (2006) wrote that it told the story of Leblebici Horhor (played by Behzat Butak) who disguises himself as his daughter in order to save her when he realizes that she is going to be kidnapped. The film, directed by Muhsin Ertuğrul, belongs to comedy in terms of genre. After this first film, audiences had to wait some years in order to watch what could be termed a cross-dressing film because, according to Özgüç (2006), a second cross-dressing film appeared with female cross-dressing featured in *Fosforlu Cevriye* (1959). After *Fosforlu Cevriye*, cinema audiences in Turkey witnessed a number of cross-dressing characters either as a main character or a supporting motif in films over the following ten years, such as *Şoför Nebahat* (1960, directed by Metin Erksan), *Gece Kuşu* (1960, directed by Hulki Saner), *Aslan Yavrusu* (1960, directed by Saner), *Belalı Torun* (1962, directed by Memduh Ün), *Fıstık Gibi Maşallah* (1964, directed by Saner), *Yalancının Mumu* (1965, directed by Semih Evin), *Babasına Bak, Oğlunu Al* (1965, directed by İnanoğlu), *Efkarlıyım Arkadaş* (1966, directed by Türker İnanoğlu), *Asker Anası* (1966, directed by Asaf Tengiz), *Kibar Haydut* (1966, directed by Yılmaz Atadeniz), *Beş Ateşli Kadın* (1968, directed by Seyfettin Tiryaki) and *Avanta Kemal* (1968, directed by Uğur Duru).

After the popularity of cross-dressing performances in Turkish films during the 1960s, a second phase of production took place in the 1980s beginning with *Deliler Almanya'da* (1980, directed by Yunus Bülbül), then *Beddua*

(1980, directed by Melih Gülgen) and *Şabaniye* (1984, directed by Kartal Tibet). Arguably the decreased number of cross-dressing film productions can be discussed with reference to contemporaneous debates about identity politics since the second wave of feminism in Turkey (unlike the second wave of feminism experienced during the 1960s and the 1970s in the western world, Turkey experienced a second wave of feminism during the 1980s). Furthermore, the growth of the LGBT movement allowed the production of 'realistic'[10] transgender movies. After a long break, a third wave of cross-dressing films appeared in the 2000s with *Komiser Şekspir* (2001, directed by Sinan Çetin), *Hababam Sınıfı Merhaba* (2007, directed by Kartal Tibet), *Plajda* (2008, directed by Murat Şeker) and *Şeytanın Pabucu* (2008, directed by Turgut Yasalar). Although I shall introduce these films later, the reason for giving this detailed chronology here is to point out the production dates of cross-dressing films. These three distinct periods of film production – the 1960s, 1980s and 2000s – coincided with not only significant turning points in Turkish political history but also times of national trauma, specifically military coups. When we look at the list of cross-dressing films in Turkish cinema, it can be easily claimed that there has been a direct relationship between military coups and cross-dressing films in the Turkish context. The topic of this study is this unexplored and undiscovered relationship.

In order to examine the relationship between cross-dressing films and military coups, I employ two theoretical approaches. First, in order to argue that there are connections to be made between military coups and cross-dressing films, I used the concept of ontological security, a concept I found appropriate to explicate this link. Second, in order to connect cross-dressing and ontological security, I used the concepts of becoming, the grotesque and the carnivalesque, which are the sources of the effects of cross-dressing performance in the films.

I am using ontological security as a connection point between military coups as times of national trauma and cross-dressing films by saying that both military coups and cross-dressing films destroy ontological security: military coups destroy it at the level of the state, whereas cross-dressing films destroy it at the level of the individual subject. Despite this similarity, however, both military coups and cross-dressing films reconstruct ontological security in different ways. According to Giddens, ontological security is a 'confidence or trust that the natural and social worlds are as they appear to be, including the basic existential parameters of self and social identity' (Giddens 1991: 374).

It involves having confidence in the routine and reliability of persons, places and things. What is 'secure' in ontological security is a psychological trust in the reliability and constancy of the world existing in the way it is 'supposed' to exist and the narrative which supports the constancy of the social construction of self-identity (Giddens 1991; Mitzen 2006). According to Giddens, questions of time, space, continuity and consistency are the actors of the ontological security of identity. In this sense, the increasing number of cross-dressing film productions during times of national trauma would not be a coincidence. In the framework of Turkey, when the ontological security of the nation was threatened by military coups, cross-dressing films appeared as an example of how individuals re-organize ontological security by means of cross-dressing.

Military coups in the history of Turkey interrupted and threatened not only the ordinary processes and continuity of the nation but also the idea of national identity. Furthermore, time and space, even language and acts of speaking, changed their ordinary meaning and usage under military rule. On the other hand, cross-dressing performances in films disrupt and fracture the source of stable identity (time, space, continuity, coherence, memory and so on) which the system of ontological security then re-organizes for the performer's own benefit which can be accepted as the dream of a citizen who has to live under the military rule. A cross-dressing character can do it in films by means of the effects of cross-dressing. However, between disrupting and re-organizing ontological security, institutions of power such as language, time, space and gender are transformed into what I term the 'playground of the subject'. I term the crises which cross-dressing causes for ontological security as 'fracturing' where the subject can travel in the geographies of power according to his/her needs. Fracturing can make both discourse and its roots visible. Therefore, the moments created by cross-dressing performance which can be called fracturing reveal not only a discourse but also a relationship between discourses. The main aim of this current study is to follow these fractures in order to understand the map of power of a particular time – in this case, times of national trauma.

This overlap between military coups and cross-dressing film productions in Turkey gives an opportunity to further discussions of cross-dressing, underlining that this is not an issue which is related only to gendered performance. Here, it is worth remembering that the idea of cross-dressing was a tradition in Ottoman culture which was based on the discourse of otherness. Although cross-dressing films begin with an examination of gender forms, they spread their examination over all forms of order, identity and socially and historically constructed representations of power. So discussing cross-dressing performance in films can be used as productive tools in order to understand 'how the system of knowledge of a film's period is designed' and 'what kinds of relationship can be found between the different discourses of the period'. All of these areas can be discussed in relation to textual questions such as: What is cross-dressing? What kinds of contribution does cross-dressing performance make to the narrative? What kinds of opportunity does cross-dressing provide to the text itself? These questions enable us to turn back to beginning of this study: the three effects of cross-dressing gender performance in Turkish films.

Within this framework, cross-dressing films provide subjects with the mobility which, as I mentioned above, is necessary for handling trauma and economic, cultural and political problems. This mobility gives an opportunity to re-organize and re-stabilize notions of subjectivity, collective identity, history, truth, continuity and coherence, routine, time and space. Furthermore, it can be claimed that cross-dressing performance provides freedom for the subject in order to escape both a panoptical society and surveillance which are created by military coups and at the same time the ability to be visible as an anchor of identity. Cross-dressing films involve and reveal components which destroy the idea of homogeneous society, culture and identity by using the idea of the gendered body in unfamiliar ways. It can therefore be claimed that cross-dressing films show how strategies and tactics for managing social anxiety are fundamentally gendered. Briefly, in all these films, cross-dressing performers can *escape* the system and at the same time express themselves *within* the system. They play with the elements of ontological security by means of the effects of cross-dressing performance on its subject. These effects can be accepted as a way of handling national trauma.

I am using Norman Fairclough's text-oriented critical discourse analysis (CDA) to address my research questions. Discourse can be accepted as a form of social practice which shapes and is shaped by institutions and power relations. According to Foucault (1972: 27), 'discourses are autonomous systems of statements structured by historically specific formation rules with particular systems of power/knowledge relations'. CDA is based on revealing these systems of statements which are accepted as natural, universal truths and foundations of human beings. CDA is one way to show how meaning is constructed and structured ideologically by power relations.

In order to analyse discourse critically, the researcher should explore relationships between the text and its language, the text and its historical, political and cultural position/location (contextuality), and the text and other texts of culture (intertextuality). By doing this, we can understand how knowledge was structured in what kind of order, which includes power, ideology and politics which change their position according to discourse. However, before following all these steps, the researcher should determine his/her texts: for the current study, the texts are films.

In order to identify my case films, I used the term 'temporary cross-dressing performance' as a filter. My interest in this study is in those cross-dressing films in which characters use cross-dressing to find a solution for similar circumstances, generally to escape enemies who are threatening them. Their cross-dressing activity is not based on sexual orientation or desire. I therefore excluded from the study realistic transgender, drag or cross-dressing films such as *Zenne* (2011), *Ruhumu Asla* (2001) and *Dönersen Islık Çal* (1992). Furthermore, I was not interested in the stage performance of cross-dressing such as Huysuz Virgin. It is films such as these which I call temporary cross-dressing performance. I chose five temporary cross-dressing films from the many available as texts which can be accepted as kinds of forms of social practice from three different military coup eras which can be accepted as turning points in the Turkish political and cultural structure: from the 1960 military coup, one male cross-dressing film, *Fıstık Gibi Maşallah* (1962) and one female cross-dressing film, *Şoför Nebahat* (1960); from the 1980 military coup, one male cross-dressing film, *Şabaniye* (1982); and from the 2007 military ultimatum, one male cross-dressing film, *Şeytanın Pabucu* (2008) and one female cross-dressing film, *Hababam Sınıfı Merhaba* (2007). I shall explain why I choose these particular films, their importance and the films themselves in more detail in Chapter 1, but here I can say that their popularity, their stars and their positions in Turkish cinema history affected my selection. In order to select my case study films, I first watched all of the cross-dressing films listed in the Introduction. After watching all of them, I eliminated some in which the cross-dressing characters only have a supporting role; these were Avanta Kemal, Kibar Haydut, Beş Ateşli Kadın, Beddua and Komser Şekspir. I then eliminated the films in which the narratives are not based on the transformation of cross-dressing characters even though a cross-dressing character is one of the main characters; this removed Aslan Yavrusu, Efkarlıyım Arkadaş and Fosforlu Cevriye. I then considered the popularity of films. Three of the films which I choose, *Hababam Sınıfı*, *Şoför Nebahat* and *Şabaniye*, all are serial films. Şaban and Şoför Nebahat are well-known characters in Turkish cinema and many films have been made which depict their various adventures. *Hababam Sınıfı* is a classic novel which has been adapted for the screen many times. I chose *Fıstık Gibi Maşallah* because it is an adaptation of *Some Like It Hot* (1959) and involves classic cross-dressing formulas. I selected *Şeytanın Pabucu* because its star Fatih Ürek is a well-known feminen singer and this could enhance the discussion because his performance of masculinity, femininity and cross-dressing involves multiple layers of performance.

After choosing the five case-study films, I examined the texts as cultural products representative of the social practices in which the discourse is both constitutive and constituted and started to carry out close textual analyses. In this study, I examine all elements of films as written texts in order to understand the structure of how discourses were embedded into them, the kinds of strategy used in order to make discourses meaningful and natural, and whether the cross-dressing films help to reproduce unequal power relations, and if so how. Hence I examine the films with regard to the characters, narratives, cinematic elements such as music, sound, colour, lighting, editing and mise en scène, and other visuals such as costuming, questioning how these aspects collectively engage with discourses. In order to do that, I watched the films several times in order to identify and catch any repeated patterns. These patterns might help me to establish any relationships which might exist between different texts and different films. In order to identify these patterns, I asked what kinds of opportunity cross-dressing performance give to the narrative and to the character(s) in each film. I discovered that some identical formulations are repeated from one film to another. I categorized these scenes which enabled me to realize that they all relate to time, space, memory, language and gender. I therefore decided to analyse them more deeply under these five headings.

After this categorization, I asked how a cross-dressing character uses these elements differently from other characters. Answering this question enabled me to discover the effects of cross-dressing performance on its performer. I then established connections between these effects and the historical, political and cultural locations of the films. In other words, in order to contextualize the study, I read these effects alongside the implications of the three selected periods of military coup. I researched the newspapers of the chosen periods and explored personal memories of times of military coups in order to understand the social relations and discourses instantiated in these texts. I explored the Turkish political, historical and cultural situation at the times when the films were produced in order to understand the relationship between cross-dressing films as discursive practices and wider social and cultural structures and in order to find continuity and determine discontinuity between texts and culture. In this way, the texts became more open and showed how they interrelated with the cultural political practices of the periods in which they were produced.

Chapter outline

The chapters which follow will highlight different questions and/or aspects of cross-dressing performance in Turkish cinema. Chapter 1 provides an overview of Turkish politics, culture and cinema and the production of cross-dressing films. The key questions which are addressed in this chapter are where and when cross-dressing films appear. This chapter presents the conceptual framework of the study and situates the case studies into debates around culture and politics in and of Turkey. In this chapter, I shall introduce cross-dressing films and at the same time I shall try to answer the question 'what does cross-dressing *do* in the films?' This chapter is, for this reason, entitled 'Framing Turkey' and this frame can be accepted as a stage of the choreography which will be produced in Chapter 2, which is based on the question 'who/what?'

In Chapter 2, I shall discuss my theoretical inclination. The terms and ideas of 'becoming' (Deleuze), 'carnivalesque' and the 'grotesque' body (Bakhtin) which can serve to explain my understanding of cross-dressing performance in the narratives are discussed. The definition of cross-dressing for the purposes of this study is given. In order to discuss cross-dressing, I have used different terms not only from different study areas but also from different cultures. Therefore, I have used 'Choreographing' as the title of this chapter, because my intention is not only to use these terms but also to explore the relationship between them. I am not interested in the single performance of these terms as stable entities, but rather I am interested in locating and designing these terms according to each other's performance. In this chapter, I try to choreograph these terms in order to make a useful theoretic map which can be used to explore Turkish cinema effectively.

This chapter discusses three effects of cross-dressing performance making use of these theories.

Chapter 3 explores ontological security. In the first two chapters, I frame Turkey and mapping the emotions of films and choreograph theory, in order to point out the theoretic position of this study, to introduce the selected films and to make a connection between national trauma and their narratives. In this chapter, I use these three actions together in order to discuss what kinds of opportunity cross-dressing performances provide for films. In other words, the previous chapter sought to discuss cross-dressing films and this chapter presents a discussion of cross-dressing *performance* in films. I therefore consider the question of how cross-dressing performance and military coups disrupt the system of knowledge which is the source of ontological security in the films.

Going back to Giddens, questions of time, space, continuity and consistency are the actors of the ontological security of identity. It can be claimed that ideologies, systems and any kind of relationship between human beings require ontological security in order to be and work efficiently. Furthermore, they require an agreement about the elements of ontological security without integration. Cross-dressing performance can be accepted as serving both the 'denaturalization' and the 're-idealization' of gender norms (Judith Butler) or misogyny (bell hooks); either way, cross-dressing encourages its audiences to re-think elements of ontological security which are usually accepted unquestioningly. I shall use my choreography of theory from Chapter 2 in order to understand how cross-dressing destroys and re-establishes ontological security. Hence, Chapter 3 discusses ontological security in relation to military coups and cross-dressing.

In the chapters which follow, I use the term 'fracturing' to describe the crises and troubles which cross-dressing causes to the idea of ontological security in films. I use different thematic concepts in order to understand the questions asked by the cross-dressing character. Each concept is addressed in a separate (but linked) chapter. Each chapter discusses how cross-dressing performances leave traces and questions behind them and how the roots of discourses can be visible through fractures which are produced by these traces and questions. Furthermore, the fractures which are made by cross-dressing performances in films overlap the fractures made by military coups in the case of Turkey. This overlapping helps us to add new dimensions to the discussion. Each chapter starts with an examination of elements of ontological security and then I shall discuss the value of each element in terms of sociology and/or philosophy. After that, I shall consider how cross-dressing fractures this element after how a military coup destroys it.

In Chapter 4, I shall discuss language, speech and voice fracturing. Cross-dressing characters also disrupt the relationship between voice and body and between the speaking subject and the listening object. The same body uses different types of voice performance at the same time. It creates soliloquy. The performer speaks with someone else with a 'cross-dressed gender' voice and style and at the same time still gives her/his own reaction to the self, using their biological given voice in a way which creates schizophrenic situations. This paradox is based on not only the different voices of woman-man but also the different ways of using language which woman and man have. In male cross-dressing films, the reluctance of male characters to lose their natural voice and speech can be seen in their performance. Many similarities can be found between the male cross-dressing character who does not want to lose his sound and his right to speak, and the citizen who wants to speak but cannot under military rule. Furthermore, cross-dressing characters also ignore the listening object – who listens to them – while they speak to themselves. These moments are lost time for the listening objects. At these moments, the listening object cannot talk, listen or even understand. Speech and sound become a bridge not only between masculinity and femininity but also between a militaristic hegemony which is not willing to listen and a civilian community who cannot be heard. In this chapter, three different but related topics will be discussed: the relationship between body and sound, the differences in language acquisition between men and women, and the fracturing between listening object and speaking subject in relation to three effects of cross-dressing performance.

In Chapters 5, I discuss time and space fracturing. I consider how cross-dressing performance affects linear time and space perception, which is the main source of ontological security and therefore a source of stable identity. Cross-dressing characters always have an opportunity to break down linear time and space perception which creates a fracture of the linear progressive way of understanding. I discuss space/time fracturing under the three headlines: leaving home and playing with past, liminal spaces and multiple nows, and an envisaged future. These three headlines shall be combined with the three effects of cross-dressing performance.

In Chapter 6, I discuss masculinity and femininity fracturing. I shall address this question: if gender is a performance what would happen if we change our performance? In order to find an answer, I explore crises of masculinity and femininity according to their periods. My argument is that cross-dressing is used for overcoming crisis of masculinity and femininity which are caused by military coups in the films. This discussion can help us to understand the relationship between gender discourse and other discourses and how they are affected by military coups as national traumas.

1

Framing Turkey and mapping cross-dressing films: Turkish modernization as cross-dressing performance

The three distinct periods of cross-dressing film production, the 1960s, the 1980s and the 2000s, coincided not only with significant milestones in Turkish political history but also with times of national trauma, in this case, military coups. Therefore, I discuss the 1960 and 1980 military coups and the 2007 military memorandum and their effects on cultural life in order to understand the main tensions of the periods and the contexts which they provided for cross-dressing performance. However, in order to understand Turkish politics and culture, the significance of the modernization process should be considered before turning to the effects of military coups. After that, the cinema of the three periods will be analysed to show the kinds of textual landscape in which cross-dressing films were located in order to understand the relationship between the texts. Gender movements and discussions of the periods will be considered next in order to understand how the gender discourses of the periods intersected with the other discourses. This chapter therefore represents a stage which is framed by the three selected military coups where the choreography of theory which is outlined in the next chapter and the case studies which will be outlined the subsequent chapters meet. I prefer to use the verb 'mapping' because 'maps are not only representations of the world, they also have the ability to change the way we think about and act upon places depicted in those maps' (Dodge *et al.* 2009: 27). Furthermore, maps not only make visible the relationships between a place and its surroundings but also help us to describe a place according to these relationships. It can therefore be claimed that maps also have a performative function. On the other hand, mapping as an action includes power over the space. Mapping a space implies not only capturing and possessing the space but also attributing value to it. These points all reflect what I want to do with the films. The questions addressed in this chapter will be 'where', 'when' and 'which' cross-dressing films show up.

Turkish modernization

The modernization process and its underpinning tension can be seen at work in all kinds of social relations, desires and anxieties and are central to Turkish political and cultural life. It can be claimed that the Turkish national identity was structured in the tension between being modern/western and being traditional/eastern, so understanding the effects of Turkish modernization on society and culture is vital for understanding the possible alternative readings of cross-dressing performance which are particular to Turkish society.

The Ottoman Empire collapsed after the First World War and Mustafa Kemal Atatürk established the westernized and modernized Turkish Republic in 1923. According to Yeşim Arat (2000), Kemalist ideology was based on three main premises: western as well as modern, rejecting the Ottoman heritage and legitimizing their modernization project with reference to the pre-Islamic Turkish past. The unique and important characteristic of Turkey's modernization which makes it different from western examples is that it is a state-centred project (Aktar 1993; Ercan 1996; İnsel 1996: 2002; Mardin 2000; Sarıbay 1982). In Turkey, the modernization politics aimed to create a modern state as dominant over society instead of transforming the citizens into modern subject/citizens (Can 1998; Durgun 1997; Keyman & İçduygu 1998; Nişancı 2001; Öğün 1995). Furthermore, 'Turkey is the only Muslim country adopting secularism as the fundamental principle of the modernization project' (Özsoy 2009). Controlling the position, visibility and appearance of women in society was regarded as the best way to show the secular, modern and western tendency of the modernization (Göle 1996; Kandiyoti 1988).

During Turkey's modernization period, women were a crucial part of the process. The legal emancipation of Turkish women constituted the vehicle for the modernization (Arat 1997; Durakbaşa 1999; Göle 1996; Kandiyoti 1988). This is not surprising and it is not specific to Turkish Kemalist modernization because, according to Nira Yuval-Davis (1997: 2), 'it is women, the bureaucracy, and the intelligentsia who reproduce nations, biologically, culturally and symbolically'. 'At the same time, discourse and struggles around the issues of "women's emancipation" or "women following tradition" (as have been expressed in various campaigns for and against women's veiling, voting, education and employment) have been at the centre of modernist and anti-modernist nationalist struggles' (Yuval-Davis 1997: 23). The emancipation of Turkish women was the centre of Kemalist modernization; in fact, it was characterized under the term of 'state-feminism'. The most important date for the emancipation of Turkish women was the adoption of the Swiss Civil Code on 4 October 1926. By means of adopting this law on western private life, women's position in family life was re-organized. This law made polygamy illegal, gave the right of divorce to women as to men, made civil marriage obligatory, and removed any difference between men and women in terms of inheritance. On the other hand, the Swiss Civil Code did not allow absolute equality between husband and wife: the husband was still the head of the family. The turban and the fez were outlawed by the Hat Law and Dress Revolution in 1925. In 1930, women gained the right to vote before most European countries had introduced it. In 1914, women started to study at universities and in 1934, the first woman judge was appointed. The image of the new woman of modern Turkey can be summarized as an educated, professional woman in the workplace, a socially active woman as a member of social clubs, a biologically reproductive woman in the family as a mother and wife, and a feminine woman entertaining men at balls and parties. The duties of modern Turkish women, according to Atatürk, were raising the next generation and being the source and social foundation of the nation (Arat 1997; Durakbaşa 1999; Göle 1996; Kandiyoti 1988). This is referred to as 'state feminism'. As a result, it can be said that the Turkish modernization/westernization sought to create emancipated woman citizens who would be the window through which one can see Turkish modernization. Carole Pateman (1988) described this process as the transformation of traditional patriarchy to civil patriarchy, thus emphasizing that civil society and citizenship are also patriarchal masculine notions and norms. So, clothing and styles of dressing served as modernist sites where the battle of conflicting ideologies took place.

Jenny B. White (2003: 149) stated, 'Dress became a cornerstone of Turkey's modernist transformation. In 1925, Atatürk travelled around the country to introduce "civilized dress" to the people. Headgear had been sign of status and distinction during Ottoman times, the different types demonstrating rank, profession and sex.' Modernization transformed bodies into the essence and symbols of nation by using clothing. Traditional and Islamic ways of dressing were forbidden in the public sphere. According to Kaya Genç (2013: 1), 'The world's first hat revolution took place in Turkey in 1925. On November 25 of that year, the parliament passed a law that made it mandatory for all men to wear Western-style hats in public places; all civil servants had to wear them, and no other type of hat would be allowed. Those who went hatless would be left alone, but if one wanted to wear a hat then one had to either wear the proposed model (and not the traditional turban or fez) or face the consequences, which could be as severe as the death penalty.' This 'Hat and Dress Revolution' initiated by Atatürk produced protests in many cities and many people were arrested. Severe and criminal sanctions were used to implement the new codes of dress, transforming dressing and the body into objects of surveillance. As can be seen easily in records of the period, the Turkish Kemalist modernization process which was based on the appearance of citizens did not take long: in a very short time, Turkish citizens were transformed from Figure 1.1 to Figure 1.2.

So it can be claimed that Turkish citizens actually *wore modernization*. If cross-dressing is accepted as a journey in the uncertain space between two poles of a binary which can be visualized by dressing, then Turkish modernization might be called a form of cross-dressing which operates across traditional

Figure 1.1 Ottoman women.

Figure 1.2 Republican women gathered around Mustafa Kemal at a ball.

to modern. Turkish national identity was formed in the fracture between traditional/east and modern/west as *both* traditional and modern and *neither* traditional nor modern. In this fracture between modern and tradition, these terms – west/east and modern/traditional – emancipate their binary opposite and produce new meaning for Turkey's national identity. Joseph R. Gusfield (1967) suggested that traditional society is not a stable and distant society like a binary opposite of modern society (unlike the claims of classic modernization theory which allow us to think about modernization as a linear symmetric phenomenon independent from historical and geographical concepts), but that traditions are invented according to the requirements of the modern world in order to legitimate modern discourses. For example, some intellectuals of the republic such as Ziya Gökalp tried to rewrite the history of pre-Islamic Turks in central Asia according to the requirements of the new modern Turkey. He argued that women had been considered equal to men among pre-Islamic Turks in central Asia, unlike during the Islamic Ottoman period. According to Gökalp (1968: 147), 'Old Turks were both democratic and feminist … In every business meeting woman and man had to be present together.' The Islamic tradition as practised by the Ottomans was accepted as the reason for excluding women and the new citizens of the Kemalist ideology were structured as the opposite of Ottoman citizens, although they were the same. According to Gökalp, democracy and feminism were the basis of ancient Turkish life, which was postponed during Ottoman Empire. The endeavours of Ziya Gökalp can be accepted as 'presentism', which is a kind of historical writing which approaches the past using the concepts and concerns of the present.

In other words, traditional and modern societies exist simultaneously and produce a hybrid society. Modern society brings an idea of the future; traditional society brings an idea of past in this relationship. To this extent, the term 'non-western modernization' indicates an impossible aim. It can be argued that modernization can be considered as a level which was structured by the west in order to determine 'other' as a position. In order to deepen the discussion on this point, Immanuel Kant's argument about time experience in the spatial sense can be used. The relationship between developed countries, developing countries and underdeveloped countries is very similar to Kant's theory of the relationship between nearing, nearness and near-hood (*nahheit*) (cited in Heidegger 1972: 15). A brief summary of near-hood is as follows: there is one point in linear time and your position is measured from this specific point. By your actions, you became near to or distant from a specific point in stratified time. In addition, this specific point changes its position according to your position. Turning back to the discussion about modernization, it can be claimed that the specific point is the measured level of modernization. The level which the west has reached historically is regarded as the criterion for modernity. Non-western countries are considered modern or 'primitive' and undeveloped based on their closeness to or remoteness from this level. However, this level constantly changes its position. Therefore, modernization for non-western nations is an endless process and a marker of the differences between the west and the non-west. The national identity of a modern state in non-western countries is structured by the tension between west and east. In Turkish modernization, however, this tension is visualized by dressing, if Indian or African countries' modernization is taken into consideration. Turkey is particular with respect to modernization discourse by using dress. It can therefore be claimed that Turkish modernization is a kind of fictional and imaginary formation.

In order to discuss the differences between western and eastern modernization, the view of Charles Baudelaire, who can be accepted as the voice of the western modernist aesthetic, might be useful. He stated that modernization inspires and produces the modernization of the citizen's soul as well. Not only cities, fashions and pastoral visions but also identity is thus not only changed but also produced by modernization. Baudelaire's argument might be applicable for the western type of modernization. On the other hand, it can be claimed that the Turkish modernization process created a modernist state without making modern individuals of its citizens. Reşat Kasaba (1999: 30) stated that Kemalist leaders took modernization to mean clean streets and cities, the modern appearance of citizens, and the type and style of institutions which matched western examples. The answer to why the modernization process in non-western countries produces a modern state rather than modern individuals would be the Enlightenment, which was experienced by western countries but not by non-western countries. 'The conception of universal individualism and modern human rights first appeared in the Enlightenment, was religiously founded by John Locke (1695), metaphysically/ethically founded by Kant (1781), economically founded as the source of the wealth of nations by Adam Smith (1776)' (Izenberg 2011: 124). So the modernization process of non-western countries without experience of the Enlightenment gives more attention to the state than to its citizens. So because the modernization of Turkey was a top-down imposition and because of its unsuccessful endeavours to create modern citizens, 'the republican leaders were realistic enough to recognize that a strong and loyal Army was vital if the young republic was to endure' (Demirel 2004: 129), and they 'saw armed forces as the main pillar of the new regime However, they were also quite aware of the fact that the military's entanglement in politics worked against both unity and discipline in the military' (Ahmad 1969: 47, 55). That is why 'after Mustafa Kemal came to power in 1923, one of his primary goals was to isolate the military command from direct involvement in partisan politics' (Lerner & Robinson 1960: 26).

As an instance of non-western modernization,[1] Turkish modernization delineates the distinction between the west and the east. Therefore, the national identity of Turkey as an example of non-western modernization can be articulated in between the two, and it constantly carries the tension of being in-between. In this journey of national identity between west and east, the military is a persistent presence. When military coups are discussed, this modernization process should also be considered. Discussions around military coups cannot be divorced from discussions around modernization. Furthermore, there are some similarities which can be found between gendered Turkish modernization experiences and the idea of cross-dressing as a journey between binary poles. The brief history of Turkish traumas should start with the Kemalist modernization project because it can be accepted as the first traumatic development of modern Turkey's history. If there had been a national cinema at that time, I am quite sure that cross-dressing films would have been popular narratives of the time. Furthermore, it can be claimed that each military coup in Turkey involved the tension of modernization. The main source of the love/ hate relationship between the military and politics in Turkey can be found in this Kemalist modernization process and its tensions. After this introduction, military coups as eras when the production of cross-dressing films increased can now be discussed.

The 1960s: Following in the footsteps of Kemalism

The 1960 military coup took place after an attempt by the multi-party system at democratization in Turkey to suppress the conservative inclination of the Democrat Party (DP) government of Adnan Menderes and Celal Bayar. It took a year, and in 1961 elections were held in order to return to the rule of a civilian government. Even though the 1960 military rule ended with the 1961 election rebuilding the sense of safety, recovering the boundaries of collective attachment and becoming accustomed to a new order took time for the Turkish people. The elections which took place immediately after military coups – in 1961– were conducted under the military coup in order to consolidate the expectation of the military powers. I therefore chose to regard the second election as the end of a time of military coup. So the 1960 military coup ended with the 1965 election. By the term 'time of a military coup', it is these periods to which I refer. During 1960 and the post-1960 period, Turkey witnessed political pluralism and the emergence of new and ideologically distinct oppositional political groups.

In 1950, the DP had won the election with 53 per cent of the vote and gained a majority in parliament. As soon as the new government was established, its first act was to change the system of assignment and reassignment in staffing. Through staffing, the new government sought to take the Kemalist power of the military and the Kemalist intelligentsia under control. After that, the language of the constitution was changed. This change was understood as a challenge to the language revolution created by Atatürk. The *dervis* lodges and Islamic associations which had been closed by Atatürk were re-opened. Although its politics were considered anti-Kemalist by some groups, the DP again won the 1957 election. The Menderes/Bayar government, which had increased its self-confidence after the second election victory, instituted the 'Inquest Commission' (*Tahkikat Komisyonu*, 1960) in order to suppress the oppositional press and groups. When an economic crisis and black market trade added to the anti-democratic and anti-Kemalist politics of the Menderes/Bayar government, the military interfered in the country's governance on 27 May 1960. Briefly, therefore, anti-Kemalist politics, anti-democratic implications and an economic crisis can be accepted as reasons for the 1960 military coup.

Studies of Turkish politics have presented different arguments about this period. According to Çağlar Keyder (1987), the 1960 military coup was a symbol of bourgeois progressivism and was undertaken in order to develop industrial capitalism as the next level of the modernization process. According to Sina Akşın (2004), the coup enhanced Kemalist ideology in modern Turkey. According to Emre Kongar (2000), the reason for the military coup was based on the tension between a statist elite who were Kemalist and supported the westernization process and lived in Istanbul, and traditional liberals such as land barons and provincial notables who lived in Anatolia. According to Keyder (1987), the roots of this tension were grounded in *Tanzimat* (1839–76), earlier attempts at modernization and westernization in the late Ottoman period. This movement of the Young Ottomans[2] was a kind of synthesis between western notions of 'progress' and a harmonious Islamic state. However, their attempts could reach only an urban, upper-class minority. After this first attempt, Kemalist Modern Turkey took its place on the stage of history as an example of a country whose citizens directly faced the effects of modernization. The 1960 military coup was based on the tension and oscillation of Turkish national identity from west to east and *vice versa*.

After the 1960 coup, the first election took place in 1961 with a new constitution under the military rule. The 1961 constitution was intended to produce a new working class in order to develop industrial capitalism. Internal migration began from rural areas to big cities, from farms to factories during this period. The 1960s was the period when the faces of the inhabitants and the voices of the city began to change. In order to develop a new working class, the new constitution allowed unionization, and this led to improving all leftist organizations. Workers' fundamental rights and liberties were guaranteed by the new constitution. Moreover, the new constitution supported artistic and cultural life financially and established an 'independent art budget commission'. Although all these attempts can be considered democratic, the military coups oppressed opposition groups and the return of the repression in 1980 was very brutal; this will be discussed in the next section of this chapter. Now, the effects of the 1960 coup in terms of the cinema industry will be discussed in order to identify the kind of cinematic universe in which the cross-dressing films were situated.

Cross-dressing films in the 1960s

The 1961 constitution and the advantages which it provided also influenced the cinema of the period. Popular cinema had its heyday during the 1960s and the early 1970s in terms of the number of productions. The popular cinema of this period is called 'Yeşilçam Cinema', named after the street in Istanbul where the film production companies were located. Internal migration and the new city-dwellers affected the demand for cinema and during these golden years, 200 films were produced every year (Büker 2002). Not only was the domestic market interested in these films, but they were also exported to other Middle Eastern countries such as Iran, Iraq and Egypt. Although melodrama and comedy were still the prominent genres of Yeşilçam cinema, socially realistic films were the key genre to describe the cinema of the period. The films dealing with social issues of the period such as internal migration, workers' rights and feudal relations can be accepted as outcomes of the 1960 military coup and the 1961 constitution. According to Daldal (2005), the lives of ordinary people against a background of major social events with a Marxist approach were the popular narratives of the period. In addition to socially realistic cinema, national cinema was discussed by Halit Refiğ (1971) who stated that the cinema of Turkey was structured by the demands of the audience without state support or private capital. Hence, for Refiğ (1971), national cinema should be socially realistic but without Marxist and leftist tendencies, and should produce home-grown perspectives and narratives. At the same time came the idea of '*milli cinema*' discussed by Mesut Uçakan in 1965. Uçakan was accepted as a neo-Ottomanist and his solution for the social anxieties of period was based on not only national identity but also Islamic identity through Ottoman culture. As can be understood from these discussions, the theory of Turkish cinema was beginning to be discussed during this period. Turkish cinema theorists began to gather around film magazines and journals such as *Sinema, Yıldız, Sinema-Tiyatro, Si-Sa, Yeni Sinema* and *Sine-film*. After magazines and journals, cinema workers and theorists began to establish associations. The other distinctive feature of the period was the emergence of auteur cinema. Lütfi Akad, Metin Erksan, Atıf Yılmaz, Memduh Ün, Halit Refiğ and Yılmaz Güney were among the outstanding directors of the period. According to Nilgün Abisel (1995), auteur cinema was trying to find a self-image of national identity which was structured by anxiety about the modernization process. There was also another type of film which was far from the period's main tendency towards socially realistic cinema: cross-dressing films.

The 1960s was a period when the number of cross-dressing film productions was much higher than during other military coup periods. The absence of an LGBT movement and the domination of heterosexual state feminism can be considered as reasons for this abundance of cross-dressing films. The complex traditions of cross-dressing and same-sex relations of Ottoman culture were rejected by the modern Turkish republic and their space was left empty until the LGBT movement took hold in the 1990s. It can be claimed that this emptiness was filled by cross-dressing films. Furthermore, the distinctive feature of this period's cross-dressing films was the number of female-to-male cross-dressing films in comparison with other periods such as the 1980s and 2000s. In order to address the relationship between military coups and cross-dressing more efficiently, the other two military coups should be discussed. First, however, I shall look at the period's cross-dressing films more deeply.

After the first cross-dressing film, *Leblebici Horhor* (1923), the first tomboy character as a female-to-male cross-dresser appeared in *Fosforlu Cevriye* (1959) and was played by Neriman Köksal; the film was directed by Aydın Arakon and adapted from a novel written by Suat Derviş (figure 1.3). The heroine is a homeless, poor girl who wants to find a real murderer in order to save her sister who is accused of being the killer. She fights like a man; uses slang words and wears men's clothes. In order to survive on the streets and hold on to life, she needs to look like a man and she pretends to be a man. In this film, gendered identity is visualized by using the relationship between bodies and places. Bodies and places exchange their meanings: in other words, they give their meanings to each other. Fosforlu Cevriye transforms into a man, not only by using clothes but also by using places, because her place is not the home but the street. She destroys the traditional place perception by using cross-dressing. Cross-dressing performance allows her to use place in her own way. By means of cross-dressing, she gains mobility and fluidity between places. As Henri Lefebvre (1974) wrote, space has been discussed as a fundamental source of social power. Ideological and political power depends on one's ability to transform and control the space and time where the social relations are located. It can be claimed that Fosforlu Cevriye, as a cross-dressing character, destroys the control of power over space. Furthermore, it can be claimed that *Fosforlu Cevriye* as a film re-identifies the city for its new inhabitants who migrated from rural areas to big cities as a result of 1960s politics which sought to enhance industry and create a new working class. The back streets of the city, police stations, pothouses and brothels are not only labelled but also gendered by film. However, Fosforlu Cevriye as a female-to-male cross-dresser is the only one who can experience all of the gendered and labelled places by means of the cross-dressing effect of being visible but not recognizable. If she is recognized as a female, she cannot experience all these spaces.

In *Fosforlu Cevriye*, cross-dressing gives an opportunity to be mobile through places, whereas *Gece Kuşu* (1960) gives its cross-dressing character an opportunity to be mobile through time. In *Gece Kuşu* (directed by Hulki Saner), Nesrin (played

Figure 1.3 *Fosforlu Cevriye* film poster – 1959.

by Belgin Doruk) is the daughter of a rich factory owner, whereas Ali (played by Eşref Kolçak) is a poor young man (figure 1.4). In Nesrin's house, family and friends speak a mixture of French and Turkish (as already explained, the French language has been accepted as a sound of modernization since Tanzimat in Turkey) and they listen to western classical music. On the other hand, Ali listens to traditional Anatolian music and uses slang and market language. He

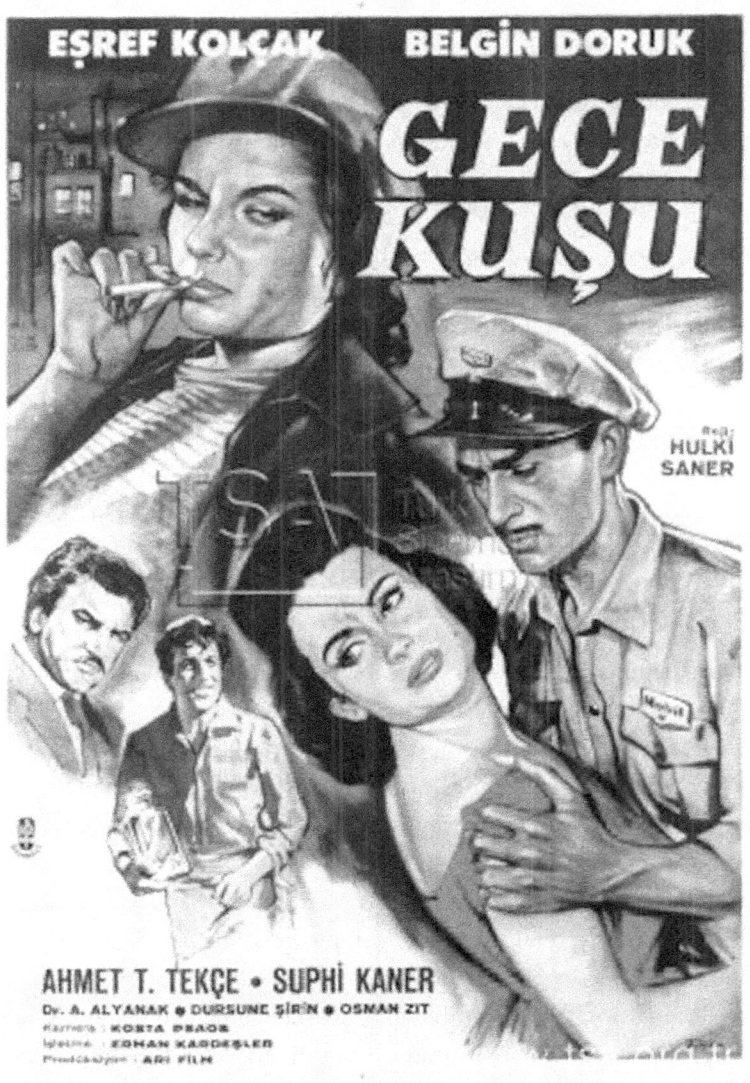

Figure 1.4 *Gece Kuşu* film poster – 1960.

is a fighter and aggressive. Nesrin falls in love with Ali. Their love is a kind of love between west and east and between modernity and tradition. Ali, who is the symbol of the east and tradition, is an unpredictable partner for Nesrin, who is the symbol of the west. This understanding of west and east belongs to the cultural politics of the 1960s and it will change by the 1980s, so I shall discuss this new understanding in the next section. In *Gece Kuşu*, in order to understand what her lover Ali does at night, Nesrin masquerades as a man and follows his night-time life. She lives as a woman during the day and becomes Ali's lover and as a man at night and becomes his friend. She gives herself a new name, Gece Kuşu ('Night Bird'). Nesrin as a cross-dresser destroys gendered time perception and becomes a mobile agency between gendered times by means of cross-dressing. According to Pierre Bourdieu (1977), time and space are special apparatuses for the coding, transforming and reproducing of social relations. Both Fosforlu Cevriye and Nesrin gain the ability to re-organize and re-produce time and space according to their needs by means of cross-dressing. Power has lost its control over time and space in these films and both women can escape the surveillance mechanism.

In *Aslan Yavrusu* (1960, directed by Hulki Saner), a cross-dressing character gains mobility between classes (figure 1.5). Although she is a woman, Neco Hanım (played by Leyla Sayer) pretends to be a man in order to work in the male-dominated rural fishery industry. Adnan (played by Orhan Günşıray) is a famous novel writer in Istanbul. A friend accuses him of creating unrealistic women characters in his novels. So he makes a bet with his friend about Neco Hanım during a holiday in the countryside. He claims that he can transform Neco Hanım into a woman whom the high society of Istanbul will admire like the women in his novels. In this film, cross-dressing is not the solution to the tension of the film, not like it is in the beginning. Her gendered cross-dressing at the beginning of the film transforms into class cross-dressing at the end of the film. However, class and gender cross-dressing performances share many of the same characteristics and feature 'a pleasure in performance, a fear of discovery, the desire to escape limits and experience a freedom denied to the "ordinary" woman' (Tasker 1998: 40).

In *Belalı Torun* (1962, directed by Memduh Ün), cross-dressing gives mobility to a character through family relations and generations. A grandfather (played by Hulusi Kentmen) wants to have a grandson, which is a very traditional wish; however, he does not have one, and his granddaughter (played by Fatma Girik) has to pretend to be a boy (as seen in Figures 1.6 and 1.7), which is very modern. In this film, the granddaughter Belalı Torun gains access to an inheritance and the rights of family representation by means of

Figure 1.5 *Aslan Yavrusu* film poster – 1960.

cross-dressing. Family and kinship can be accepted as a symbol of normative identities and relations. Family can be considered as either an institution (Foucault 1990) or an ideological state apparatus (Althusser 1970), where not only labour power but also agreement and acceptance of power relations have been reproduced. Belalı Torun as a cross-dressing character fractures the idea of family and uses family relations as a space in which power is destroyed by

Figure 1.6 Fatma Girik in *Belalı Torun*.

Figure 1.7 Fatma Girik in *Belalı Torun*.

its own weapon. Briefly, by means of cross-dressing, Belalı Torun gains the sovereign power of fathers and husbands for herself. Victor Turner (1969: 38) suggested that 'every society is confronted by four tasks: the reproduction of populations in time, the regulation of bodies in space, the restraint of the interior body through discipline and the representation of the exterior body in social space and time'. Cross-dressing characters in all of these films destroy the tasks which confront society. This film also differs from other female cross-dressing films because in this film the cross-dressing character completely transforms into a man. All other characters think that she is male. However, in *Fosforlu Cevriye* and *Gece Kuşu*, the other characters know that they are women because they still wear some women's clothes and accessories. Their performance rather than their costume makes the cross-dressers men in *Fosforlu Cevriye* and *Gece Kuşu*.

As already discussed, the modernization process forced women to be seen in the public sphere as a symbol of the modern state. These female-to-male cross-dressing films which were produced in the 1960s taught women how to be a modern woman in the public sphere. On the other hand, however, cross-dressing performances usually require an alternative reading, as the cross-dressing performance itself asks a question of the system of knowledge and the idea of categorization. The presence of a woman in the public sphere was under surveillance by means of the aims of modernization. It can be claimed that cross-dressing performance provides a chance for a woman character to be mobile and to create her way of re-connecting the sources of ontological security – such as time, space, continuity and coherent routine – which were threatened by either modernization or military coups in these female cross-dressing films. In these films, the cross-dressing women characters are free to experience themselves because of the cross-dressing against the surveillance of modernization.

Turning to male-to-female cross-dressing films, *Efkarlıyım Arkadaş* (1966, directed by Türker İnanoğlu) attracts attention by involving three different forms of cross-dressing: gender cross-dressing, class cross-dressing and modern/traditional cross-dressing. This film reminds us of Marjorie Garber's (1992) point about the inseparability of gender dress codes from other dress codes such as race, class and ethnicity. Although she is a rich novel writer, Fatoş (played by Filiz Akın) pretends to be a poor girl in order to find a topic for her new novel about poverty. She comes across Gönlübol (played by Sadri Alışık), a poor young man, and they begin working together in a band. Then they fall in love. When she finishes her novel, she returns to her rich life. Gönlübol, who cannot understand what is going on, masquerades as a modern blonde woman (being blonde is accepted as being western and modern in Turkish culture) and goes to Fatoş's house. Fatoş's grandfather, however, falls in love with Gönlübol (as shown in Figure 1.8) and proposes to 'her'. In this film, how class and modernity are gendered and how they intersect with each other can be read by means of cross-dressing.

Figure 1.8 Sadri Alışık in *Efkarlıyım Arkadaş*: Hulisi Kentman as Fatoş's grandfather tries to seduce Sadri Alışık as Gönlübol.

In addition to these films, there are several examples in which the cross-dressing character can be seen as a supporting motif. For example in *Avanta Kemal* (1968), Fikret Hakan masquerades as a woman in order to be close to his lover. In *Beş Ateşli Kadın* (1968), Cüneyt Arkın masquerades as a woman in order to arrest a group of women who are laundering illicit money. In *Kibar Haydut* (1966), Yılmaz Güney masquerades as a woman in order to help his lover. As can be seen from these examples, the 1960s cross-dressing films described space, time, class and so on by using the tension between west/modern and east/traditional which was also the tension behind the 1960 coup. Moreover, cross-dressing films provided mobility between these terms, unlike the military coup. It can also be claimed that the cross-dressing films of the 1960s described the big city with its specific time, space and class to its new inhabitants who were encouraged to immigrate by the 1960 coup, and its aim to create a new working class.

I chose two films which belong to the 1960s political, cultural and cinematic environment for this study: *Fıstık Gibi Maşallah* (1964) and *Şoför Nebahat* (1960). *Fıstık Gibi Maşallah* was adapted from the western cross-dressing film *Some Like It Hot* (1959). This adaptation from western cinema (Hollywood) makes it valuable for discussing not only questions about what kinds of difference can be found between western and eastern representations of

Figure 1.9 Sadri Alışık and İzzet Günay in *Fıstık Gibi Maşallah* – 1964.

Figure 1.10 Sezer Sezin in *Şoför Nebahat* – 1960.

cross-dressing, but also how cross-dressing fractures the idea of the gendered westernization/modernization process of Turkey. Furthermore, *Fıstık Gibi Maşallah* can be used as a source in order to understand Turkification[3] strategies (figure 1.9). *Şoför Nebahat* (1960) (figure 1.10) became a very popular narrative in Turkish cinema so it was extended into a series and many *Şoför Nebahat* films were made. It was chosen for this current study because of its popularity. I shall now relate the stories of these two films in greater detail.

Fıstık Gibi Maşallah, directed by Hulki Saner, was an outcome of the 1960s cultural and political environment. A pair of out-of-work musician and comedian (Naci, played by İzzet Günay, is handsome and a womanizer; on the other hand, Fikri, played by Sadri Alışık, is a comic and responsible member of the group called 'Wasps' (*Eşek Arıları*)) who accidentally witness a mob killing are obliged by poverty and self-preservation to disguise themselves as women in order to get jobs with an all-female band about to leave Istanbul. The soloist of the band, which is called 'Blue Butterflies' (*Mavi Kelebekler*), is Gülten (played by Türkan Şoray) and she is seeking a rich husband to marry. Although Gülten believes/knows that Naciye[4] is a *woman*, Naci falls in love with her. Naci has to play three different characters in the film, Naci as himself, Naciye as a woman in the band and Kemal, a rich yacht-owner, in order to win Gülten. On the other hand, a real rich old man falls in love with Fikriye without knowing that she is a man. At the same time, the killers are seeking the two men who witnessed the mob killing. These mixed relationships between the characters create comedy which takes place between knowing, unknowing and misunderstandings. Furthermore, comedy underlies the journey from being a *wasp* to being a *butterfly*.

The female-to-male cross-dressing film of this period which will be discussed in this study is *Şoför Nebahat* 'Driver Nebahat and Her Daughter', made in 1964 by Sürreya Duru. After her father dies, Nebahat (played by Sezer Sezin) has to be a driver like him; in order to survive in a man's world she pretends to be a man. She is a divorced woman with a teenage daughter Hülya (played by Filiz Akın). Although everyone knows that Nebahat is a woman, Nebahat prefers to dress like a man. She behaves like a man. The main question underlying this situation is that if everyone knows that Nebahat is a woman, why does everyone behave as if she is a man? Briefly, it can be said that performance determines gender. No matter what an individual's biological sex, if a person acts like a man, everyone accepts that the person is in the frame of masculinity.

The 1980s: Neo-liberal transformation

After the 1960s, cross-dressing film production stopped until the 1980s. Then, after the 1980 military coup, cross-dressing characters showed up again in Turkish cinema. Therefore, the 1980 military coup and its effect are discussed in this section. This discussion can also help us to understand changes in cross-dressing performance over two decades. Even though the 1980 military coup ended with the 1983 election, rebuilding the sense of safety, recovering the boundaries of collective attachment and becoming accustomed to a new order took time for the Turkish people. The elections which took place immediately after military coups – in 1983 – were conducted under the military coup in order to consolidate the expectation of the military powers. For example, in the first election after the 1980 military coup, the party members who stood in the election had to be approved by the National Security Council. For the 1983 election, the army imposed a rule that none of the parties was permitted to criticize the military. I therefore chose to regard the second election as the end of a time of military coup. So the 1980 military coup ended with the 1987 election.

The army intervened in politics on 12 September 1980 when General Kenan Evren, the chief of the Turkish General Staff, led the military against the government of Süleyman Demirel. The army saw the reason for the 1980 military coup as being domestic disorder. The summer of 1980 was a chaotic time in Turkey. Political violence between left and right increased in the big cities and spread through rural areas. The work of parliament almost came to a standstill. Many writers and journalists were assassinated. As a result, in the early hours of 12 September 1980, the armed forces seized control of the country.

All political activities were banned and leaders were arrested. The activities of labour unions, the press, universities and voluntary institutions were restricted with the explicit aim of depoliticizing the polity. The Turkish parliament was closed by the army. All diplomatic immunities were invalidated. The Constitution was temporarily suspended. Fundamental rights and liberties were ignored and many people were arrested without judgment and tortured.[5] 'YÖK' (the Council of Higher Education) was established in order to take control of the universities and the academic world. The process of de-politicization undermined the traditional left and right. The 'emptiness' of political life led to an increase in identity politics such as ethnicity, religion and gender.

After the 1980 military coup, neo-liberal politics took hold by means of Turgut Özal's and the Motherland Party's (ANAP) politics. ANAP gained a major victory in the election of November 1983 which marked Turkey's return to parliamentary democracy, contrary to the wishes of the military elites, and Turgut Özal became a critical figure in Turkey's transition to a neo-liberal development model in the 1980s. The political party which he helped to create was based on a hybrid ideology combining elements of liberalism, conservatism with strong Islamist connotations, nationalism and welfarism. By means of Özal's neo-liberal politics, the middle class began to disappear. The service sector became more important than industry. A consumption culture and

Türk Silahlı Kuvvetleri bu sabaha karşı yayınladığı bir bildiriyle ülke yönetimine el koyduğunu açıklamıştır. Genelkurmay ve Milli Güvenlik Konseyi Başkanı Kenan Evren imzasıyla yayınlanan bildiride şöyle denilmektedir:

«Yüce Türk milleti. Büyük Atatürk'ün bize emanet ettiği, ülkesi ve milleti ile bölünmez olan Türkiye Cumhuriyeti devleti son yıllarda izlediğiniz gibi iç ve dış düşmanların tahriki ile varlığına rejimine ve bağımsızlığına yönelik fikri ve fiziki haince saldırılar içindedir. Devlet başlıca organlarıyla işlemez duruma getirilmiş, anayasal kuruluşlar tezat veya suskunluğa bürünmüş, siyasi partiler kısır çekişmeler ve uzlaşmaz tutumlarıyla devleti kurtaracak birlik ve beraberliği sağlayamamışlar ve lüzumlu tedbirleri almamışlardır. Böylece yıkıcı ve bölücü mihraklar faaliyetlerini alabildiğine artırmışlar ve vatandaşların can ve mal güvenliği tehlikeye düşürülmüştür. Atatürkçülük yerine irticayı ve diğer sapık ideolojik fikirler üreterek sistemli bir şekilde ve haince ilkokullardan üniversitelere kadar eğitim kuruluşları, idare sistemi, yargı organları, iç güvenlik teşkilatı, işçi kuruluşları, siyasi partiler ve nihayet yurdumuzun en masum köşelerindeki yurttaşlarımız dahi saldırı ve baskı altında tutularak bölünme ve iç harbin eşiğine getirilmişlerdir. Kısaca devlet güçsüz bırakılmış, ve acze düşürülmüştür.

Aziz Türk milleti, işte bu ortam içinde Türk Silahlı Kuvvetleri İç Hizmet Kanununun verdiği Türkiye Cumhuriyetini kollama ve koruma görevini yüce Türk milleti adına emir ve komuta zinciri içinde, ve emirle yerine getirme kararını almış ve ülke yönetimine bütünüyle el koymuştur. Girişilen harekâtın amacı, ülke bütünlüğünü koruma, milli birlik ve beraberliği sağlama, muhtemel bir iç savaşı ve kardeş kavgasını önlemek devlet otoritesini ve varlığını yeniden tesis etmek ve demokratik düzenin işlemesine mani olan sebepleri ortadan kaldırmaktır.

Parlamento ve hükümet feshedilmiştir.
Parlamento üyelerinin dokunulmazlığı kaldırılmıştır.
Bütün yurtta Sıkıyönetim ilan edilmiştir.
Yurt dışına çıkışlar yasaklanmıştır.
Vatandaşların can ve mal güvenliğini süratle sağlamak bakımından saat 5'ten itibaren ikinci bir emre kadar sokağa çıkma yasağı konulmuştur.

Bu kollama ve koruma harekâtı hakkında teferruatlı açıklama bugün saat 13'teki Türkiye Radyoları ve Televizyonu'nun haber bülteninde tarafımdan yapılacaktır. Vatandaşların sükunet içinde radyo ve televizyonları başında yayınlanacak bildirileri izlemelerini ve bunlara tam uymalarını ve bağrından çıkan Türk Silahlı Kuvvetlerine güvenmelerini beklerim.»

KENAN EVREN
Orgeneral, Genelkurmay ve
Milli Güvenlik Konseyi
Başkanı

Figure 1.11 1980 Military coup press release, broadcast on Radio TRT; the reasons for the coup are explained as public disorder, the insecurity of citizens, and the fact that parliament and institutions are at a standstill. The implications of the military coup are explained; curfews after 5.00 p.m., travelling abroad is banned, martial law is announced, parliament and government are repealed.

individualism became widespread. Squatter settlements (*gecekondu*) changed the face of the city and became a topic for academic discussion. The IMF and the World Bank became major agencies in the Turkish economy: thus, the path to a foreign-dependent economy was opened. Privatization was used to prevent state intervention in the economy. Culture became an industry.

When the 1960 and 1980 military coups are compared, it can be easily seen that the 1960 coup was progressivist and based on a social state, whereas the 1980 coup was reactionist and based on a liberal state. After the 1960 coup, a political generation began to grow; on the other hand, the generation of the 1980 coup was apolitical. The 1980 coup aimed at a centralist governance (Arcayürek 1986; Boratav 2000; Kongar 2000). These changes also influenced the cultural sphere and the cinema industry. That is why discussing the cultural changes of the 1980s is important for understanding the cross-dressing films of the period.

The cultural environment of the 1980s can be separated into two parts. The early 1980s were under military control with oppression. The second part of the 1980s was marked by neo-liberalism which gave people a false sense of freedom along with the freedom of consumption. The 1980s was a time of contradictions. According to Nurdan Gürbilek (1992), the 1980s was the era when those who were repressed returned. However, Turkey witnessed the fact that the things which returned were not the same as the things which had been repressed before. In order to understand this change, the term 'discontinuity' can be used and Foucault's writing can enhance this discussion. For Foucault (1972: 217), discontinuity meant that 'in a transition from one historical era to another, things are no longer perceived, described, expressed, characterised, classified, and known in the same way'. The new things, which had been repressed by the 1960 coup and returned in the 1980s, involved anger at the modernization that had repressed them and an insistent desire for power. Therefore, the new arabesque culture became a popular culture of the era. According to Meral Özbek (2012), arabesque music began in the 1970s as music for people who had left their traditional life in rural areas but never found their place as new dwellers in the cities. In other words, arabesque music was made by and for inhabitants who were neither/both traditional nor/and modern: who were in between. This first wave of arabesque was proud and satiated. However, the second wave of arabesque in the 1980s began to call modernization to account for its repression and demanded that their desires be satisfied (Gürbilek 1992; 2001; Özbek 2012).

The second half of the 1980s was a time when the 'meta/grand/master narratives' (Lyotard 1979) which had been believed to be the sources of Turkish national identity collapsed. Kemalism and its modernizing and westernizing ideas as meta-narratives which had been used to legitimize who would be excluded and who would be included gave way to pluralities and marginalities. Not only Kemalism and its meta-narratives but also Marxism and the Turkish revolutionist movement settled in fragmented narratives through eclecticism as a nostalgic image. They took their part in the new pop history. Desires which were different from each other came together and Turkish citizens witnessed the migration of ideas as nomadic. Collapse, non-continuation, temporariness and chaos are words to be used to describe the 1980s cultural environment. Briefly, it can be said that the contemporary discussion of postmodernism can be seen easily in Turkish cultural life of the 1980s.

The other distinctive feature of the culture of the period was the politics of naming and categorization. According to Gürbilek (1992), the culture of the 1980s was based on the labelling of parole, gestures, desires and anxieties. It can therefore be claimed that the 1980s both repressed and provoked parole (Gürbilek 1992). For example, on the one hand, homosexuality was labelled an illness in the 1980s; on the other hand, its label made it possible to talk about it (Gürbilek 1992). After the first few years of the 1980s, there was a move to examine, classify and encourage people to confess their intimate personal life, all in the desire to learn the 'truth' about others. Weekly magazines which contained the confessions of unknown people were a popular genre of the period (Gürbilek 1992). These cultural changes not only influenced but also shaped the cinema of the period.

The depoliticizing effects of the 1980s, arabesque culture and the politics of naming influenced cinema, and a run of sex films was followed by a run of arabesque films. In 1981, thirty-three films out of seventy-two were arabesque (45.8 per cent) (Esen 2000: 146). Furthermore, the social realistic films of the 1960s gave way to psychological individualistic films which included identity crisis in relation to the naming and categorizing politics of the period. With these changing narratives, a new formulation for film language had to be found. Long shots, less dialogue, less music and more silence were the popular conventions of the period's cinema. On the other hand, a distinctive feature of the cinema of the 1980s was women's films. According to Eylem Atakav,

> Turkish cinema was profoundly affected by the coup and its aftermath. Filmmakers could not present overtly political material [...] Prominent among

the film trends of the 1980s were films dealing with the coup's psychological effects on individuals (especially intellectuals) and women's films (in parallel with the rise of feminism in Turkey) with their depiction of female characters engaged in a search for identity and independence.

(2013: 48)

In order to understand the background to women's films in Turkish cinema, feminism and academic discussion about gendered identity should be discussed next. Under the de-politicization effects of the 1980s coup, politics had to be articulated within a new paradigm. Although second-wave feminism had flourished around the world since the 1960s, for Turkey, second-wave feminism began in the 1980s. Feminist rhetoric found fertile ground in the 1980s. The post-coup period witnessed the emergence of organizations which defined themselves as feminist for the first time.

This second-wave feminism is based on a critique of Kemalist *state-feminism*. 'Feminists discussed the meaning of Republican reforms for women and basically argued that these reforms did not aim at women's liberation for they essentially defined women as breeder and educator of the new generations: enlightened mothers of the nation' (Tekeli 1988: 22). In Kandiyoti's (1987) words, women in Turkey were emancipated but unliberated and now, as in the west, they sought both emancipation and liberation independent of the state. 'Educated, mostly professional, middle class women organized consciousness raising groups, petition campaigns, protest walks to highlight women's problems, wrote papers and published two feminist journals, instituted a women's library and a foundation against the beating of women' (Arat 1994: 241). A younger and more radical feminist group began publishing the journal *Feminist* in 1987. Another group identified with socialist feminism published the journal *Kaktüs* during the same period. About 100 women who called themselves feminist were involved in organizing activities. From the mid-1980s, colourful campaigns were launched such as the 'Purple Needle' campaign against sexual harassment in the street and in workplaces, and a 'Women's Circle' based on gathering women was founded in 1984 as a company instead of an association in order to escape the surveillance of the state, which was very strict at that time. For these new feminist movements, class was not the social basis. Issues of identity and identity discussion gained importance. The scope of the movement extended into individual experiences and everyday life. The movement became less hierarchical and less centralized, and became an alternative to conventional channels of political participation.

In scholarly works, discussion of feminism in the 1980s began with the writings of feminist scholars such as Şirin Tekeli, Deniz Kandiyoti, Nükhet Sirman and Yeşim Arat. For example, Şirin Tekeli's book *Kadın Bakış Açısından 1980'ler Türkiye' sinde Kadınlar* (Women in the 1980s: Turkey from the Women's Perspective) first appeared in 1990, providing space for a number of leftist women scholars to discuss women's issues in modern Turkey. At the same time, popular feminism took its place in the Turkish political arena by means of the writings of Duygu Asena, who edited the popular feminist magazine *Kadınca* ('Womanly'), which had nationwide distribution and a great impact on the dissemination of feminist issues at the popular level in the period 1979–95. Scholars such as Ramazan Gülendam and Ayşe Gelgeç Gürpınar claimed that feminism could be discussed by means of the 1980 coup. 'They believe that if the leftist movement had not been hit so severely by the coup, women would not have been able to question the hegemony of the male leaders' (Gülendam & Gürpınar, cited in Atakav 2013: 26). Fatmagül Berktay (1990) discussed women's position in left-wing organizations before the 1980 coup. According to Berktay (1990), women could speak out not only to the traditional patriarchy but also to the patriarchal left in Turkey only after the 1980 coup. In Turkey, first-wave feminism occurred in the early twentieth century around civic and political rights in the Kemalist ideology, and second-wave feminism took place after the 1980 coup (instead of in the 1960s) by bringing up issues such as patriarchy, violence against women and the use of sexuality in the media, and the motto of second-wave feminism was 'the personal is political'. This feminist movement and academic discussion about gendered identity in 1980s Turkey require a different reading of cross-dressing films from that of the previous period. For example, when discussing the modernization anxieties of 1980s cross-dressing films, it is worth remembering the feminist critique of modernization.

A huge decline in cross-dressing film production can be observed in the 1980s. There are many reasons for this decline. First, the depoliticizing effect of the 1980 coup influenced not only cinema but also the production of all art forms in Turkey. Also, the agenda of the feminist movement in Turkey affected cinema. The increase in the number of women's films was related to the de-politicization as film directors were trying to avoid the overtly political and women's issues or gender issues were not perceived as politically significant. This is also, why the feminist movement managed to emerge as a political movement within a period of de-politicization. Gender issues began to be discussed in cinema in different ways by means of the feminist movement, but not in cross-dressing films. Even so, it can be claimed that 1980s cross-dressing films were influenced by the politics of naming and classification. This can be shown in relation to the question why Şaban – a well-known film character in Turkish cinema – was chosen as a cross-dressing character in the film *Şabaniye*. In this film, Şaban-iye as a cross-dressed character challenges Şaban's labels as a foolish but wise, clumsy but virtuous character. The other dominant topics in Turkish cinema of the period, migration and identity politics, were also topics of cross-dressing films. I shall now discuss these films in greater depth.

Cross-dressing films in the 1980s

Coming to the 1980s, *Deliler Almanya'da* (1980) was the first cross-dressing film of the period. Directed by Yavuz Figenli, it depicts the trouble between two musicians who go on tour to Germany, Keko (Yunus Bülbül) and Zeko (Yusuf Sezgin), and a group of insane people who think that they are members of the mafia. Cross-dressing gives an opportunity for its characters to be mobile between rationality and insanity in this film. However, the description of west and east in this film is completely different from that in the 1960s cross-dressing films. Germany is described in the film as a place of insanity where the exploitation of eastern naiveté takes place, whereas in the 1960s the west was described as a place of modernism and reason. As explained above, the culture of the period can be described as an era when the repressed returned. The film depicts the adventures of two characters – Keko and Zeko – in Germany. Keko and Zeko as names have complex and deep connotations in Turkish culture. Keko was used for people who live in the east part of Turkey – especially Kurdish people – in order to humiliate them and emphasize how eastern people are vulgar, far from being modern and western, savage and primitive. Zeko is the abbreviation of the name Zeki, which means intelligent. Now, it is transformed into the name Zeko in order to humiliate the reason of the age of modernism. The names in the film give the characters an opportunity to be heroes for people who were excluded by the modernization process. The traditional east (Keko and Zeko) is going to Europe (Germany) and mapping the place, which therefore re-produces the place as the west's knowledge of the east. Cross-dressing gives a chance to escape being labelled as easterners. Blonde hair, modern women's costumes and their modern behaviour in the public sphere make them western (as the film poster in Figure 1.12 shows) and no-one understands their roots. They are visible – as western – but not recognizable – as eastern. It can be claimed that by means of cross-dressing mobility, they

Figure 1.12 *Deliler Almanya'da* film poster – 1980.

produce their own knowledge about the west, which had been presented as an imaginary land by the modernization process. In relation to the politics of the period, those who had been repressed by the grand narratives of Kemalist modernization now return, and by means of the effects of cross-dressing produce their own knowledge. It is thus not surprising that arabesque music is the soundtrack of the film, as the sound of the repressed.

Figure 1.13 *Beddua* film poster – 1980.

The other important film of the period is *Beddua* (1980) (directed by Melih Gülgen). However, its importance is based on a different gender confusion. The star of the film is Bülent Ersoy[6] (*see* Figure 1.13), a well-known transgender singer in Turkey. Before the film, she underwent an operation, so she was officially a woman and this was her first film with her new identity. However, she played a male character in the film, although the protagonist is a woman

Figure 1.14 *Şabaniye* film poster – 1984.

at the end of the film. This film might not be accepted as a cross-dressing film; however, it gives a clue about the new direction of the period in discussing gender issues. Transgender issues came out and began to be discussed and to appear in popular movies. Furthermore, the rise of underground movies in addition to Yeşilçam cinema can be a reason for the decline in cross-dressing films mentioned previously. However, one film which belongs to this period reached the peak: *Şabaniye* (1984) (see figure 1.14). It is probably true that there is no-one in Turkey who has not seen this film. Therefore, in this study *Şabaniye* is used from the 1980s.

Şabaniye was directed by Kartal Tibet in 1984 after the 1980 military coup. Şaban (Kemal Sunal), who lives with his mother (Adile Naşit), escapes a blood feud and moves to the city. Moving into the big city as a narrative motif parallels the urbanization process of the period. Şaban and his mother work in a music hall. One day, their enemy family traces them. In order to hide, Şaban and his mother decide to make Şaban into a woman, because a blood feud takes place between male members of families. Şehmuz (Erdal Özyağcılar), the son of the enemy family, falls in love with the 'new woman', Şabaniye. Şabaniye herself falls in love with Nazlı (Çiğdem Tunç), the daughter of the enemy family. Şaban introduces himself as a man whose name is Bayram to her. Therefore, Şaban has to play three different characters in the film, Şaban as himself, Şabaniye as a woman singer in the music hall, and Bayram as a brave and talented man in order to win Nazlı. Şabaniye becomes a famous singer and a rich woman. The rich, old owner of the music hall falls in love with Şabaniye and wants to give everything he owns to Şaban if s/he accepts his proposal. At the same time, Şaban's mother falls in love with the owner of the music hall.

Şaban is a famous character in Turkish cinema history created by Kemal Sunal and now in this film he becomes a woman and is named 'Şabaniye'. According to Savaş Arslan (2011),

> Şaban's films are different in that they rely primarily on the foolish but wise, clumsy but virtuous Şaban character who stays honest and true to his lower-class and often rural background (…) Şaban's character provides a nostalgic connection to what has been lost in the process of modernization. Frequently Şaban fights against greedy businessmen, landlords or merchants who want to change the environment of the small country small town or lower-class neighbourhoods.

According to Engin Ayça (2001), Kemal Sunal continued the culture of fairy tales. *Şabaniye* as a cross-dressing film encourages us to ask the same question: if a subject changes its position on the map of power relations by using cross-dressing, how are other forms of identity, forms of oppression and relationships between discourses affected and then relocated by this change? Şaban not only changes his gendered position, he also changes his class and jumps to the upper class by means of his cross-dressing gender performance. This change gains another meaning according to neo-liberal politics of period. Although Şaban is 'foolish but wise, clumsy but virtuous' and proud of his lower-class origins like the first-wave arabesque of the 1970s, Şabaniye wears not only women's clothes but also the tension of the period, and she desires back what modernization took from her.

The 2000s: The period of Islamic conservativism

The 2000s is the other distinct political era in Turkish history and an era in which cross-dressing characters appeared in Turkish cinema again for the first time since the 1980s. The final part of this chapter is therefore devoted to a discussion of the 2000s, when Islamic conservatism took the place of the modernist secularism of Kemalist ideology. According to Begüm Burak (2011: 144), 'From the mid-1990s up to the early 2000s, the Turkish Army placed far greater emphasis on its role as guardian of the basic principles of the Turkish state'. 'On 3 November 2002, Turkey's fifteenth general parliamentary election was won by the Justice and Development Party (AKP) … an avowedly Islamic-oriented party that had evolved from several previously extant Islamic parties. Since that election, few would dispute that the character of religion/state relations in Turkey had changed' (Warhola & Bezci 2010: 432). The AKP became the first one-party government in seventeen years, after a series of coalition governments.

The AKP used harmonization reforms for EU membership as a strategy to reduce the military's sphere of political influence. The military made its last attempt for power on 27 April 2007. Turkey experienced three memorandums (1971, 1997 and 2007) but I have focused on only that of 2007. I excluded the 1971 and 1997 memorandums because they can be accepted as only interventions in Turkish politics and did not affect everyday life in the way that the 1960 and 1980 coups did. On the other hand, 2007 was the turning point of the relationship between the military and politics. The 2007 memorandum is accepted as a breaking point by many scholars (Aydınlı 2009; 2011; Balcı 2007; Cınar 2011; Ozbudun & Hale 2010). The shadow of the military as guardian of Kemalist secularism had lain over Turkish politics from the beginning of the modernization process until it was lifted by this memorandum. The power of military forces began to decrease against the rise of Islamic conservatism after this memorandum. The political climate of Turkey changed, which is why I distinguished this memorandum as more significant than those of 1971 and 1997. The memorandum was announced on the internet, which is why it is called an *e-memorandum*, which was a very different way to exercise military power. In this ultimatum, a military force warned and secretly threatened the government against an Islamic shift in Turkish politics. The AKP government behaved very differently from other governments, which had been faced with military force of this kind. It reacted very aggressively and gave a counter-threat, saying that military force is only one part of government and that the military cannot behave separately as it had in previous military coups. After this memorandum, the relationship between the military and the state changed completely. This marked the end of the military's power as the guardian of Kemalist ideology and secularism in Turkey. It can be said that the 1960 coup was an extension of the Kemalist secular ideology, the 1980 coup was neoliberal, and the 2007 ultimatum opened the door for Islamic conservatism, which also influenced gendered identity discussions in Turkey. Although the 1960 and 1980 military coups both had specific dates, the 2007 ultimatum spread right across the 2000s. It started with the election of the AKP and its politics against Kemalist military service. That is why I prefer not to look at the date of the ultimatum but at the whole era as a complete political shift in Turkish politics.

In order to understand the relationship between gender discourse and other discourses of a period which created the system of knowledge of the period, the gender movements and tendencies of the period have to be discussed first. In Turkey, first-wave feminism occurred in the early twentieth century, second-wave feminism took place after the 1980 coup, and since the 1990s, new discussions and tendencies have been taking place in Turkish gender studies. Three main tendencies can be observed in the Turkish women's movement: the Kurdish women's movement itself, the Islamic women's movement and the LGBT movement. Many similarities can be found between these tendencies and the Black and lesbian feminism of the west. Similarities between Black feminism and Kurdish feminism can be gathered under three headings: representation problems in institutional practices such as academia and the labour movement; sources of knowledge such as history and culture; and the subjugated and ignored experiences of Kurdish women such as war trauma or subordination trauma. The Kurdish women's movement raised criticism against Turkish mainstream feminism for being ethnocentric and excluding 'other' identities. At the same time, the Kurdish feminist movement challenged traditional patriarchal Kurdish nationalism. Since 1984, the Kurdish Workers' Party (PKK) and the Turkish Army had been at war. Therefore, one of the topics on the Kurdish feminist agenda was the trauma of women because of the war. Contrary to the Turkish feminist movement, it can be said that Kurdish feminism involves women who come from the peripheral backgrounds of a lower social and economic class and are uneducated.

Another challenge to mainstream feminism in Turkey has come from political Islam. Islamists seem to have adopted identity politics since the 1990s. New lslamist intellectuals have emerged along with a pro-Islamic bourgeoisie, and Kemalist ideology and the path of Turkish modernization have been criticized because of their secular and somewhat authoritarian nature. Islamic feminism tries to interpret the Qur'an with a feminist eye in order to discuss the status of women in Islam. However, Islamic feminism can be critiqued for being stuck in a discussion about the veiling of women which has been conducted by men.[7]

Turning to cinema, it is necessary to talk about the new Turkish cinema of the 2000s. In the mid-1990s, Turkey experienced two different revivals in the cinema industry: commercial films with Hollywood style and box-office success, and art films with minimalist style and international success. In addition, one of the most important new aspects of the new cinema was an increase in the level of 'testosterone' (Güçlü 2011: 60). Some scholars have described this period as 'macho cinema' (Dönmez-Colin 2004) or named examples of the new cinema as 'male films' (Ulusay 2004) and 'weepy male films' (Akbal Sualp 2010). During this period, auteurs became stars to their niche spectators. Nuri Bilge Ceylan, Zeki Demirkubuz, Reha Erdem, Fatih Akın and Yeşim Ustaoğlu are considered to be the significant directors of the period. As Asuman Suner (2005) pointed out, in this new cinema, identity, memory and a sense of belonging were the new aspects of narration. The cinema of the 1960s had depicted the city in relation to modernization, whereas the cinema of the 1980s had depicted migration from rural areas to the city and the new face of the city in relation to neo-liberalism. According to Suner (2005), 2000s cinema depicted a rural life which remained for the new city dweller as a promise of happiness. For Suner (2005), the idea of the 'ghost house' is the centre of the narrative of the new Turkish cinema: a house which contains nostalgia and an idealization of what has been lost. Therefore, journeys and searching are the dominant and important themes of the new Turkish cinema. On the other hand, there is a conservative inclination in the cinema parallel to the politics of Turkey. Television series and films which depict the idea of new Ottomanism have been very popular not only in Turkey's domestic market but also in other Middle Eastern countries.

Furthermore, from the mid-1990s, LGBT people became more visible in cinema. In particular, Turkish directors who lived abroad, such as Ferzan

Özpetek, Kutluğ Ataman and Fatih Akın, made the discussion of such issues possible. Even so, in this period, sexuality was perceived in an essentialist way. Kutluğ Ataman can be considered as distinctive. He is proud of being the only openly gay film-maker in Turkish cinema. For this reason, the auteur's role in film can be discussed for LGBT and cross-dressing films by means of Ataman in Turkey by making reference to Richard Dyer's argument that 'It matters who specifically made a film, whose performance a film is. The lesbian/gay film makers had access to lesbian/gay sign systems that would have been like foreign languages to straight film makers' (Dyer 1986: 188).

Turkey went through a very interesting and previously unexperienced political shift which affected all aspects of cultural and daily life. The new AKP government demanded and expected a new type of citizenship which was completely different from the Kemalist ideal. The 2000s can be accepted as a time of transformation between these two different types of citizen. Cross-dressing films appeared again in this entirely new political environment of the 2000s.

Cross-dressing films in the 2000s

Cross-dressing characters appeared in 2001 for the first time since *Şabaniye* (1984) with *Komiser Şekspir* (2001, directed by Sinan Çetin) as a form of journey from a Repressive State Apparatus (RSA) to an Ideological State Apparatus (ISA) (Althusser 1970) (figure 1.15). A traditional and conservative father (Kadir İnanır, the main actor in the film, is a well-known star in Turkey famous for his macho character. Therefore, the film was launched using the image of Kadir İnanır in women's clothes), who is a police superintendent, masquerades in the police station as a malevolent queen for his daughter, who is dying: her last wish is to be a princess in a play. The superintendent uses the police station (RSA) as a stage (ISA) and its occupants as actors. The cross-dressing character explodes into an ideological state institution by taking occupants who are labelled as others into his service and creating a critique and comedy of the system. The superintendent's father is a bad-tempered and inconsiderate old man who cannot be spoken to. So the superintendent's best friend is a sculpture of Atatürk, and he constantly confides in this sculpture. Sculptures of Atatürk can be considered as the tower of panoptic architecture as a surveillance tool of modernization. Sculptures of Atatürk and sculptures of the war of independence can be seen in every government institution in order to create not only an historical feeling but also a surveillance tool. Furthermore, these sculptures not only keep alive but also support national identity by using a dialogue between past and present. This is because the sculptures capture and dislocate a particular moment in time, then re-locate it into the present. In one scene, he cries and calls out: 'How lonely we are, my ancestor. My Mustafa, my father where are you?' This scene can be read based on the conservative tendency of Turkey in the 2000s. The superintendent's image in his woman's clothes is far from the ideal militaristic masculinity of both Kemalist modernization/westernization and Islamic conservatism/ easternization. However, he needs a father because his metaphorical idealization is destroyed. His power domain – the police station – is a stage, and his body, where the masculine power can be seen, is a woman's. The destruction of his metaphorical masculine idealization can be considered as the destruction of Kemalist modernization. In this destruction process, the father is both a lacuna as an imaginary and a surplus because a real and cross-dressing character travels between them, because he is a father as well. He represents both lack and surplus as a cross-dressing father. In the film, the cross-dressing character changes the meaning and function of the state apparatus according to the shift in Turkish politics.

Plajda (2008, directed by Murat Şeker) is the other popular cross-dressing film of the period (see in figure 1.16). A pair of actors who play a lion and a robot in a children's play (Ali, played by Sarp Apak, is handsome and a womanizer; on the other hand, Can, played by Gürgen Öz, is a comic and responsible member of the group) who accidentally witness a mob killing and are obliged by poverty and self-preservation to disguise themselves as women in order to get jobs in a television serial. The narrative is almost the same as *Some Like It Hot* and its Turkish version, *Fıstık Gibi Maşallah* discussed above. A key question underlies these repetitions.

I chose two films of the 2000s to discuss in-depth in this study: *Şeytanın Pabucu* (2008) and *Hababam Sınıfı Merhaba* (2007). *Hababam Sınıfı* is a well-known cinema series in Turkey which was written by Rıfat Ilgaz as a novel. The first film of the series was directed by Ertem Eğilmez in 1974. After the success of the first film, nine further films have so far been made. Furthermore, the novel version of *Hababam Sınıfı* has been transformed into a stage play several times. This film was chosen because of its value for Turkish culture. Many generations grew up with the characters of *Hababam Sınıfı* and it is highly likely that there is no-one in Turkey who has not watched this series. *Şeyatnın Pabucu* was chosen because of its star, a well-known feminen singer in Turkey: Fatih Ürek. He is famous for his make-up, his exaggerated costume and his belly dance. This reputation makes the film more productive for discussing gender performance. These two films will now be introduced.

Figure 1.15 *Komiser Şekspir* film poster – 2008.

Şeytanın Pabucu (2008) was directed by Turgut Yasalar and Hilal Bakkaloğlu (figure 1.17). Burhan (Fatih Ürek) is an alcoholic swindler who is in debt to the street mafia and lives with his older sister. After a dream, he decides to escape, and he and his sister go on '*Hac*' (pilgrimage). His sister disappears suddenly and he decides to pretend to be her in order to hide from his creditors. At the same time, five other swindlers rent his basement. They pretend to be musicians;

Figure 1.16 *Plajda* film poster – 2001.

however, they dig in the basement in order to reach a bank vault. While they are digging, they play records in order to avoid being heard and caught. Burhan falls in love with his neighbour, Aysun Kayacı. The grandfather of one swindler falls in love with the cross-dressed Burhan. Another of the swindlers falls in love with the neighbour as well. In *Şeytanın Pabucu*, the cross-dressing character gains mobility between being religious and an atheist. In this cross-dressing

Figure 1.17 *Şeytanın Pabucu* film poster.

Figure 1.18 Nehir Erdoğan in *Hababam Sınıfı*.

film, the cross-dressing character changes not only his gendered position but also his religious status. He pretends not only to be a woman but also a religious, conservative moralist. In *Şabaniye*, Şaban changed his class in relation to the period's neo-liberal politics; in *Şeytanın Pabucu*, Burhan changes his religion according to the period's Islamic conservative line. Both of these situations coincide with the politics of the periods.

Hababam Sınıfı depicts the adventures of a group of male students at a boarding school. Each film in the series is based on a different topic. *Hababam Sınıfı Merhaba* was directed by Kartal Tibet in 2006, the first time with new actors. In this film, a woman named Arzu (played by Nehir Erdoğan), (*see* Figure 1.18) from outside the school, falls in love with the one of the students (played by Mehmet Ali Alobora) and masquerades as a male student and moves into the male dormitory to control him and his private life without his knowledge. In the film, the cross-dressing character gains mobility between adult and childhood/young life. By being at school, children are excluded from society; they cannot be seen in the public sphere. 'Once he had passed the age of five or seven, the child was immediately absorbed into the world of adults' (Aries 1962: 331). Referring to the work of Louis Althusser, 'no other ideological state apparatus has the obligatory audiences of the totality of the children of the social capitalist formation, eight hours a day for five or six days out of seven' (Althusser 2008: 30). By means of education, childhood and adult life are separated until students are 'ejected into production' (Althusser 2008). 'This can be considered as a "temporary restricted marginalization", a means intended to reach normality, that is de-marginalization, by way of temporal isolation and marginalization' (Dekker-Lechner 1999: 40). Arzu as a female can join adult life which takes place outside the school, and as a cross-dressing character she can stay in the dormitory whenever she wants. Her cross-dressing journey involves transitions between adult and child/young lives.

School is a place where all kinds of relationship between who knows and who does not know/knowledge and ignorance take place. In other words, school always involves a hierarchy which is produced by knowledge. Therefore, school and its power have always been accepted as a tool of ideology. In a book entitled *Erdoğan Ne Diyor?* ('What Is Erdoğan Saying?') (2012), which collected Prime Minister Recep Tayyip Erdoğan's speeches since 2001, the two most repeated sentences of Erdoğan's politics were 'we know' and 'we know well'. It can be claimed that the relationship between the citizens and the prime minister of Turkey is very similar to the teacher/student relationship. Therefore, after a gap of thirty years, it is not surprising that it was decided to release a *Hababam Sınıfı* film again.

In summary, in all these selected films, cross-dressing performers can escape from the system and at the same time express themselves within the system. After introducing the films, telling their stories and explaining their position in their genre, we can now discuss these five films in greater depth in order to clarify the relationship between Turkish politics and cross-dressing films and understand the relationship between the discourses by asking what cross-dressing does in the films in the next chapters.

After this broad overview of Turkish politics, culture and cinema according to when and how cross-dressing films and characters have appeared, two basic questions have been raised which will be discussed in two separate chapters. First, what does cross-dressing do in the films in order to provide a popular narrative of the time of military coups as a national trauma? Second, how does cross-dressing do that? The first question will involve choreographing theory. In the next chapter, I shall discuss three effects of cross-dressing in films in their particular political and cultural environment. The second chapter seeks to expand the discussion and the analysis of the films by using the idea of fractures in ontological security – gender, identity, body, language, time and space, which are the supporters of elements of ontological security, and continuity, contingency and routine – which are destroyed by cross-dressing performance. In other words, the discussion will explore how cross-dressing performance makes the intersections between forms or systems of oppression and discourses visible. I address this question by using Turkish cinema as a case study, examining whether the subject changes its position on the map of power relations by using cross-dressing, and how other forms of identity, forms of oppression and relationships between discourses are affected and then relocated by this change. In other words, how a subject becomes *a tourist in the geographies of power* by means of cross-dressing will be discussed. Films themselves will be used in order to discuss cross-dressing.

2

Choreographing theory

A **Tourist** is someone
who comes but does not stay,
who is both/neither foreign and/nor an inhabitant,
who is nomadic and placeless,
whose space is her/his performance: being on a road,
who is in between,
who knows at the beginning of the journey that s/he will return,
who seeks his/her own alienation,
then, who disappears suddenly.

Being tourist on the map of power relations

Cross-dressing is a performance which disrupts structures wherever it is located. I call this disruptive action 'fracturing'. Cross-dressing fractures ontological security, which is our sense of confidence and trust about things, persons, time, space and the world as they appear to be. My analysis of films has been focused on finding out what kinds of opportunity cross-dressing provides to its performer/character as this allowed me to examine the ways in which cross-dressing characters in films fracture ontological security. This discussion is important for this book because I use the outcomes of this discussion to answer the question of why cross-dressing films were popular in two specific times of military coup and one memorandum in the chapters which follow. After analysing the selected films scene by scene, I discovered three effects of cross-dressing gender performance on its subject/performer which fracture ontological security. In this chapter, I discuss these three principal effects of cross-dressing performance on its subject. First, cross-dressing provides an ability to be mobile on the map of not only gendered identities but also all relations between subjects and power. Cross-dressing characters in the Turkish films change not only their gendered identity but also n/either their other form of identity n/or their different connection points with power relations. The mobility of a cross-dressing character disrupts the stability of identities, time, space and language which are the connection points of the subject with power relations. For example, Şaban in *Şabaniye* not only becomes a woman but also changes his class identity; Burhan in *Şeytanın Pabucu* not only changes his gendered appearance but also becomes religious; and Cevriye in *Fosforlu Cevriye* not only becomes a man but also gains mobility between spaces which are structured by power relations. Her mobility changes the use of space and therefore she disturbs her connection points with power. Second, cross-dressing can be accepted as a way of satisfying a desire to be visible while at the same time escaping panoptic social mechanisms. Cross-dressing characters in films can escape surveillance because they cannot be recognized. They are visible with their new gendered identity as cross-dressers but not recognizable as self. Şaban in *Şabaniye* is visible as Şabaniye so the son of the enemy family falls in love with her, but not recognizable as Şaban so he can escape the surveillance of the enemy family even though they are always together; Nesrin in *Gece Kuşu* is visible as a man so she can experience life at night but she cannot be recognized as a woman so no-one abuses her; and Arzu in *Hababam Sınıfı* can stay in a male dormitory because she is still visible but not recognizable as Arzu and can escape the surveillance of school control. Third, cross-dressing is a means of escaping the fear of being other and at the same time experiencing otherness. All cross-dressing characters in Turkish films take pleasure in being other, penetrating other's time and space, looking with other's eyes, because they know that they are not completely transformed into other.

In order to discuss these three actions which fracture ontological security, in this choreography, the term 'becoming' is at the centre. I therefore begin the discussion with Deleuze and his concept of 'becoming'. After this, I examine the notion of the grotesque body. Finally, at the end of the chapter, I discuss the idea of the carnivalesque in relation to the 'experiencing otherness without being other' effect of cross-dressing.

Becoming and mobility

Cross-dressing characters in Turkish films are mobile both between different forms of identity – class, ethnicity, religion and so on – and the institutions of power – time, space, language and so on. This mobility of cross-dressing gains new meanings when we put it in the Turkish context. The captivity implications

Figure 2.1 The front page of the Hürriyet newspaper (12 September 1980) announcing the military coup and its implications. It was announced that the curfew started at 5:00 p.m. and that travelling abroad was banned.

of military coups restricted the mobility of citizens in time and space. Curfews, restrictions on travel between cities and a ban on travelling abroad were imposed by a military regime in the coups of both 1960 and 1980 (see figure 2.1 and 2.2).

Cross-dressing films in this period gave an opportunity to be mobile against the particular practice of the military regime for controlling subjects.

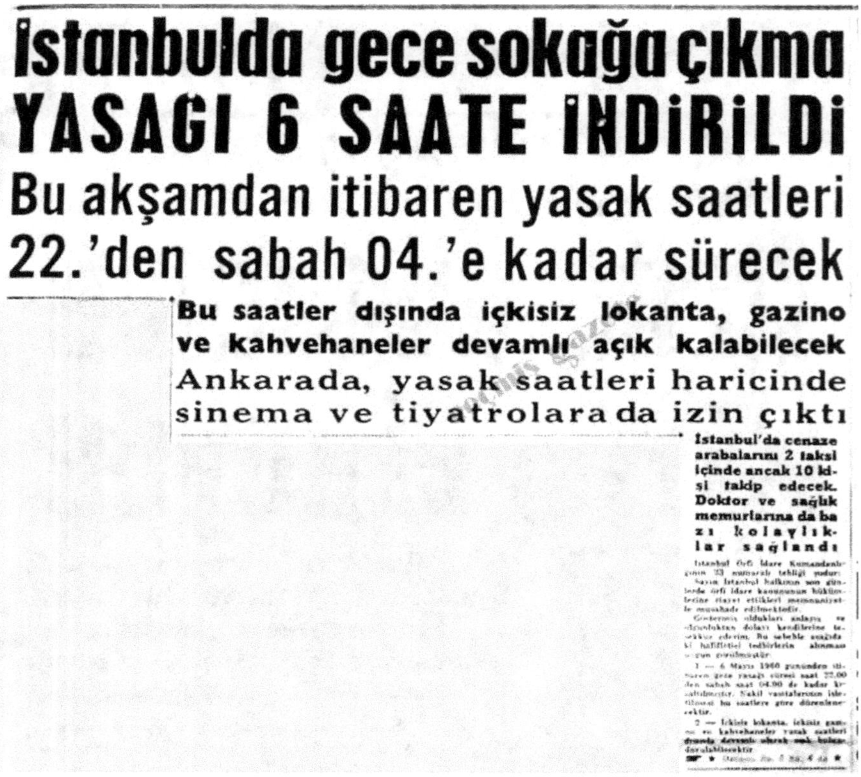

İstanbulda gece sokağa çıkma YASAĞI 6 SAATE İNDİRİLDİ
Bu akşamdan itibaren yasak saatleri 22.'den sabah 04.'e kadar sürecek

Bu saatler dışında içkisiz lokanta, gazino ve kahvehaneler devamlı açık kalabilecek
Ankarada, yasak saatleri haricinde sinema ve tiyatrolara da izin çıktı

İstanbul'da cenaze arabalarını 2 taksi içinde ancak 10 kişi takip edecek. Doktor ve sağlık memurlarına da bazı kolaylıklar sağlandı

Figure 2.2 News item in the *Hürriyet* about the new curfew regulation announced in 1960 after the military coup. Under the new regulation, the curfew started at 10:00 p.m.

Furthermore, military coups restricted the mobility of citizens by re-organizing the use of time, space and language. A cross-dressing character is mobile in the use of time, space and language. This mobility which cross-dressing performance accords to its subject can be accepted as one of the sources of this act of fracturing. It also fractures the implications of military coups. I discuss the idea of 'becoming' in relation to cross-dressing in order to discover the core of the mobility which is provided to the subject by the act of cross-dressing by arguing that cross-dressing is the visible face of the processes of becoming. In order to suggest that cross-dressing performance in Turkish cinema is an example of becoming, I first examine not only the idea of becoming but also some other terms around the idea of becoming, such as rhizome zigzag, and then I shall identify the connection points between becoming and cross-dressing performance in Turkish cinema.

Cross-dressing as a becoming

The notion of becoming provides a way of discussing the relationship between being, power and the body. In order to understand what becoming is, it is necessary to compare the idea of 'becoming' with 'being'. Whereas there is a stable, unchanging, unified, eternal and monism of being, becoming involves flux, process, multiplicity and change. In contrast to the enclosed system of being, becoming is dislocated, displaced and untimely. It can therefore be said that becoming forces the subject to experience a journey of possibilities beyond the limits and boundaries which separate human from animal, man from woman, child from adult, self from other. In other words, becoming is a process which takes place between combinations of self and other and therefore disrupts subjects and objects because it disrupts stable terms. So every becoming should begin with deterritorialization of self as a stable form of being. This deterritorialization is the movement of stable identity from an organization which has been structured by power to an anarchy which has no structure. The interest of being and of becoming is also different. Being focuses on a beginning and end point whereas becoming focuses on the in-between and on moving along a road which has no end point. Basically and briefly, becoming implies identity which is always in motion in-between.

Because of the mobility and relationality, which is involved in becoming, the notion of becoming refers to being in between but not in the middle. 'Middle' is the specific point between at least two points and determines the direction of movement. In fact, becoming is the way of erasing these two points which imply a beginning and end point. Becoming is not only moving along a road, but is also itself a road which is 'no-man's land' (Deleuze & Guattari 1987: 293) where there cannot be found any more points, which refers to stable beings and meanings. One becomes another but this becoming changes the meaning of being another and therefore another becomes different from itself in relation to one's becoming. A becomes B but at the same time B becomes C. Eventually there is no A, B or C. The doubling begins with a renouncing of the subject position. In *Dialogues*, Deleuze (2002: 6–7) pointed out that

> becoming is not one term which becomes the other, but encounters the other, a single becoming which is not common to the two, since they have nothing to do with one another, but which is between, which has its own direction ... not even something which would be in the other, even if it had to be exchanged, be mingled, but something which is between the two, outside the two and which flows in another direction.

This movement of becoming takes place in a 'rhizome', which is the other productive notion of Deleuzian philosophy set out in *A Thousand Plateaus*. Deleuze and Guattari used this botanical term in order to critique the tree metaphor used within the western philosophic tradition of linear, progressive, ordered systems. However, they did not want to use rhizome as a binary opposite to the western philosophical tradition since to do so would be a way of reproducing the model of binary thinking. In fact, they tried to destroy the western philosophical tradition and re-organize our way of thinking by using the term rhizome, in which one thing involves many possible meanings. Rhizome is a kind of anti-method which allows us to think many possibilities which cannot be represented.

According to Deleuze and Guattari (1987: 21), the rhizome connects any point to any other point, and its traits are not necessarily linked to traits of the same nature; it brings into play very different regimes of signs, and even non-sign states. Unlike a structure, which is defined by a set of points and positions, the rhizome is made only of lines; lines of segmentarity and stratification as its dimensions, and the line of flight or deterritorialization as the maximum dimension after which the multiplicity undergoes metamorphosis, changes in nature. Each becoming touches each other's becoming and changes not only the positions of the beginning and end points but also changes the meaning of becoming itself in a rhizome. Unlike a vertical and linear connections, a 'rhizome is a network of multiple branching roots and shoots with no central axis, no unified point of origin and no given direction of growth – a proliferating somewhat chaotic and diversified system of growths' (Grosz 1994:199). However, how can we use these arguments to discuss and understand the effects of cross-dressing performance in Turkish cinema? And why are becoming, rhizome zigzag and deterritorialization important for understanding cross-dressing?

Mobility of becoming can be a protractive tool for discussing cross-dressing in Turkish cinema which can be located in the relationship between body, power and being as well. Cross-dressing can be accepted as a process where the stable, fixed, univocal gendered identity begins its journey in a rhizome. During a cross-dressing act, one gender does not become the opposite gender, but encounters it. It is a journey and one cannot transform into the other completely. This action changes the meaning and structure of the beginning and end points. In other words, a man who wear a woman's clothes and pretends to be a woman can only change the idea of *being a woman* and make visible becoming a woman. On the other hand, the same man also changes the meaning and structure of *being a man*. In this way being a man gets closer to becoming other. There are two points here; first, eventually there is no more being woman and being man because the action of cross-dressing changes the meaning and structure of the beginning and end points; and second, cross-dressing is not in the middle of being woman and being man but can be at any point in between. Therefore, the positions of each cross-dressing are different from each other's. So a 'thousand tiny sexes' (Grosz 1994) can be freed from these two gendered stable identities by using an act of cross-dressing, which might be discussed as an example of becoming which is an open door to possible lives. Cross-dressing cannot therefore be discussed as a final product or form, but in this study it will be accepted as a journey and a process in which imitation and pretending cannot exist because becoming challenges the idea of an inner self. For Deleuze and Guattari,

> becoming is never a process of imitating, yet the one who becomes finds himself before another who ends up being in oneself. With the other in me, however, I am not substituting myself for another; the structure of becoming is not reciprocal. It is a zigzag in which I become other so that the other may become something else, but this becoming something else is possible only if a work (œuvre) is produced.
>
> (Lawlor 2008: 170)

In *Dialogues* (1977: 2), Deleuze wrote that

> to become is never to imitate nor to do like nor to conform to a model, whether it's of justice or of truth. There is no terminus from which you set out, none which you arrive at or at which you ought to arrive. Nor are the two terms exchanged. For as someone becomes, what he is becoming changes as much as he does himself.

So while discussing cross-dressing in this book, it should be remembered that there is a deterritorialization of gendered identity in the rhizome and this deterritorialization affects many other forms and other becomings which take place in the rhizome.

On the other hand, the rhizome, as discussed above, is where the open-ended linkages create possibilities of life and is the place of destabilization of social order politics and ontologies in relation to each other's becoming process. In other words, each movement on the rhizome creates new possibilities. When the cross-dressing deterritorializes gendered identity in the rhizome, this movement affects other forms of identity's structure. So, when we discuss cross-dressing, we should accept that it is not an issue which relates only to gendered identity. It affects and is affected not only on/by gendered position in power relations but also other on/by forms of relation between subject and power. For example,

Şaban in *Şabaniye* not only becomes a woman but also jumps to the upper class. The deterritorialization of his gendered identity allows the creation of a new rhizomatic formation so he not only changes his gendered identity but also his class identity. In *Şeytanın Pabucu*, Burhan not only becomes a woman but also becomes a *hacı* (pilgrim) even though he is an alcoholic. These two characters become tourists on the map of power relations by means of cross-dressing. Cross-dressing as a becoming allows questioning the existing power relations in the subject and reminds us that multiple possibilities are hiding in this power relationship. It therefore liberates its subject by providing mobility on this map of power relations. Cross-dressing characters who start their journey by transforming their stable, fixed univocal gendered identity into dislocated, displaced and untimely becoming can travel on this map. I shall give more examples of this situation and discuss it in greater depth in the case study chapters where the films and the cross-dressing performances in them will be discussed. Here, however, briefly, if the subject changes its position on the rhizome by using the mobility of becoming, this change affects other forms of identity because of the multiple linkages and connections between them on the rhizome. This change also affects the usage of institutions of power such as time, space, language because identities are structured by them. In other words, the becoming which is practised by the cross-dressing subject fractures the idea of stable identity.

On the other hand, against the mobility and anarchy which is produced by this mobility of becoming, power has its own weapon which can be called culture which is used for the reterritorialization of the subject. This weapon also uses time, space, memory, history, language and identity in order to destabilize becomings. Deleuze and Guattari explained this by the metaphor of the Global Positioning System (GPS). They suggested that culture and the elements of power help one to locate oneself again after the multiplicity of becoming and restless changes of identity. On the other hand, becoming challenges this GPS of culture and power. For example, becoming frees space because it takes place on a threshold which was termed the 'zone of proximity' by Deleuze and Guattari. For example, cross-dressing can be in three different spaces at the same time. They have their own time and their own story. These different spaces and times sometimes run parallel and sometimes they cross one another. These fractures highlight and make visible our fictional relationship with time and space, which cannot be discussed without a power relation. Cross-dressing characters destroy the continuity which is required for being but which is the enemy of becoming. Becoming destroys the linear perception of space-time. Furthermore, destroying the perception of time and space destroys the control of power over the subject. By means of destroying the perception of linear time and space, the subject gains flexibility. Cross-dressing disrupts the dominant value of presence, the here and now. Furthermore, becoming has no history because, according to Deleuze (1996), human beings have no essence but history. History makes us human. History is the way of producing a stable world and fixed identities. As Deleuze (1987) noted, 'becoming isn't a part of history; history amounts only [to] the set of preconditions, however recent, that one leaves behind in order to "become", that is, to create something new'. Identity is the story about ourselves which we tell others, and memory is the main element of that history. Cross-dressing characters in films must find their own way to create a new memory of their new gendered identities, so in cross-dressing films there are several scenes detailing how cross-dressing characters create new memories for their new gendered identities, because becoming escapes from the present and moves in the past and the future at the same time. These new memories can be accepted as sources of new identities. The ways in which cross-dressing characters invent memories include knowledge about the perception of social order, social interactions and the value system. Creating memory transforms a cross-dressing character into an active agent in the discourse, which is why these strategies give us a great opportunity to discuss the system of knowledge of a specific period. By creating memory, cross-dressing characters fracture history on both the individual and the social levels. When we consider cross-dressing movement in the frame of the rhizome, there is always a conflict between culture/weapons of power and cross-dressing performance – the visible face of becoming. As is obvious, I refer to the outcomes of this conflict as fractures. I contend that cross-dressing performance fractures time, space, memory, history, language and so on which are the main sources of power. In these fractures 'all forms come undone'. The mobility of cross-dressing on the rhizome provided by the idea of becoming is one of the main sources of fractures.

Visible but not recognizable

In examining examples of cross-dressing films from Turkish cinema, I argue that the cross-dressing character is forced by the narrative to change his/her gendered position on the map of power relation and to cross-dress in order to escape the surveillance of an enemy person, group or institution. The narratives of cross-dressing films usually create a need for the character to change his/her appearance. Thus, the cross-dressing characters are responding to particular circumstances. A kind of panoptic society is created for the characters which force them to cross-dress. The characters always know that they are being observed but are never sure when they encounter their observer. However, although they escape from the surveillance, they are not hiding and they do not disappear. On the contrary, they are still visible, and they are protecting their presence. Although they are still visible, they are with their enemy even more than at the beginning of the films; cross-dressing characters are not recognized by their observers precisely because of their cross-dressing gender performance. This situation constitutes the second effect of cross-dressing performance on its body: that cross-dressing can be accepted as a way of satisfying the desire to be visible as cross-dressed and at the same time escaping from the panoptic social mechanisms, because cross-dressed characters are unrecognizable as the self. Cross-dressing characters can escape the all-seeing social mechanism because although they are still visible, which can be accepted as the source of self, they cannot be recognizable, because their bodies are in the frame of undecidability and because cross-dressing makes the body and its performance artificial. This circumstance gains a different meaning in the Turkish context. As discussed throughout the previous chapter, cross-dressing films have been popular narratives at times of military coup in Turkey. Curfews, control over everything, even people's history and language and even banning words which are related to oppositional ideas, and rigid controls of daily routines as part of the implementation of a military coup all contribute to the same panoptic, all-seeing environment for the citizens. Fictional characters can escape this panoptic control of narrative only if they change their subject position on the map of power relations, which is also the desire of all citizens who live under a military take-over. *Being visible but not recognizable* is a crucial effect of cross-dressing in relation to military coups.

In order to understand the force behind this argument, I shall use the concept of the grotesque body. I have chosen to use the grotesque because this concept discusses the body and its position in relation to power. The grotesque body is both *being with other* and *being in other*. The differentiation between visibility and recognizability can be discussed as a tension between *being with other*, which is the main source of visibility because it shows the relationship between being and other which involves representations and hence produces visibility for cross-dressing and *being in other*, which is the main source of unrecognizability because it destroys both being and other and therefore involves unrecognizability for self. So the question of why and how cross-dressing characters can escape surveillance without losing their visibility can be discussed by reference to the grotesque body. Furthermore, the grotesque body can be discussed under the umbrella of the idea of becoming. I shall therefore discuss the grotesque body in relation to cross-dressing in order to explain the visible but not recognizable aspect of cross-dressing.

Cross-dressing as a grotesque performance

The grotesque body represented a powerful force. It is a body which is always in process. Russo (1994: 63) described the grotesque body as one which is 'open, protruding and extended, the body of becoming, process and change'. A grotesque body transgresses the boundaries between bodies. Extenuated or escalated, the distortional and shapeless body of a grotesque challenges the stable and unchangeable body. It is exaggerated and immeasurable: 'Grotesque played with a double image which belongs to both the upper and the lower sphere ... There is a swing in grotesque' (Morris 1996: 215). In this sense, a grotesque body is a degradation of what is accepted as a normal body. The grotesque body is an uncanny body which swings between life and death, subject and object, one and many by eluding borders. According to Bakhtin (1984: 26),

> the grotesque body is not separated from the rest of the world. It is not a closed, completed unit; it is unfinished, outgrows itself, and transgresses its own limits. The stress is laid on those parts of the body that are open to the outside world, that is, the parts through which the world enters the body or emerges from it, or through which the body itself goes out to meet the world.

It can be said that the grotesque is like a cross-dressing performance as both an outcome of binary oppositions and at the same time by destroying the boundaries between binary poles by opening its body to outside them. Cross-dressing, like the grotesque body, creates an uncanny body which is not finished.

The grotesque raises a crisis about the hierarchy and categories of the body. According to Bakhtin (1984: 352), in the grotesque, organs become independent from the body and are released from the organization of the body. Our faces can show our ethnicity or our skin can show our class, our reproductive organs can show our gender, and overall, the social organization of our organs shows us the limits and limitations of our bodies. On the other hand, the grotesque is a process of becoming where the body is freed from its limits. The grotesque destroys the field of body where the organs follow norms, values and meaning according to their functions and in relation to each other as social formations for giving their meanings to whole body, which is the main subject of power. The grotesque is the way of making body both visible – because it is still there – and unrecognizable – because it is freed from its linguistic and multiple codes and limits such as class, race, age and gender, and therefore this body does not belong to me or you or someone else. Bakhtin (1984) suggested that by means of the grotesque, objects and organs exchange their meaning. The grotesque eliminates not only the limits of the body but also the hierarchy between subjects and objects, and uses the body as an intersubjective and interobjective space. In the grotesque, for example, a table leg can be used as a human leg and this creates a new understanding of both a human leg and a table leg because there is no more human or table leg and the meaning of both is always double. This creates an unbounded, uncompleted body in transformation, a body with links to its past and its future in the present, not individual but the people's body, not private but collective bodies, open-ended, irregular and shame-free bodies. In cross-dressing performance, there is no limit between object and subject, organs and body just like in the grotesque. For example, a ball of wool can be a breast and transform a man's body into a woman's body. A ball can create a pregnant body. A wig transforms a man into a woman. So the cross-dressed body pushes the limits of itself just as the grotesque does. So cross-dressing can be discussed as an outcome of this semantic shift between organs and objects. The relationship between body, identity and a ball of wool is established by the exaggerated performance. For example, in *Şeytanın Pabucu*, Burhan uses balls of wool to produce breasts and buttocks for himself. However, they do not achieve the desired effect, so he exaggerates his walk to underline his new bottom. His exaggerated performance establishes a relationship between his body, his new gendered identity and the object which he uses to achieve it – in this case balls of wool.

The grotesque is not only about the limits of the body and the relationship between the body and objects but is also about the performance of *this* body. The grotesque is the way of challenging the power relation by using its own weapon, the body, because the term is interested in not what the body is – because it is about the limits of body – but what the body can do. Therefore, grotesque is based on doing, on performance. The main source of the existence of the grotesque body is based on not only becoming, but also doing and showing. The performance of the grotesque body transforms into something which is rendered nothing, artificial, unrecognizable or undone. That is why bodily exposure is the main feature of the grotesque. It can be said that performance takes the place of the organs in the cross-dressed body as well as in films, and that it is not organs but performance which identifies the body. The hierarchy of the body, which is produced by using the cultural and historical organization of organs, is destroyed by performance. There are no more penises, vaginas, breasts, hair or anything else which make us woman or man. Instead, doing takes place in order to express body.

I shall now move away from my key focus for a while in order to discuss Judith Butler's argument about performativity, which is another productive notion by which to discuss cross-dressing and its visible but unrecognizable quality. I read Butler's performativity theory and Richard Schechner's performance theory together and reciprocally for understanding the exaggerated performance of the cross-dressing body, because cross-dressing as a gender orientation involves performativity and as a grotesque body it involves performance. Performance can be considered a way of doing and of showing what the body is doing. Performance requires a long-term education process which began before us and will continue after us in order to be human and to learn the appropriate behaviour for daily life. 'Performance behaviour is not free and easy. Performance behaviour is known and practised by osmosis since early childhood' (Schechner 1985: 118). Performance covers all human life and all actions of human beings as a whole, because all human actions are repeated. These repeated features make actions into performance. No human action can be the first. The body as a performer resists the space which is surrounding it and by doing so it makes itself the doer. Performance takes place between the body and the space (Schechner 1985). Therefore all human actions as a performance exist in the space between individuals and can be visible in the relationship between individuals. They have interchanging values. Individuals value their performance according to someone else's reaction. They relay information about us, about our gender, religion, pleasure, desire. In this sense, performances show continuity and it is this continuity which makes people 'normal'. Performance is the restoration of human action (Turner 1982: 7). Performance certificates, preserves, regulates and straightens human action.

Gender is performance. In other worlds, we perform our gender. As Butler argues: 'What we take to be an "internal" feature of ourselves is one that we anticipate and produce through certain bodily acts, at an extreme, a hallucinatory effect of naturalized gestures' (Butler 2006: 15). Gender is constructed by repeated acts; it is not being but doing. However all doing also includes showing. Showing structures act as a performance. 'Gender with performance is based on external evidence and outward behaviour where gender exists as perception: the very components of perceived gender – gait, stance, gesture, deportment, vocal pitch and intonation, costume, accessories, coiffure – indicate the performative nature of the construct' (Senelick 1992: 9). Therefore, gender as a performance takes place in the gap between individuals. In other words, gender is exchanged between them. Gendered identity is based on doing, showing, seeing and exchanging.

> Performativity is a matter of reiterating or repeating the norms by which one is constituted: it is not a radical fabrication of a gendered self. It is compulsory repetition of prior and subjectification norms, ones which cannot be thrown off at will but which work, animate, constraining the gendered subject and which are also the resources from which resistance, subversion, displacements are to be forged.
>
> (Butler 1997: 17)

According to Butler, there was performance before performer. One does not only *do* one's gender; at the same time one makes an agreement with particular sanctions and prescriptions of discourse and in doing so one contributes to keeping the discourse alive. 'Gender is an act which has been rehearsed, much as a script survives the particular actors who make use of it, but which requires individual actors in order to be actualized and reproduced as reality once again' (Butler 1997: 277). 'Because performance behaviour is not free and easy it never wholly belongs to the performer' (Schechner 1985: 118). If we read Butler and Schechner together, we can conclude that not only gender but all forms of identity are performance.

Cross-dressing is the performance where repeated and stylized gender acting can be destroyed. Cross-dressing performance has two lines: biological-given-sex performance and cross-dressing performance. According to Butler (2006), 'Cross-dressing is not as real to copy or copy to real, drag is copy to copy.' The cross-dresser is both man and woman and neither man nor woman. In cross-dressing activity, body, performance and clothes create a new way of being which is beyond the category of sex and which is in the process of becoming. By means of cross-dressing performance, gender performances become artificial and annihilated. Repeated and stylized gender acting becomes unrecognizable. That is why cross-dressing performance seems to be exaggerated.

Turning back to the grotesque, according to Bakhtin (1984), exaggeration is a fundamental element of grotesque realism and implies the positive and assertive aspect of the term. Exaggeration of the grotesque is based on accepting that the body is not an individualistic entity but rather taking the body in a relation with the collective idea of body which involves not only people but also

Figure 2.3 The exaggerated body of Şabaniye in the poster of the film.

other living things and the material world in the grotesque. In the grotesque, 'an object can transgress not only its quantitative but also its qualitative limits, that it can outgrow itself and be fused with other object' (Bakhtin 1984: 308). The cross-dressed body exaggerates the representation of the sexual orientation of the body in order to highlight the new orientation of new bodies and this sense cross-dressing comes close to the grotesque body. The sexual fragmentation of the body (breasts, buttocks, hair) is highlighted. The elements of human anatomy can be seen to be in conflict and are caricatured. Cross-dressing might be perceived as a significant distortion of the known or recognized regulatory forms of the body. In the film poster for *Şabaniye* (*see* Figure 2.3), the body seems to be in conflict, with an extra thin waist, extra big head, extra short arms. The muscles imply being a man but the dress, hair and make-up imply being a woman. The sexual orientation of the body is caricatured. The body of Şabaniye expands its limits. The grotesque body of Şabaniye makes the Şaban unrecognizable but he is still visible.

The exaggeration of the grotesque can be seen not only in the exaggerated form of the body but also in the exaggerated performance of the cross-dressed body. The exaggeration of the grotesque can be read as an effort to accommodate the subject to new possible meanings or the meaninglessness of organs which give us our identity. In order to be a cross-dresser, first, the organs which identify the gendered body have to lose their meaning. However, losing meaning is followed by organizing new meanings for organs by using their exaggerated performance in order to establish their new relations with the body. No other women swaggers, guffaws or flirts like a cross-dressed character. When the old man sees Naci and Fikri in *Fıstık Gibi Maşallah* as cross-dressed characters, he falls in love with Fikriye and says 'I have seen many other women but I have never seen a woman like you. Look at your appearance (*boyuna posuna*), look at your wiles and coquetry. Look at your hilarity. *Hay Maşallah.*' He is unwittingly speaking the literal truth: there really is no other woman like Fikri because Fikri is not a woman, and Fikriye is not a woman either. In order to highlight his new sexual orientation, Fikri-ye exaggerates his performance and his appearance and the old man reacts to a woman of a kind that he has never seen before.

The idea of degradation in the term 'grotesque' is based on the relationship between the upper and lower spheres by combining positive and negative, in other words the relationship between self and other. The direction of movement of the grotesque begins from self, which can be accepted as upper and positive, and moves to other, which can be accepted as lower and negative. The exaggeration and degradation destroy the official certainty of the body: a body as entirely finished, completed, strictly limited and individual, labelled by language, which speaks for itself, a closed sphere, a single meaning.

The terms imply a body which is in the process of becoming. According to Bakhtin (1984: 317), 'The grotesque body, as we often stressed, is a body in the act of becoming. It is never finished, never completed; it is continually building and creating another body.' Therefore, the necessary conditions for the grotesque are deterritorialization and de-subjectification. The grotesque creates double. A transforms into B and B transforms into C, and eventually there is no more A, B or C. It can be said that the grotesque uses the body as a weapon against the idea of stable beings and definitions and resists the centralized organization of the body. Cross-dressing lodges itself on a stratum between two gendered poles and uses the opportunities provided by being in-between. It deterritorializes first gendered identity and then other forms of identity in an intersectional way and creates new conjunctions between them. Because cross-dressing is also the deterritorialization and desubjectification of identity, which is the main starting point of the act of crossing, it also has a double meaning as was explained above: man becomes a woman, and the meaning of becoming both woman and man are changed. Cross-dressing creates an open-ended, irregular, unbounded body which is constantly in the process of becoming. Cross-dressing uses the body as a weapon as well as a form of artificial performance.

A new question arises from this discussion about cross-dressing, the grotesque body and damaged performance: what will happen to cross-dressing if we accept that it is a grotesque body? In order to discuss this question, I shall use the term *undecidability* which was coined by Jacques Derrida. Discussing cross-dressing as a grotesque can help us to understand its undecidability and hence its unrecognizable nature.

The grotesque and cross-dressing are the frame of undecidability: 'Undecidables are characterized by their virtue of being able to function within certain oppositions that are essential for a certain argumentation, but undermine these oppositions at the same time because of their double meaning' (Derrida 1987: 40). Derrida (1987: 43) described 'undecidables as verbal properties that can no longer be included within philosophical (binary) oppositions; they resist and disorganize such oppositions without ever constituting a third term and without ever leaving room for a solution in the form of speculative dialectics'. Undecidable implies things which can never be mediated, mastered or dialecticized. In other words, the locus of undecidability is in between binary poles: such as cross-dressing between woman/man, as a centaur or mermaids between animal/human, as zombies between death/life, as the terminator between human/machine and so on. 'Undecidables graft one meaning onto another; they take up a key role as they bring together and separate possible meanings at the same time. Their meaning cannot be presented as "this and that" or "this or that". It is "and" and "or" at the same time' (Derrida 1987: 40). Undecidables are in the process of becoming, hence they are mobile: 'a process where opposites merge in a constant undecidable exchange of attributes' (Norris 1987: 35). According to Derrida (1987: 86), things of undecidability 'situate perhaps better than others the places where discourses can no longer dominate, judge, decide: between the positive and the negative, the good and the bad, the true and the false'. Derrida called undecidability a virus which threatens the thinking system and takes place as a slippery thing in the uncertain space which is the zone of indetermination between binary poles. Cross-dressing as a grotesque body can be understood as an undecidable body. Not only self and other but also self and objects produce one body together. Therefore, this body eliminates the hierarchy and limits of the body which give it official and institutional recognizability. The exaggerated performance of this body destroys repeated and stylized gender acting and creates a new way of being which is beyond the categories. Therefore, they cannot be always recognized.

Although the grotesque body and the cross-dressed body are there, they are visible but they cannot be recognizable. They are out of the meaning, materiality and reality which are produced by language. Linguistic reality states that 'this body is female', which also shows the limit of body. The reality and materiality of this statement come from the success of discourses which erase and conceal it and which mediate our knowledge about a body. On the other hand, cross-dressing destroys this reality and materiality of language and enables an escape from the prison of language to some extent. The cross-dressing subject is not a passive entity which is constructed by linguistic determination and limits but is an active agent situated outside linguistic monism and binary opposition. Hence, they are undecidables. However, at this point again a new question must be asked: what does cross-dressing do with this unrecognizability in films?

As discussed at length above, cross-dressing can be accepted as a way of satisfying the desire to be visible and at the same time to escape panoptic social mechanisms. The narratives of cross-dressing films usually create a need for a character to change his/her appearance. The characters can escape this all-seeing society of the narrative only if they change their position on the map of power relations. In *Fıstık Gibi Maşallah*, Fikri and Naci accidentally witness a gangland killing and the killers seek them everywhere: in order to escape surveillance, they change their subject position and dress as women. In *Şabaniye*, Şaban escapes from a blood feud. He is under the surveillance of the enemy family. In *Şeytanın Pabucu*, Burhan owes money to the mafia and in order to escape them he pretends to be his sister. In *Şoför Nebahat*, the male gaze and heterosexual masculine organization of society is the origin of the surveillance. Panoptic society is the centre of the narrative in *Hababam Sınıfı Merhaba* because the film's main location is a male dormitory which can be accepted as an extension of the school's disciplinary regime. The character can escape the panoptic social mechanism without disappearing or hiding because s/he is still there, s/he is visible, living, eating, falling in love and being loved but cannot be recognized, because the body is freed from its linguistic determination and multiple codes. By means of cross-dressing, the performance of identities becomes artificial and then annihilated. Because they are in the process of becoming, their bodies are the frame of undecidability because the system of power cannot label or mark them, cannot categorize them. This escaping from a panoptic social mechanism gains deeper meaning when the politics of the era of the films are considered. As already established, cross-dressing films and military coups have overlapped in Turkey. The implications of military coups are based on surveillance and make the panoptic social mechanism visible; the all-seeing sees all. The authoritarianism of a military regime observes its citizen everywhere, even in their homes. The streets are full of military personnel. Everywhere and at any time a citizen's ID card can be demanded and controlled (see in figure 2.4 and 2.5).

In the coup of 1980, 650,000 people were taken into custody, 230,000 were tried, fifty were executed and 229 'died of unnatural causes' while in custody. Under these circumstances, cross-dressing films have provided emancipation from panoptic surveillance. The films play out a fantasy scenario in which characters are emancipated in this way.

Figure 2.4 Military coups in action; archive photographs from *Hürriyet*.

Figure 2.5 Military coups in action; archive photographs from *Hürriyet*.

In addition, cross-dressing characters not only escape their enemies or guardians but also escape the obligations of society such as military service, bank debt, school attendance, exams (Burhan in *Şeytanın Pabucu, Hababam Sınıfı Merhaba*), and peer and neighbourhood social pressure (Şaban in *Şabaniye*). However, the type of authority figure which creates the need to escape changes according to each separate time period. In *Fıstık Gibi Maşallah*, the situation is not the cross-dressing characters' fault; they are accidentally stuck in the middle. In *Şoför Nebahat*, her father dies suddenly and she has to work as a taxi driver. The cross-dressing characters' situations in both films are very similar to the situation of the Ottoman citizens who came face to face with Kemalist modernization and westernization suddenly and in an unexpected way. In *Şabaniye*, the reason of the authority is the inheritance left by the father as a reification of tradition. If the neo-liberal politics of the post-1980 period are considered, the situation in *Şabaniye* gains another meaning. The post-1980 period can be read as a disengagement from Kemalist (Atatürk as the father of the Turks) tradition and an attempt to open the country to foreign capital. As already discussed, the 1980s culture can be read as a return of those repressed by Kemalist modernization. In *Şeytanın Pabucu*, obligation is structured by the cross-dressing character's faults. He is an alcoholic swindler and his authority derives from the mafia. In order to escape surveillance, he changes not only his gender but also his religious position. In other words, he becomes not only *she* but also *hacı*, a pilgrim. This makes sense if the Islamic conservatism of Turkey is taken into consideration. Briefly, against the authoritative figures in films who create the panoptic society, the characters use the period's dominant discourse as a weapon. They are countering the dominant culture.

On the other hand, after escaping surveillance, they re-produce themselves and their new identities as their own surveillance tool. All of these cross-dressing films feature characters who are able to penetrate spaces which are forbidden to them: the women's dormitory, the men's/women's bathroom, the men's/women's dressing room, without others' knowledge. In *Fıstık Gibi Maşallah*, Naci and Fikri penetrate the women's sleeping quarters (see in figure 2.6), whereas in *Hababam Sınıfı Merhaba*, Arzu moves into the male dormitory (see in figure 2.7). In *Şeytanın Pabucu*, Burhan uses the same changing room as Aysun. Knowledge shared with the audience about the true gender of the characters gives power to the cross-dressing character to be an observer. As well as penetrating forbidden spaces, they also become the observer of their enemy. Şaban in *Şabaniye* falls in love with the daughter of the enemy family and the enemy family's son falls in love with Şabaniye, so Şaban and the enemy family spend all their time together. Thus Şaban has access to all the information about them. In *Hababam Sınıfı*, Arzu becomes the observer of her lover by means of a cross-dressing performance and creates a panoptic situation for him. It is worth reminding ourselves that all of these films were made under and/or after a military coup, a time which can be described as militaristic surveillance. Citizens who live under a military hegemony try to create their own civil-based power domain and surveillance system where they can regain the power taken away by the military.

This part of the chapter is based on the recognition of the ability of cross-dressing characters to escape the panoptic social mechanism without losing their visibility. Furthermore, while they are escaping from the panoptical social mechanism, at the same time, they can be free from social obligations and they can produce their own surveillance systems. I have claimed that this power of cross-dressing characters is rooted in their undecidability. They are in the frame of undecidability because cross-dressing performance frees the body from the linguistic and multiple codes which are expressed by performance and organs and therefore destroys performance and the organization of organs. In order to discuss these two issues together, I have used the analogy with the grotesque body. In the next section, I shall discuss carnivalesque in relation to cross-dressing performance.

Figure 2.6 Fikri-ye in the women's sleeping quarters in *Fıstık Gibi Maşallah*.

Figure 2.7 Arzu in the male dormitory in *Hababam Sınıfı Merhaba*.

Life in a carnival: Experiencing otherness without being the other

Cross-dressing is the means of enabling the body to become mobile and undecidable just like the grotesque experiences otherness without being other. As I have argued throughout this chapter, cross-dressing provides mobility against the captivity of a military regime and a means of escaping the surveillance inherent in a panoptic military regime: a cross-dressed body who experiences otherness without being other creates a carnival against the discriminatory politics of a military regime. In this section, the idea of carnivalesque – in Bakhtinian terms – will be discussed in order to understand how a cross-dressed body as a grotesque body communicates with other bodies and how this communication enables the carnival in films. When the cross-dressed body experiences otherness without being other, how are other bodies affected? I shall argue that this effect of cross-dressing creates a carnival environment in the films. In order to establish the relationality between bodies and to determine the position of the grotesque body in this relation, carnival will be discussed next.

Cross-dressing and the carnivalesque

Bakhtin acknowledged the carnivalesque to refer to the varied popular festive life of the Middle Ages and the Renaissance. According to Bakhtin (1984), the folk culture of the Middle Ages and the Renaissance can be divided into three parts: 'ritual spectacles: carnivals, comic verbal compositions, various genres of Billingsgate'. 'Carnival' is Bakhtin's term for a bewildering constellation of rituals, games, symbols and various carnal excesses which together constitute an alternative social space of freedom, abundance and equality. Carnival brings together, unifies, weds and combines the sacred with the profane, the lofty with the low, the great with the significant, the wise with the stupid.

According to Bakhtin (1984), carnivals were sharply distinct from the serious official, feudal, political cult forms and ceremonies. They offered a completely different, non-official aspect of the world and a second life. They belong to an entirely different sphere. Carnival belongs to the borderline between art and life, but there is not a stage; there is no distinction between actors and spectacle. Everyone participates in it. During a carnival, there is only one law – the law of freedom. Carnival is organized by laughter, but this is festive laughter, not an individual reaction to some isolated comic event. Carnival laughter is the laughter for all people, and it is deeply ambivalent.

The suspension of all hierarchical precedence during carnival time was of particular significance. Liberating energy is an anti-authoritarian force which can be mobilized against the official culture. Carnival enables open-ended, irregular bodies and undermines boundaries. Carnival is a shame-free space. There are no mistakes in a carnival. Carnival refuses to accept fixed, pre-given social roles; it is a de-alienation of social life. The language of carnival is the patois of the marketplace, the language of a fish-market, what Bakhtin has called 'Billingsgate' language. A new type of communication always creates new forms of speech or new meanings given to old forms. Carnival has always provided an excuse to profane and parody sacred texts. Briefly, the power of carnival to turn things upside down is not only facilitated by bringing it into a dialogic relation with official forms but also 'it liberates people not only from external censorship but also from great interior censorship' (Bakhtin 1984: 94).

According to Bakhtin (1984), carnivals declined after the sixteenth century. Displaced from the public sphere to the bourgeois home, carnival ceased to be a site of actual struggle. Castle (1986) suggested that the reason for the decline of carnival could have been the crucial shift to rationalism and bureaucracy in the eighteenth century. The carnivalesque survived but only in marginal genres such as children's fables. I claim that cross-dressing films are a new space of the carnival.

On the other hand, Bakhtin's image of carnival has been criticized as a utopian fantasy. Carl Emerson (1997) stated that the weakest, least consistent and most dangerous category in Bakhtin's arsenal is the concept of 'carnival'. The degradation implicit in carnival is also an affirmation linked to the regeneration and renewal of authority. Carnival is a part of culture which is structured by power relations. In other words, the way in which authority is turned upside down during carnival allows its temporary suspension. Simon Dentith (1995) commented that the inversion which carnival allows was clearly not aimed at loosening people's sense of the rightness of the rules which kept the world the right way up, but at reinforcing them because the carnival space was also a space of violence and crime. Peter Stallybrass and Allon White (1986) criticized Bakhtin for his extremely positive evaluation of carnival and for ignoring that it was part of the process of civilization. However, carnival, like the cross-dressed body, fractures the official forms of time, space, language and gender. In the carnival between affirmation and the temporary suspension of official authority, the planes of power are fractured.

Grotesque realism and the body are the main elements of carnival. Normally, grotesque is related to the notion of the distortion and deformity of the way in which things are normally used for the purpose of creating irony. Bakhtin developed his own term 'grotesque body' as an inseparable part of carnival. As a hysterical celebration of the corporality of the body which eats, digests, copulates and defecates, grotesque is one of the main elements of carnival. In other words, carnival is the space where the grotesque body is encountered. As stressed above, the main feature of grotesque is its in-between-ness: subject/object, body/world, self/other. The space of this in-between is carnival. As has already been discussed, the rhizome is the space where all becomings encounter each other. Therefore, if we discuss the grotesque as an example of becoming, then we can make an analogy between carnival and the rhizome.

Cross-dressing, like a grotesque body, usually creates a carnival atmosphere in the films when the cross-dressed body encounters other bodies. Ackroyd's comment is relevant here, that 'cross-dressing is so deeply rooted in festive celebration and anarchic display that it survived centuries of persecution. It passed from the pagan rites of antiquity into medieval folk ceremonies and seasonal festivities' (1979: 51). Cross-dressing characters experience otherness without being other and in doing so they reject the pre-given roles. Cross-dressing liberates its performer not only from what is officially forbidden but also from inner taboos. Cross-dressing provides for the performer a shame-free time, a language-free space. One particular scene in *Fıstık Gibi Maşallah* illustrates this (see in figure 2.8):

> Fikri: I'm engaged.
> Naci: Who's the lucky girl?
> Fikri: I am.
> Naci: What?
> Fikri: I am. Why not?
> Naci: It's not possible. Please repeat: 'I am a man', 'I am a man', 'I am a man'.
> Fikri: I am a man, I am a man, I am a man – but being a woman is wonderful.
> I don't want to be a man any more. I will never find another man who is so good to me.

In this scene, Fikri experiences being woman without taboo, self-control or prejudice. He not only gains an advantage but also gets pleasure from being other. The experiences of cross-dressing characters affect other characters' points of view as well when a cross-dressed character encounters other characters. In *Fıstık Gibi Maşallah*, when the rich old man realizes that Fikri is not a woman

Figure 2.8 Frames from *Fıstık Gibi Maşallah*.

but a man, he says, 'No problem at all, it's OK for me. No-one is perfect.' The cross-dressing character also frees other bodies from their own inner taboos.

When cross-dressing characters who experience otherness without being other meet other characters who are freed from inner taboos and control, the carnival spirit becomes visible in the films. In cross-dressing films, usually at least one scene can be found in which the turning of things upside down is facilitated by bringing it into a dialogic relation with official forms. These carnivalized scenes take on the carnival spirit and reproduce their own structures, practices, parodies and inversions. These scenes enable open-ended, irregular bodies by creating the suspension of all hierarchical precedence. Anti-authoritarian forces can be mobilized against the official culture in these scenes. These scenes are sharply distinct from the serious official, feudal, political cult forms and ceremonies which take place in other scenes. In these anarchic scenes, cross-dressing performers experience otherness without taking the risk of being other. Furthermore, these scenes are meeting places for official and non-official bodies which are also provided by carnival. I call these scenes 'gathering scenes' because in them, all the various sides which belong to completely different spheres of conflict in the narrative gather and create chaos and temporary suspension.

For example, at the end of *Fıstık Gibi Maşallah*, one of these gathering scenes can be found. In this scene, police officers, killers, lovers and cross-dressed characters all meet in the bolo room where they eat, drink, dance and get drunk. Police officers dance with the killers, one male cross-dressed character kisses his lover (although the audience sees a lesbian kiss on the screen), and at the same time, another male cross-dressed character tries to escape both the killers and the old man who has fallen in love with him. The members of the audience watch the chaos of carnival where a special type of communication which might be impossible in everyday life takes place and they can join in the laughter of carnival. Everyone who takes part in this gathering is involved in the wholeness of the situation and this destroys the hierarchical distinction between police and killers, man and woman, old and young, moral and immoral by using very exaggerated actions. Such scenes can be read as 'a second life of people, who for a time enter the utopian realm of community, freedom, equality and abundance' (Bakhtin 1984: 9). In this chaotic environment, only the cross-dressed characters know the individual people's unofficial and official truths which lead to fear and oppression. They know who is who and whose character is formed by what kind of tension between fear and desire. It can therefore be claimed that they are just as much an element of this carnival as anyone else; in other words, they are the other of carnival, but they are not other, they know the system which is behind the chaos. This carnival which is provided by cross-dressed characters is the opposite of the solid official form of a military coup. At the time of a military coup, meetings, protests and even a gathering of more than five people are forbidden, whereas cross-dressing characters can simply create carnival.

The three effects of cross-dressing fracture the institution of power and any kind of power relations. Fractures can be considered, like the rabbit-hole in *Alice in Wonderland* (Lewis Carroll 1865), as a door to playfulness, transformation and a space where ordinary conventions have collapsed and where not only the construction strategies of representations but also the relationship between discourses on these representations which previously eluded them suddenly become visible. We can say that cross-dressing is a 'positive device for making trouble' and 'a traumatic response to political certainties' (Collins & Mayblin 2011: 4).

After reflecting on the key concepts related to the study of cross-dressing performance above, I explored the effects of cross-dressing performance in particular narratives. I identified three effects of cross-dressing performance on its subject: cross-dressing gives mobility to its subject not only between gendered identities but also on the map where all relations between subjects and power are located; and a cross-dressed performer gains mobility within the sources of power, such as time, space, language and memory. In order to discuss this effect, I used the idea of 'becoming' in the Deleuzian sense. I have suggested that cross-dressing can be accepted as a body which is in the process of becoming which provides mobility to the subject. In the context of a military coup, I argue that cross-dressing provides mobility against the solid constraints of a military regime. The second effect is that cross-dressing can be accepted as a way of satisfying the desire to be visible and at the same time escaping panoptic social mechanisms because the cross-dressed body is in the frame of undecidability. I structured this argument between visibility and recognizability. In order to discuss the relationship between them, I have used the term 'grotesque' and considered how this form of the body in relation to cross-dressing affects the determination of the body. Third, I have suggested that cross-dressing is a way of escaping the fear of being other and at the same time experiencing otherness against the discrimination politic of military coups. In order to discuss this argument, I had to establish the relationality between the cross-dressed body and other bodies, and to do this I have used the idea of carnival. After discussing the effects of cross-dressing on its subject, I suggest that these three effects fracture the institutions of power. In the following chapters, I shall explore the ways in which film texts are fractured and how these are related to military coups. In doing so, I will go back to the concept of ontological security.

3

Ontological security: Meeting point between cross-dressing and national traumas

I discuss the term 'ontological security' in order to establish a relation between military coup and cross-dressing gender performance in the Turkish context. I shall first discuss what ontological security is in the way that Giddens used it, what the elements of ontological security are and what kinds of relationship can be found between cross-dressing and ontological security. After that, I shall discuss ontological security in relation to military coups. This discussion might help us to determine the strategy of power which is used to stabilize subjects and the relations between them and how cross-dressing disrupts them. This discussion will take us to a point where state, military and cross-dressing performance meet.

Ontological security and cross-dressing

From the beginning of this study I have argued that cross-dressing characters in films fracture the institutions of power such as time, space and language which are the sources of stable identity. They are not only sources of stable identity but also provide security for this identity by creating a basic trust system of confidence, routine, continuity and relationality. It is this understanding which makes ontological security relevant to this study. I argue that the understanding of ontological security which refers to 'a person's fundamental sense of safety in the world and includes a basic trust of other people' (Giddens 1990:92) correlates with cross-dressing performance in films.

Giddens (1990) defined ontological security in the same way as Erik Erikson (1950), whose approach reflected identity as an 'anxiety-controlling mechanism' consisting of biographic continuity reinforced by a sense of trust, predictability, confidence and control, in the following way:

> [Ontological security] refers to the confidence that most human beings have in the continuity of their self-identity and in the constancy of the surroundings social and material environments of action. A sense of the reliability of persons and things, so central to the notion of trust, is basic to feelings of ontological security; hence, the two are psychologically related. Ontological security has to do with 'being' or, in the terms of phenomenology, 'being-in-the-world'. But it is an emotional, rather than a cognitive, phenomenon, and it is rooted in the unconscious.
>
> (Giddens 1990: 92)

Although the needs and the character of ontological security have been constantly changing, some elements do remain stable and we can call these stable features 'elements of ontological security'. They are a stable sense of being, confidence in the continuity of self and other, and trust in the constancy of surroundings, persons and things. All these feelings can be structured by the routines which are supplied by time, space and language, each of which is discussed in this study. Ontological security can exist and controlling daily life can be possible by using these elements and their sources. Each of these elements and their sources work as institutions of power for identity formation. All these elements which are conditions of ontological security produce not only the singularity of norms but also knowledge about norms. A person who is ontologically secure is expected to admit and reproduce this singularity and knowledge.

Ontological security is based on a stable identity, continuity of self and the experience of self as a real whole, and being alive to controlling anxiety. A man who masquerades as a woman (and vice versa) disrupts stability and continuity of being a man. This means that ontological security can be possible for *being* but not for *becoming*. Cross-dressing performance in Turkish films fractures the continuity and stability of self, because identity moves away from 'be' and comes close to 'becoming' by means of cross-dressing. As discussed above, the subject is accepted as stable by ontological security, and ontological security enables the subject to be discussed as 'being', whereas, on the other hand, cross-dressing shows the process of 'becoming' as discussed in Chapter 2. Cross-dressing underlines the impossibility of stable narratives of identity which is the main point of ontological security and 'opens the mesh of possibilities, gaps, overlaps' (Sedgwick 1990: 8) which are regarded as chaos, unpredictability and uncertainty in ontological security theories. It can therefore be said that cross-dressing simply by its existence disproves ontological security theories. Furthermore, because of the mobility which is provided by becoming, the process of cross-dressing deterritorializes not only gendered identity but also all the stable identities which the cross-dressed body has, because becoming dislocates, displaces and un-times all the categorizations which give identity to the subject. By means of becoming, the cross-dressing body gains the ability to be mobile not only between gender binary but also on the map of power relations. It can transform and change its relations with the power, and it is another way which disrupts ontological security. Cross-dressed bodies begin their journey in the rhizome and this journey allows them to transform all meanings of stable identities not only gendered identity. They can change, for example, their class identity (as in *Şabaniye*) but in this changing the definition and categorization of class identity also transforms into a completely new understanding; there is no more upper or lower class in this transformation because this action changes the meaning of classes. They can also change their religious identity (as in *Şeytanın Pabucu*) but this changing makes religious identity an area open to discussion. Because of their mobility in the rhizome, all meanings and categorizations become mobile; there is no more stable meaning or continuity of stable identities. Therefore, there is no more ontological security for the cross-dressing performer.

Another element of ontological security, in addition to stability and continuity of identity, is a sense of the reliability of other persons, things and material and social environments. To be ontologically secure, people need a basic trust system with roots going back to their early childhood. Basic trust is a trust in the continuity of others and in the object world. Erikson (1950) stated that early childhood development provides a basic trust system and he explained ego identity by using this system.

Ontological security is a kind of trust system which includes a danger-warning system implicit in the term itself without actually referring to it and which applies to all cultures and eras. It is the form of feelings of trust which help the continuity of not only self-identities but also the identities of others and communities. Ontological security and its trust system make it possible to answer questions such as not only 'Do I really exist?' 'Am I same person today as I was yesterday?' but also 'Do other people really exist?' 'Does what I see in front of me continue to be there when I turn my back on it?' 'Does what is perceived really exist?' (Giddens 1990). The flux of everyday life is the necessary order of things, persons and relations and this order can be supplied by traditions, rituals, routines and taken-for-granted activities all of which help individuals to avoid the panic which is rooted in the unknown, the pain which is rooted in loss, the horror which is rooted in the uncanny, and the chaos which is rooted in undecidability, and protects their identities against these negative forms of feeling. This eschewal of dangers which threatens the stable agency and its relations with its surroundings is provided by institutions of power such as the family, education, community, nation, religion and the active engagement of the agency with these institutions. Acquiring such trust becomes necessary in order for a person to maintain a sense of psychological well-being and avoid existential anxiety (Giddens 1991: 38–9). Ontological security is the way of controlling everyday life and it does this by the trust which is provided and supported by these institutions. The cross-dressing character destroys the reliability of persons and the trust system of ontological security in films. As already discussed, the cross-dresser is both man and woman and neither man nor woman and this paradox disrupts the feeling of trust in the stability and continuity of other persons. In cross-dressing activity, body, performance and clothes create a new way of being which is beyond the category of stable norms. By means of cross-dressing performance, gender performances become artificial and annihilated. Repeated and stylized gender acting becomes unrecognizable. It is this which allows us to discuss the grotesque body. It can therefore be said that cross-dressing is a way of destroying the basic trust system because it is structured by repeated acts which are the main sources of performativity. As discussed above, the basic trust system is the main shelter in which a subject can escape the dangers, risks and unknowability of social life. In this sense, the artificial and annihilated performance of cross-dressing as an undecidable grotesque performance destroys the trust system of ontological security. In cross-dressing performance, no-one looks real or whole, no-one ensures the continuity of identities and no-one is as s/he appears.

The basic trust system helps the subject to create routine by blocking out the fear of not knowing what dangers are lying in wait and this routine ensures the continuity and consistency of identity as narrative which we tell about ourselves by blocking out the chaos in which anything is possible. According to Jennifer Mitzen (2006: 342), 'ontological security is achieved by routinizing' which 'drives to minimize hard uncertainty' (*ibid.* 346). Routines regularize social life and produce self-knowledge about this social life. Therefore, these routines sustain identity and make it the active agency of daily practice. Routines work like cement between actors and social structure because our daily life is structured by routines. It is obvious when we should wake up, when we should go to work or school, when we should stay at home. In parallel with daily life, our whole life is routinized. People know when they last voted, when they got married, when they had children and how often they do such activities. So routine is used as a tool for social control. If the daily practice of human beings can be controlled, at the same time so could their way of thinking be controlled. Giddens explained routine as follows;

> If the subject cannot be grasped save through the reflexive constitution of daily activities in social practices, we cannot understand the mechanics of personality apart from the routines of day-to-day life …. Routine is integral both to the continuity of the personality of the agent as he or she moves along the paths of daily activities and to the institutions of society, which are such only through their continued reproduction.
>
> (Giddens 1984: 60)

'The maintaining of habits and routine is a crucial bulwark against threatening anxieties, yet by that very token it is a tensionful phenomenon in and of itself' (Giddens 1991: 39). Routine is therefore an action of bracketing the infinite possibilities of daily life and this bracketing makes social relations possible, otherwise human beings could not take in the infinite possibilities. Cross-dressing performance in the case studies opens the door onto the infinite possibilities of daily life and in doing so, it destroys ontological security because, as determined in Chapter 2, cross-dressing as a grotesque body usually creates a carnival atmosphere in the films. The power of carnival is based on carrying those infinite possibilities. Carnival times are sharply distinct from the serious, official, feudal and political cult forms, ceremonies and daily routines. Carnival refuses fixed pre-ordained social routines, it is outside daily life. The grotesque body and carnivalesque aspects of cross-dressing gender performance threaten routines by disrupting the basic trust system of ontological security. In the world of the cross-dresser, things and persons are not always what they are or what they seem to be. Things and persons are not monolithic. That is why almost all cross-dressing films end with a gathering scene, as was discussed in Chapter 2, to create a carnivalesque atmosphere. For example, in *Fıstık Gibi Maşallah*, all the characters and the different characters of the same persons gather at a dance; Fikri/Fikriye/Kemal, Naci/Naciye, Gülten, killers, policemen, old men, young men, rich clients, poor workers and so on. Each one's knowledge about the others is different. All hierarchies and official forms of identity and routines of these identities have collapsed. Ontological security could not work in these scenes. In the carnivalesque life of the cross-dressing body in the films, there is no routine any more. Conversely, cross-dressing performance can be possible only when the routines of daily life are fractured.

Cross-dressing performance in narrative fractures the element of ontological security: as an example of *becoming* it fractures the stability and continuity of identities; as an example of the grotesque body and performance it fractures the basic trust system towards others and things as they appear to be; and as a producer of carnival it fractures the routine of daily life. On the other hand, some institutions of power are needed to routinize daily life, stabilize identities and create a feeling of trust towards the world in general, such as time, space and language. Without organizing and trusting the organization of time and space and language which are the principal sources of meaning which enable us to be rational agencies, a subject cannot be ontologically secure. My contention in this book is that time, space and language are the principal sources of ontological security and are the connection points which take place between subject and power. Furthermore, they are the conditions of being.

In ontological security, a fixed subject and its fixed position are discussed according to changeable discourses, dangers and others. In other words, ontological security aims to protect the stability of the subject in power relations. We can therefore say that ontological security is for being, not for becoming. Cross-dressing is not being but becoming. Therefore, cross-dressing performance is itself inherently against the term 'ontological security'. This will be expanded in the following chapters when I examine how the process of fracturing functions.

Cross-dressing can be claimed as a way of expressing the connection of ontological security and insecurity together. Cross-dressing performance makes this connection visible by means of the fractures created by films. However, these fractures, such as becoming, carnival and grotesque, are labelled with power relations in order to inject them into the discourse as a safeguarding system. That is why they involve both the collapse and the renewal of systems. All of these terms help us to explain the subject's way of being mobile by using cross-dressing. Almost all cross-dressing characters in Turkish films can escape from the system and at the same time express themselves within the system. They can perform these two actions simultaneously because of their mobility, which is the tool for re-establishing ontological security in their own way. On the other hand, performing both actions together fractures reality and the order of the system: re-establishing ontological security which is threatened by military coups is a renewing of the system; fracturing the reality and order is collapsing the system, like the carnival and the grotesque. Cross-dressing's randomness, unpredictability, facelessness and undecidability in performance transform everyday life into a space of chaos which is the enemy of ontological security but which also involves possibilities of transforming everyday life into a space of resistance and renewal. However, between these two spaces, fractures take place. Fractures are the places

> where dominant standards of success so frequently reflect particular configurations of (capitalist, heteronormative, patriarchal) power ... failing, losing, forgetting, unmaking, undoing, unbecoming, not knowing may in fact offer more creative, more cooperative, more surprising ways of being in the world ... failure allows us to escape the punishing norms that discipline behaviour and manage human development with the goal of delivering us from unruly childhoods to orderly and predictable adulthoods.
> (Halberstam 2011: 2–3)

Against the demands for a good, coherent story about ourselves, for authenticity and for stability, Jack Halberstam invited us to take (and even enjoy) our ontological failures as starting points for an alternative ethics of the self (Rossdale 2015: 380). It can be said that, like Halberstam's point, cross-dressing gender performance also invites us to see the possibilities which take place between ontological security and insecurity which I call fracturing.

Ontological security and military coup

In the section above, I sought to make a connection between cross-dressing and military coup by using the term 'ontological security'. I shall now discuss military coup in terms of ontological security in the same way as I discussed ontological security and cross-dressing in the previous section.

So far, I have discussed ontological security in terms of subject, but the term has also been used in reference to the state. Mitzen (2006), among several commentators,[1] developed and discussed ontological security for international relations and claimed that ontological security can be discussed not only for individuals but also for states. Ontological security is needed by both individuals and states 'in order to realize a sense of agency' (Mitzen 2006: 342). According to Mitzen (2006: 342), states, like individuals,

> need to feel secure in who they are, as identities or selves. Some deep forms of uncertainty threaten this identity security. The reason is that agency requires a stable cognitive environment. Where an actor has no idea what to expect, she cannot systematically relate ends to means, and it becomes unclear how to pursue her ends. Since ends are constitutive of identity, in turn, deep uncertainty renders the actor's identity insecure. Individuals are therefore motivated to create cognitive and behavioural certainty, which they do by establishing routines.

States, like individuals, need their trust system, their routine, and their stable relations and they need their stable narratives for their identity which can be called national history, and in this history as narrative states are positioned in a particular time and space. States, like individual, can therefore face a crisis of ontological insecurity. 'By analogy, in the cases of states-as-persons, traumatic social encounters and other experiences such as major wars or other disruptive events, especially those related to the founding or constitution of these states, should undermine their basic trust and place them in a state of ontological security-seeking. This condition, in turn, translates into a strong attachment to routinized behavior' (Krolikowski 2008: 116).

Military coups are one action which threatens the ontological security of a state. According to Eric Carlton (1997: 16–17), a coup is a 'particular type of assault on the state and is an action made by government not of oppositions and it is kind of ideological orientation'. The definition of a *coup d'état* given by the Oxford English Dictionary is a 'sudden and decisive stroke of state policy which is carried out violently or illegally by the ruling power'. A military coup, according to Edward Luttwak (1968: 11), is 'violence controlled by militarism'.

> militarism is not just war as such. It is a social hierarchy of order givers and order takers. It is obedience, domination and submission. It is the capacity to perceive other human beings as abstractions, mere numbers, death counts. It is, at the same time, the domination of strategic considerations and efficiency for its own sake over life and the willingness to sacrifice oneself for a 'Great Cause' that one has been taught to believe in.
>
> (Landstreicher 2009: 85)

According to these definitions of military coup and militarism, it can be said that a military coup is an actor which destroys the ontological security of the state in many ways. First, a military coup re-organizes not only conceptualizations of social groups and categories, but also their positions in the past and accordingly in the future. Groups and identities move away from the centre, which becomes the space of the military. Group identities are shaken and questioned. For example, the 1960 military coup in Turkey brought leftist groups to the forefront whereas the 1980 coup re-organized the relationship between the groups of the left and the right and featured the right-wing groups. The military rulers after the 1980 coup sought to use Islam as a conservative force against the resurgence of the strong leftist movement of the 1960s. Military coups in Turkey disrupted the continuity and stability of groups and by doing so they disrupted the state's ontological security.

Second, military coups blocked the freedom of information and speech by preventing the ordinary circulation of newspapers. When there is insufficient information or explanation of circumstances, groups and events become unsettled and the basic trust system collapses. For example, 'between 12 September 1980 and 12 March 1984, the number of publishers, journalists, writers and artists who were interrogated, arrested and brought into court totaled 181, and 82 of these were convicted'; 'Newspapers were not published for 300 days' and 'On November 11, the moderate leftist newspaper *Cumhuriyet* was closed down by martial law command for "exaggerated and baseless" reports' (Çağdaş *Gazeteciler Derneği. Basın '80–84* Ankara: CGD *Yayınları* (1984: 197)). On 6 February 1980, Martial Law headquarters announced that foreign press reports critical of the regime must not be quoted or reprinted in Turkey. Under the uncertainty created by the blocked freedom of information and speech, people and groups suffered anxiety about what was happening and what was going to happen. It can therefore be said that the military coup changed the basic trust system of the state which was the basis of the state's ontological security.

So the actions which followed the military coup destroyed the daily routine of not only social groups and individuals, but also the state itself. Space, time, history, memory and language were re-structured beyond their daily, normal and ordinary usage and meaning. Spaces were used in different out-of-routine ways, for example, schools, sport arenas and stadiums were closed and transformed into prisons, many streets were closed and workplaces were regulated. Time was also re-organized by the military beyond the ordinary usage; for example a night-time curfew was imposed and people could only do specific actions at specific times. Acts of speaking were restricted; individuals and groups could not speak and use language in their routine way. For example, after the 1980 military coup, the use of the word *inkilap* ('transformation' or 'reform') was imposed instead of 'revolution' because the military rulers thought that the word 'revolution' had a direct relationship with the left-wing groups. School books were withdrawn and then were published again with the new word *inkilap*. The military made decisions on behalf of individuals and groups about what events could be remembered and what could be forgotten. In short, not only was the routine of now re-organized, but also the routines of the future and the past. Military coups broke down the routine of social order, which created ontological insecurity and destroyed taken-for-granted values, collective identities and groups.

A military coup imposes machine-like behaviour and a greater degree of discipline than normal. In military coups, the perspective of militarism determines what is proper and what is not. A military coup is a process of making and controlling meaning. In addition, in order to control the level of obedience, the imposition of a system of surveillance gains great importance. After the 1980 military coup, on 22 September,

> the Martial Law Commanders, who had taken over the administration in virtually every location in Turkey, were given broad authority in a revision to the Martial Law Act, law number 1402. The powers vested in the Martial Law Commanders included: censorship of the press, radio, television, books, pamphlets, placards; a complete halt or ban on all union activities; a ban or permits required for all meetings or demonstrations; close, restrict or control operating hours of all restaurants, theatres, night-clubs and other such places of entertainment; and double the pre-coup fines and penalties for infractions of the law.

Both military coup and cross-dressing gender performance destroy ontological security on two levels: the individual and the state. However, the way of destroying it and what is put in the place of ontological security of the two spheres are different. A military coup restructures the surveillance system of daily life, and on the other hand, the visibility but not recognizability which is provided by cross-dressing gender performance to its body gives an opportunity for the cross-dresser to escape this surveillance system. Cross-dressing provides the opportunity for its performer to be visible but not recognizable because it is a body which is in the grotesque form, so by means of a cross-dressing gender performance, the subject can escape the panoptic surveillance created by a military coup without losing his/her visibility. A military coup limits the movement of bodies and ideas, but on the other hand cross-dressing gives mobility to its body because its body is in the process of becoming. A military coup shakes and breaks down groups' identities and gives new meaning to being other, but on the other hand, cross-dressing gives an opportunity to experience otherness without being other by creating a carnivalesque environment for its subject. A military coup solidifies daily life and identities but on the other hand cross-dressing fragments them.

Taking all this into consideration, it can be said that the increasing number of cross-dressing films during the times of military coup in Turkey cannot be a coincidence. Both fracture the elements of ontological security, routine, the basic trust system, confidence and continuity of time, space, language, memory, the act of speaking, and the relationship between self and other. However, they each fracture and re-organize these elements in very different ways. There is something between the disrupting and re-organizing of ontological security which I have called fracturing. It can be said that cross-dressing eases the tension created by a military coup and by doing so gives free space to individuals to be ontologically secure.

Another question is what these three actions do in films in relation to military coups. These three actions disrupt ontological security just as military coups do and then re-organize it. In the Turkish context, not only cross-dressing performance but also military coups destroy the ontological security of both the citizens and the state by affecting the ordinary workings of these institutions. Both military coups and cross-dressing characters in films threaten the continuity of self, the constancy of surroundings and the material world, the reliability of others and the stability of social life by disrupting the institutions of power, time, space and language, and then re-organize them. This brings us to my main argument. Between these two actions of disrupting and re-organizing reality, power relations, order and systems fracture. Questions which are asked by cross-dressing performance remain in the air and are never fully lost. This shows us the questionability of categories, normality, order and power relations; it does not matter whether it re-organizes them or not. I use the term 'fracturing' to describe these moments and enable them to be discussed. These fractures take place on the elements of ontological security.

If ontological security is understood as a state of confidence in 'who I am and what everything is, and that everyone around me is how they seem to be', then, cross-dressing destroys the idea of believing that the person with whom I am is not how s/he seems to be. Therefore, cross-dressing destroys the ontological security of other and its audiences in terms of relationality and at the same time enables its body to re-organize its ontological security. A military coup destroys ontological security as well, but in a different way. It destroys routines and the basic trust system at state level whereas cross-dressing works on the individual level. That is why, when ontological security is threatened by a military coup at state level, cross-dressing films appear in order to relieve the anxiety. And that is why I have used the term 'ontological security', because military coups and cross-dressing can be discussed together and can be bound to each other by using the concept of ontological security. On the other hand, military coups curtail these possibilities openly and it is this which makes them visible.

4

Fracturing language, voice and speech: Whose voice, whose language, who speaks? I cannot hear

The cross-dressing body in films allows multiple interpretations of language which show us the way in which the world is contracted by language. I call these moments fracturing in language, where the ontological security is disrupted and therefore the discourses which involve language and the relationships between them can be seen. Cross-dressing films contain a typical scene strategy about sound/voice, language and speech. The strategies of these scenes are usually the same: cross-dressing characters come face-to-face with various un-ordinary situations: for example, s/he comes across sexual abuse or is attracted by a woman, or enters a dangerous situation such as encountering killers. In situations like these, cross-dressing characters express their feelings in their 'original' voice and style for a moment, and then realize their position and revert to their cross-dressed performance. These moments of forgetfulness cannot be recognized by other characters in the film, and even if they can be heard by other characters, they cannot be understood. These moments are usually treated as a source of comedy and irony in the films. In this chapter, I explore scenes like these under the idea of language fracturing by asking why these scenes are repeated, what kinds of opportunity they provide to us and how they fracture ontological security in relation to military coups.

Everything which is unheard, misunderstood or repeated but with different voices, words or sounds can be accepted as a kind of citation borrowed by a cross-dressing character from another text. This multiple-voiced utterance allows us to recognize that multiple layers of identity of self and other may be present in a single body. In these fracturing moments, the cross-dressing body opens itself to at least two different speakers. These two speakers express themselves by using different voices and intonations at the same time from the same body. The audience can hear at least two voices, two pieces of information, two points of view, two languages which all talk with each other dialogically. One body is a space of dialogic relationship between multiple voices which address different listeners with different aims. These scenes can therefore be accepted as a conversation of different discourses of the period which embody a gendered way. In other words, one discourse can be understood and interpreted only through the other system of discourses. This encounter between discourses takes place at the level of language, voice, sound and speech in these scenes. Because of these encounters, the consistency, stability and ability to hide the structure as a natural truth of language, voice, speech or sound are collapsed, and it is this which I call the fracturing of language/voice/sound/speech. These fractures make the relationship between power and them visible. This inter-relation between the two creates fractures not only on acoustic and linguistic levels but also in oncologic security, as discussed above.

When we look at examples in the Turkish context, we can identify three different usages: (1) the 'original' voice of the cross-dressed character which cannot be heard; (2) even if it is heard it cannot be understood; and (3) the cross-dressed character can use language freely from different gender employments. I shall therefore discuss three different forms of fracturing in relation to the three effects of cross-dressing performance on its subject. First, I discuss voice and body fracturing. The same body uses different types of voice performance at the same time. The cross-dressed characters speak with someone else using the 'cross-dressed gender' voice and style but at the same time they give their own reaction to themselves using their 'biologically given' voice. This destroys the unity of body and fractures the organic relations between body and voice. Hence it destroys the relationship between sound and image. This fracturing relieves the anxiety of citizens who do not want to lose their voice under military rule. Second, I discuss, fracturing between listening object and speaking subject. Cross-dressing characters also ignore the listening object when they speak to themselves. These moments are lost time for the listening objects. At these moments, the listening objects cannot talk, and although they are hearing the voice of the cross-dressed character they cannot understand it. This situation is related to the *visible but not recognizable* discussion. Under the effect of this fracture, cross-dressing can speak freely without being judged by others. They can escape the surveillance because no-one can hear them, and even if they do hear they cannot understand. These fractures help citizens who are exposed to the restriction of freedom of speech by military rule. In the final section, I discuss the language employment of femininity and masculinity fracturing. This situation is based not only on the different voices of woman and man but also on the different ways in which women and men use language, and I combine this idea with the *experiencing otherness without being other* effect of cross-dressing performance in its subject in relation to the discrimination politics of military coups.

Voice and body fracturing

Cross-dressing involves not only body performance but also voice performance, but this is commonly passed over in discussions of cross-dressing. Cross-dressing characters use voices to disrupt and then re-organize ontological security by breaking the bond between voice and gender which is accepted as organic and natural. Not only are the body and the identities of cross-dressing characters mobile but their voice which is provided by becoming is also mobile. This mobility of voice fractures ontological security because it creates ambiguity about the stability and continuity of a person who speaks with different voices for the listener. This fracturing gives the speaker an opportunity to speak freely, which is one of the main demands of citizens who live under military rule. However, firstly I should provide an overview of the possible meanings of voice as a discourse for this study. After discussing voice, I shall examine what happens in these voice alteration scenes.

When we look at theories about the body, we can easily see that the concept of voice has been largely ignored and excluded from these discussions. The body has usually been theorized without voice as silent. Even in her groundbreaking study *Gender Trouble*, Judith Butler (2006) discussed body and gender performativity in terms of the visual aspect and gave less consideration to the vocal act and performativity of the body. And it is not only gender studies which have made this error: linguistic studies too have overlooked theorizing the voice to a great extent. According to Jonathan Sterne (2003: 13), however, 'voice is an important artefact of the political human sphere'. If this is so, why has voice been ignored and excluded from discussions? Asking this question and trying to find some possible reasons can help us to understand the unique values of voice.

Adriana Cavarero (2005: 14) stated that 'the metaphysical tradition tends towards a "devocalization" of speech, a method, or strategic decision to thematise speech while neglecting the vocality of speakers'. Mladen Dolar (2006: 15) explained the reason for this ignoring of voice by saying, 'voice is that which cannot be said'. That is why voice has been discussed only in relation to language, speech, utterance, singing and reproductions but has not been discussed for its own sake because it is outside enunciation. It can be said that voice is associated with time and, in contrast, writing is spatial organization. Because of its spatiality, writing has always been accepted as the condition of language. An idea must be repeated, expressed and constituted in order to categorize and measure it. That is why, until the development of recording technologies, writing and gaze had been the subject of philosophy. Turning to the question which I set out in the previous paragraph, from these discussions three aspects of voice can be found: it is a temporal organization; it is here and now; it is outside language and cannot be said.

On the other hand, I suggest that there is another reason for the fact that voice has been ignored, and it is related to the non-resident nature of voice. Voice is a nomadic act: it does not completely belong to the body and it does not completely belong to language. Voice in terms of body can be accepted as being both inside and outside not only the body but also language. Voice is always in-between, so is cross-dressing. In other words, voice is a transgressive production which is produced by the body and its outside, and language and its outside together. Voice is therefore a relation between outside and inside both the body and its surroundings, and language and its surroundings. In this relationship, the body orients itself according to its surroundings by using voice. This is why voice is the source of orientation for the body. Then, we can say that voice is not only a temporal activity but also a spatial activity, countering Cavarero's argument.

Because voice is in-between and therefore relational, as one element of the orientation of the body, voice, as Michelle Duncan (2004: 291) put it, 'produces effects of the body on the other bodies', which is why voice can disrupt ontological security. For example, in *Hababam Sınıfı Merhaba*, the effects of the cross-dressed character's ambiguity of voice create anxiety in the other bodies. In this scene (see in figure 4.1), Arzu, a female-to-male cross-dressing character, reacts to being given presents in a woman's voice. After hearing this voice, the other students in the class react, and one of them says, 'You are such a nice, kind man, but when you speak with a woman's voice I am afraid of you and it makes me nervous. Is there any cure for your voice?' The reason for the other student's discomfort is not the woman's voice, because they are living in a male dormitory and the main topic of conversation among them in the film is anything which is about women. The alteration of her voice creates 'horror' because it destroys the positions of the other students relative to the cross-dressed character as a classmate. This situation goes beyond the ordinary relations between all the male classmates and breaks their routine. No-one knows how he (or she) should react because this ambiguity destroys their ontological security. As discussed above, voice is an element of ontological security and its ambiguity casts doubt on the reality and truth about the world which has to be accepted without doubt in order to survive, according to arguments of ontological security. In other words, the ambiguity of the other's voice destroys ontological security and opens the door to the uncanny because the truth about the other, which also determines us, loses its safety, which creates anxiety about the reliability of our surroundings.

In another example, in *Şabaniye*, while Şabaniye is walking down a road as a cross-dressed character, street workmen use slang words to abuse at her (see in figure 4.2). Şabaniye needs to re-organize relations between her/himself and them and in order to protect her/himself uses a man's voice. It is not this male voice but the alteration of the voice in relation to the body which creates ambiguity and stops the workmen's abuse because the alteration of Şabaniye's voice breaks the basic trust systems about the stability and continuity of others and the routine which is created by this basic trust systems, and because workmen know how to abuse at a women and how a woman who receives such treatment will react in the routine of ordinary life. A body's voice is a kind of boundary between bodily interiorities and exteriorities, but this boundary is also a meeting point of inside and outside, which is why voice is a relational phenomenon in which political, cultural and gendered and social routines are

Figure 4.1 A frame from *Hababam Sınıfı Merhaba:* Arzu in the male dormitory.

Figure 4.2 A frame from *Şabaniye*; Şabaniye reacts to the workmen's catcalls.

embedded. That is why voice is not a basic container of language and discourse, but also itself is a discourse which determines any kind of relation between self and other. Hence a cross-dressing character can use his/her voice in order to re-structure the relationship between his/her body and the bodies of others. A cross-dressing character can break the ontological security of others by using voice, in which any kind of identity is embedded, to protect his/her identity and can reconstruct this fractured ontological security according to his/her desires and needs at the time. If we reconsider that these films were popular narratives at times of military coups, we can easily say that this situation is the necessary relief of citizens whose ontological security has broken down in a sudden and unexpected way, and who do not want to lose their voice under military rule.

Voice performativity as a materialization of body is a social construct which contains an exchange value. This exchange value makes it a discursive practice because not only does the body produce voice but also voice produces the body as well. This is why voice cannot be discussed without body/gender performance. Although 'the voice manifests the unique being of each human being' and 'this uniqueness makes itself heard as voice' (Cavarero 2005: 173), Nina Eidsheim (2008: 178) suggested that 'a source is heard according to schemas of racialized, gendered or otherwise categorized bodies in accordance with the values of the given society … (In turn), the sound as so perceived is considered evidences of the existence of these categories'. In other words, social agreements and conditions classify the voice and this classification makes the categories, social agreements and conditions natural. However, as discussed above, voice involves various intersecting discursive practices and regimes. For example, when we think about gender and voice it is obvious that, as John Durham Peters stated (2004: 88), 'voice is a site where sexual differentiation is most clearly and most routinely accomplished'. Voice should be understood culturally rather than biologically within the normative regimes of gender.

> As feminist linguistic research since the 1970s has shown, there are no basic differences in male/female intonation patterns in English, which are exclusively one or the other. Gender differences in the use of the voice, such as pitch and timbre, are rather socially formed than anatomically determined. Even the change in boys' voices during puberty as a result of hormone changes is not fully explained by biology alone.
>
> (Key, cited in Hendricks 1998: 115)

Pamela Hendricks (1998: 116) argued that vocalization in itself does not provide enough information to the listener about the speaker's gender: 'Only when voice and gesture are combined and repeated in more detailed patterns do they result in an impression of 'masculine" and "feminine"'. In short, voice as a social product gives meaning and any sort of identity to body and *vice versa*, and their combination makes both of them visible and audible. These arguments can help us to answer the question of why voice ambiguity creates incomprehensible speech in many scenes.

I would like to give another example from *Fıstık Gibi Maşallah*. In one scene, Gülten goes into Fikriye's bedroom in order to thank her for something (see in figure 4.3). She realizes that Fikriye is very cold and in order to help her to get warmer, she gets into bed with Fikriye. In order to warm Fikriye up, she begins to rub herself against Fikriye's body. After various noises, Fikri-ye begins to talk to himself in a man's voice, saying 'I am a woman, I am a woman, calm down, I am a woman; am I a woman? Oooo, God, can you see whether I am a woman or a man?' This monologue cannot be heard by Gülten even though it goes on for a long time because the connection between body performance and voice performance has been destroyed. These private words are shared as information about the situation between Fikri-ye and the audience who know the 'original' gender of Fikri-ye.

The speech which is produced by the 'original' voice of the cross-dressed characters either cannot be heard or, if it is heard, cannot be understood. The reason for this is the separation of body and voice performance. When the body and gestures are not combined with voice, voice becomes undone;

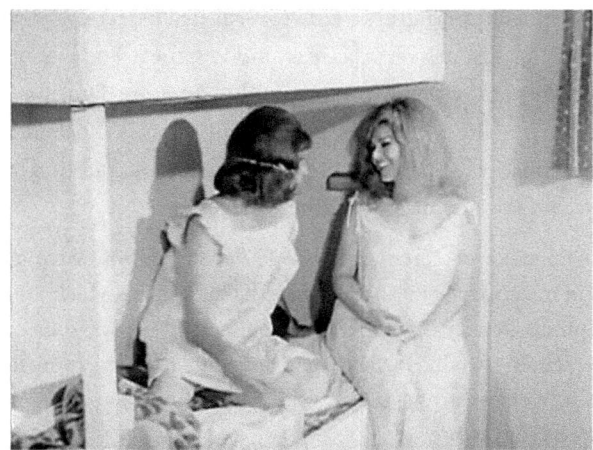
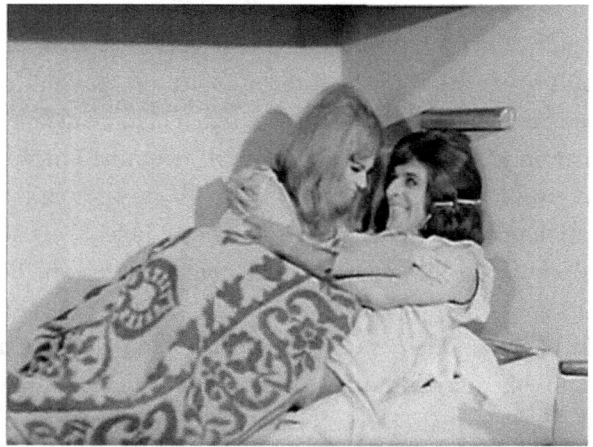

Figure 4.3 Gülten tries to warm Fikriye up in bed.

in other words, voice loses its locus and the locus loses the voice because, as discussed above, the relationship between body and voice is reciprocal and has been structured as a discursive practice socially, historically and culturally. When the voice and body relation is destroyed, both body and voice move outside any categorization and become inaudible. This inaudible space gives an opportunity to the cross-dressed character to exercise the right of free speech, which is impossible under a military coup.

If the cross-dressed body is a body which is in the process of becoming, and if the voice and body have a reciprocal relationship during the process of their construction, then we can say that the voice of a cross-dressing performer is also in the process of becoming. The voice of cross-dressing performance is also mobile not only in between gender poles but also on the map of power relations. The voice of the 'first gender' becomes another, but this becoming changes the meaning of being another and therefore another becomes different from itself in relation to the first voice's becoming. In other words, trying to make one voice masculine or feminine in the performance highlights the discursive regimes which are embedded in voice. The cross-dressing performer has at least two voices which dispute each other: the feminine voice calls into question the masculine voice and *vice versa*. The cross-dressed voice therefore disrupts the binary opposition which is embedded in voice and which shows this binary as a natural truth about gender. Between the two voices which are produced by cross-dressing performance, the consistency of hegemonic discourses about the categorization of voice disperses and fractures occur on the plane of voice. Fractures make visible the construction strategies of voice as an institution and the way of affecting the subject of this institution. We can regard fractures as an empty and therefore slippery space where the subject and any kind of relationships which produce the subject as a subject and a metaphysical concept of being are deterritorialized. In cross-dressing performance, voice, as one of the metaphysical concepts of being, is deterritorialized because, in cross-dressing films, the cross-dressed character can produce different vocal utterances, some of whose source cannot be seen in the frame, and some images whose sound cannot be heard.[2]

Voice as a discursive practice is kind of label which is used for categorizing bodies. It is a social construct, which is why although all voices are unique, we can nevertheless hear them with their label: women/men, Black/white, human/non-human. The cross-dressed voice in films as a voice of body of becoming fractures the system of categorization which both produces and is produced by voice. This is why, when the body and voice relationship breaks down, voice becomes inaudible, or audible but not understood. This feature of voice which is discovered by cross-dressing characters gives them an opportunity to express themselves freely and to re-organize the relationships between self and other; it also re-orients their body according to their needs. They can use at least two different texts/discourses/voices together and by doing so, they disrupt ontological security which is based on trust in the continuity and stability of others. Furthermore, disrupting ontological security and re-organizing it again give them the right to free speech, unlike the citizens under military rule. The mobility of the cross-dressed voice which is produced by the body which is in the process of becoming fractures not only the relationship between body and voice but also the film's surface. This fracture which takes place on the film's surface creates a third dimension which is directly related to the audience. At this point, we can discuss how the alteration of voice opens up a new discussion about listening and speaking. I shall explore this new question in the following section.

Speaking and listening fracturing

Ontological security is a relationship which takes place between the self and its surroundings in order to create confidence and trust for the self that the natural and social worlds are as they appear to be. Language is one of the most important elements of ontological security because we understand our surroundings through language. Dialogue as a relational part of language is a place where the power and orientation of self not only take place but also are exercised. Unheard and misunderstood parts of the dialogue of characters which are produced by the alteration of a cross-dressed character's voice also fracture the dialogue between the speaking and listening subjects in film. Cross-dressing characters ignore the listening subject when they speak with their 'original' voice. These voices belong to someone who is not there and speak to someone who is not there. However, the voice's place is still in the dialogue and its value can be understood only if or when the relationship between this monologue and the dialogue can be understood. In this section, I shall discuss the possible meanings of fractured dialogues. How do these fractures of dialogue 'talk' and what do they say to us? In order to analyse them, I shall first consider the functions of the acts of listening and speaking in dialogue.

There are two actions in a dialogue: one is speaking and the other is listening. Both actions work together and colligate each other's action and reaction like a rope. Therefore, the direction of a dialogue is usually forwards. One monologue not only creates its counter-monologue but also determines its own position according to this new counter-monologue. By means of listening and speaking, a person as a part of one dialogue becomes a part of the broader situation. This is why Sterne (2012: 9) pointed out that 'Speaking, listening and hearing places you inside an event but seeing gives you a perspective on the event'. It is almost impossible to place yourself in what you see. On the other hand, your listening activity carries you into the event and your speaking activity gives you the opportunity to be on the other side of the dialogue in order to re-orient yourself according to your reaction which is embedded in your speaking. This is why it is important to ask why some parts of the dialogue in cross-dressing films are not understood or are misunderstood, what the possible reasons are for these situations and why it happens so often.

There are some possible explanations for this situation. First, in these scenes the direction of the attempt at communication differs from the real recipient of the dialogue. The intention of the cross-dressed character is to open a new dialogue with someone else who is not in the frame, who is the viewer of the film, the audience. This new dialogue is therefore not bounded by the context of the dialogue which takes place between the characters (very similar to the voice which is an unbounded body). The text which is not bounded by its context

Figure 4.4 Aysel massaging Burhan's back in *Şeytanın Pabucu*.

creates a sense of nonsense. These new dialogues which take place between the audience and a cross-dressed character are unbounded from the context of the dialogue which takes place between two characters. Destroying the relationship between text and context could be a reason for the misunderstanding. One example from *Şeytanın Pabucu* can be given for the unbounded relationship between text and context.

In this scene, Aysel massages Burhan's back (Burhan is a male-to-female cross-dressing character) without knowing that she is a he (see in figure 4.4). She thinks that she is helping to ease the health problem of an old, religious woman. Her mistaken thinking provides the context for her in the scene. Burhan, however, gets an erection after her massage. Aysel says, 'How stiff your back is' (*Sırtın ne kadar sert*). Burhan answers with a man's voice, 'There is somewhere else which is more stiff than my back!' (Implying his erection). Although she can hear what Burhan says, Aysel cannot understand the meaning of the sentence because it is not bonded with her context. The interlocutor of this dialogue is not Aysel: the dialogue is not between Aysel and Burhan but between Burhan and the audience. This shared information between Burhan and the audience empowers Burhan over Aysel.

Another reason could be the intentions of the speaker and the listener. Claire Humphreys-Jones observed that 'The relationship between what the speaker intends and what the hearer understands essentially determines the outcome of a communication attempt (1986: 43). If what the hearer understands to have been expressed differs from what the speaker intended to express, misunderstanding or not understanding has occurred'. In another example from *Şeytanın Pabucu*, while Aysel is servicing tea to Burhan, he looks directly at her breasts and says, 'Ahh, ahh, Aysel, thank you, Aysel, wonderful Aysel, ahh, Aysel' (see in figure 4.5). Although he uses a very erotic masculine voice, Aysel interprets these sentences as if he really is thanking her because she has served him tea. Their two different intentions affect the communication process and fracture the plane which exists between listener and speaker. By this fracture, the cross-dressed character appeals to the desire of the audience, that is the intention of the cross-dressed character.

Furthermore, the intention of a cross-dressing character as a speaking subject not only establishes a direct relationship with the audience but also establishes direct access to his/her way of thinking which is also full of secret information which is shared between the audience and the cross-dressing character. The alteration of voices gives them the right to free speech, now causing a fracture between listener and speaker and giving them an opportunity to share their way

Figure 4.5 Aysel serves Burhan tea in *Şeytanın Pabucu*.

of thinking with whoever they want to and to hide it from those who they do not want to share it with. While they are doing that, they escape any kinds of censorship or self-control. In other words, they can escape surveillance, unlike the citizens who live under military rule.

At this point, the effect of the visible but unrecognizable body of the cross-dressed character can be recalled. In some examples, even though context and text relations are not bonded and even though the intentions are same, some utterances of cross-dressing characters still cannot be understood. In a previous chapter, I suggested that cross-dressing can be accepted as a way of satisfying the desire to be visible and at the same time of escaping panoptic social mechanisms. Cross-dressing characters can escape a panoptic social mechanism because although they are still visible, which can be accepted as a source of self, they cannot be recognizable, because their bodies are in the frame of undecidability, because cross-dressing makes the bodies and the performances of bodies artificial and annihilated. We can use this argument for the voice performance of cross-dressing characters. The original voice of a cross-dressed body is audible but incomprehensible, like being visible but unrecognizable; because it is liberated from its linguistic and multiple codes such as class, race, age and gender, this voice therefore does not belong to the character. It belongs to someone who is not in the frame. In this fracture by cross-dressing, characters can escape acoustic panoptic surveillance and can say whatever they think and want without any fear.

In the scene from *Şabaniye* shown in Figure 4.6, we see a dialogue between Şabaniye and his old and rich boss who falls in love with Şabaniye. The boss talks about how masculine Şabaniye is and says 'I like hard women'. Şabaniye answers him by saying, 'Yes, I like hard women too' in a man's voice. The boss is surprised and says, 'Pardon, I didn't understand', then Şabaniye realizes what she has done and corrects herself, saying 'I mean men, hard men'. In this scene, the counter-part of the dialogue (the boss) can hear the voice but he cannot understand it. Although it is still in the same context and probably the same

Figure 4.6 Şabaniye and her boss fail to understand one another.

intention is shared between speaker and listener (informing the other about what s/he likes), the monologue of the cross-dressed character cannot be understood. Military coups impose a panoptic social mechanism not only for bodies and the identities which these bodies have, they also impose surveillance on speaking and on the sharing of information. They also control who speaks, what is spoken and to whom it is spoken. Audible but incomprehensible monologues, like the visible but not recognizable body of the cross-dresser, enable cross-dressing characters to escape the solid surveillance of a military regime without losing their voice.

Dialogues are not only a relationship between two speakers, they are also the way of spatializing and temporalizing narratives and events. So where and when do these acts of unheard or non-understood speech take place on the film's surface? These moments are lost time for the listening objects; at these moments listening objects cannot speak and although they can hear the voice of the cross-dressed character they cannot understand it. These monologues are placed outside the frame by being addressing directly to the audience, so we can call these newly placed utterances 'lost space' because in this space, these voices cannot be heard or even if they can be heard they cannot be understood by the other film characters. These scenes therefore fracture the spatiality and temporality of films as well. This misunderstood or not understood part of a dialogue makes time and room for them on the film's surface where it becomes lost space and lost time for the counter-character who has no opportunity to access this lost space and time. In this lost time and space where the cross-dressing character exercises her/his power as a speaking subject, he/she takes control over the listener. R.S. White stated in *The Art of Listening*, 'What we hear is what enables us to speak, and what we say is what enables the other to hear and speak, and so on' (1986: 124). So the unheard or misunderstood part of the dialogue does produce a reaction and a response, thereby establishing the right for a counter-part of the dialogue to be spoken. This produces a hierarchy between two characters. Moreover, by using the new window which is opened directly to audience, the cross-dressed character takes control of the narrative. In the example described above, for instance, Aysel cannot understand that she is being abused and so cannot give a reaction to the situation. Here, it is worth remembering the crises of masculinity which are caused by military coups and which were discussed in the previous chapter. A military coup changes the hierarchy between masculinities by putting militaristic masculinity at the top. I suggested that military coups change the relationships between masculinities and relocate them. This is what creates a crisis of masculinity. Here, the lost time and space which is produced by the unheard and un-understood parts of a dialogue enable the cross-dressed character to recover his/her dominance which is taken from him by a military coup over others/women because masculinity is a practice over others and it needs this practice in order to be enunciable.

What happens in this lost time and space? What are the politics of these lost utterances? These lost utterances correlate the text with other texts which are the hegemonic discourses of the era. They can be accepted as a response to other texts of the era. These lost utterances usually involve at least two different structures. For example, if one of them involves action, the other involves emotion; if one of them carries the truth, the other carries falsehood; if one of them is masculine, the other is feminine; if one of them is full of power, the other is not. So the two different utterances, one of which addresses the audience and the other addresses another character, form a hierarchy which might give us the correlation between the discourses of the era.

An example can be given from *Şeytanın Pabucu*. One scene, shown in Figure 4.7, depicts the ritual after a funeral. Although rituals of this kind involve gender segregation and men are not allowed to be present, Burhan is a cross-dressed character who is pretending to be his sister, so he is present in the women's ritual space. He joins in the mourning by saying, 'Ahh, my sister where are you? I hope and I know you are with God as a good Muslim' by using religious terms in a woman's voice. Then, after he sees the underwear of the woman sitting opposite, he says 'Ayy Maşallah'[3] in a man's voice in a form of abuse towards her. He then realizes what he has done and corrects himself by saying same words, 'Ayy, Maşallah' in a woman's voice in order to express his-as-her religious feelings, and then continues, 'My sister was always a good Muslim and she died in Kaaba'. The first 'Ayy Maşallah' cannot be heard by any others who are at the wake. He uses exactly the same term differently according to his/her gender. The two poles of the gender binary speak together in the utterance of 'Ayy Maşallah'. On the other hand, the first 'Ayy Maşallah' contains a sentiment of abuse whereas the second contains a religious sentiment; the first one is masculine and the second is feminine, the first is a way of conquering and establishing a hierarchy over the object which the exclamation 'Ayy Maşallah' addresses and the second expresses devotion. In short, the first can be read as active, male and invasive, and the second can be read as passive, emotional, feminine and devotional, but both of them contain clues about the gender discourses of the situation and they come outspoken from the same body. Scenes such as this are double-voiced discourse.

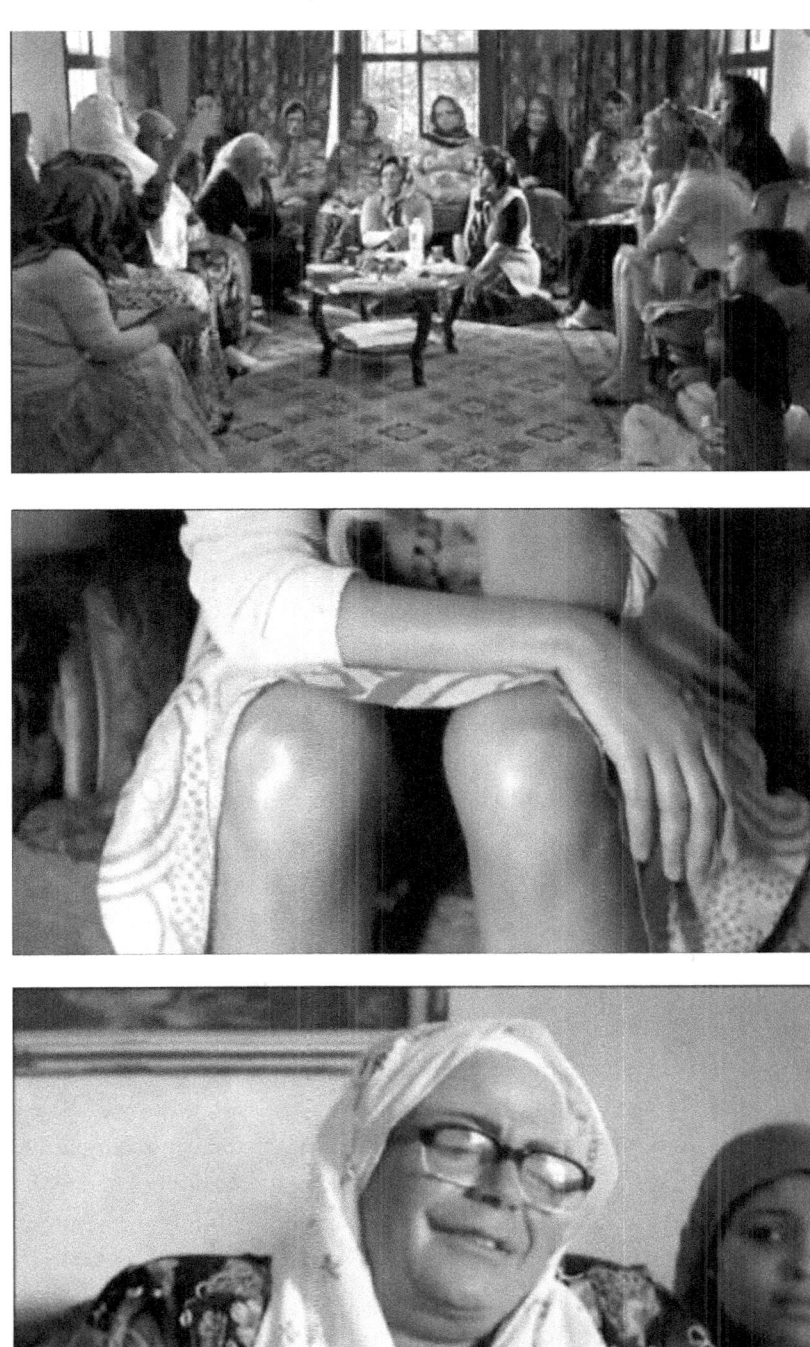

Figure 4.7 Burhan's experience at a funeral in *Şeytanın Pabucu*.

Şeytanın Pabucu is a film which was made in 2008, at the beginning of the era of Islamic conservatism when conservatism and Kemalist modernism were talking at the same time with different voices. In this 'Ay Maşallah' dialogue, we can observe not only how two different genders can speak from the same body but also how two different political discourses of the era can speak together from the same body. Another key issue is these politics of inner utterances. These monologues of a cross-dressed character make the binary oppositions of the discourses of the era visible. These utterances are produced by a body which can be visible but non-recognizable, so they are audible but incomprehensible, and can therefore help cross-dressing characters to escape acoustic surveillance, unlike the citizens of the period, and give them back the right to free speech.

Both voices of a cross-dressing character use at least two different texts. One voice whose body is not in the frame makes a reference to another text which is not the subject of the frame. One body uses two different texts and therefore two different discourses which talk to each other at the same time. One of them can be accepted as an echo of the other. Words which are repeated as exactly the same but with different connotations function as a political invention which can find its place in its repeated form. They make visible the power and the discursive dimension which lie inside the language. Language destroys itself by resisting within itself. Cross-dressing characters and the fractures which they create make this situation visible.

A dialogue which temporalizes and spatializes language is one of the elements of ontological security because dialogues provide temporal and spatial continuity, locate subject and others inside an event, and convince the subject of the stability and continuity of the self/other and of the event. Cross-dressing characters fracture the relationship between the two sides of a dialogue, the listener and the speaker, and therefore disrupt the temporal and spatial continuity and stability of self, other and the surroundings. There can be several reasons for this fracturing. One of them is that the monologue which fractures the relationship between listener and speaker is not bonded with the context of the scene. Another explanation can be the different intentions of speaker and listener. These monologues of cross-dressing characters produce lost time and space for the counter-part of the dialogue. From this lost time and space, cross-dressing characters call to the audience and share their way of thinking freely with whoever they want, because this lost space and time are kind of a door which opens directly onto the way that the cross-dressing character is thinking.

Language occupation fracturing

The fracturing of language occupation is based on not only the different voices of woman/man but also the different ways which women and men have of using language. Cross-dressing performance provides opportunities to hear two different usages according to gender in the same body. In this way, cross-dressing characters can experience otherness without being other. Language gives opportunities for this experience. I discuss the differences between men's and women's ways of using language under the specific conditions of cross-dressing performance by using sexual difference theory in terms of language. I discuss this fracturing by reference to the third effect of cross-dressing performance; experiencing otherness without being other.

As we know from post-structuralist discussions about the subject, it is a process of formation which is based on the differences between subject positions. This system of differences is a result of power relations which shows that the system is natural. These asymmetrical power relations construct woman as the other of the dominant subject, which is male. Language, as discussed above, is not a tool of communication but the space where the subject is constructed. In order to get access to language, the subject has to take up her/his gendered position. The significant divide of masculine/feminine determines the content of language. Wittig (1992) stated that culture, history, memory, truth and gender are all products of language which are structured by and structure the system of differences, carrying the hetero-normative, straight thinking within them. In the last three decades of the twentieth century, attention began to be given to how and why speakers use language in relation to their identities. Within this study area, one of the most important discussions has addressed questions about 'how people use language to express gender, how a person's gender affects the choices they make in how they speak, and how their talk is received' (Kiesling 2007: 653).

'The founding of the field of language and gender studies is often traced to Robin Lakoff's (1975) *Language and Woman's Place*, which focuses on how women are expected to use language and how their linguistic usages perpetuate their subordinate position in society' (Kiesling 2007: 653). Language came to be thought of as a site of differences and dominance. After the 1960s, feminists writers began to discuss language in different ways compared with second-wave feminism. For example, Julia Kristeva (1980) suggested that to speak is necessarily to occupy a male position and that even the maternal voice can be heard only through the male voice. According to Luce Irigaray (1985), unlike the male organ the female sex is not one but several. Her vision of feminine language hangs on this model of multiplicity, contiguity and simultaneity, giving greater value to the sense of touch over sight. Irigaray stated that a woman speaks by wandering off in different directions, touching upon rather than focusing. For Helene Cixous (1976), 'women have historically been silenced: made to assume the role of physicality and materiality as a counter to masculine reason and discourse, women have been denied access to language and writing'. Kaja Silverman (1988) then argued that, for the reasons suggested by Irigaray, Cixous and Kristeva, the female voice cannot be rational, coherent or concentrated in films.

In cross-dressing films, the differences between male and female employment of language are highlighted in many scenes. In these scenes, cross-dressing characters are free to enter the other's way of thinking by using the other's way of employing language because language is where the self is produced. For example, in *Şoför Nebahat*, when Nebahat (the female-to-male cross-dressing character) begins to talk like a man, her driver friends say, 'Welcome to our world now; right now you are beginning to be a real man, a real driver'. They are all aware that being masculine is not only related to dress but also to the way of employing language. Even though men and masculinity are in the gender relationship, they are subject to a different organization. We cannot say that all men are masculine or that all masculine things belong to men: 'Men are the corporeal beings identified as such, usually ultimately based on genitalia and body; however, maleness is also socially constructed' (Bing & Bergvall 1996). 'Masculinity is a quality or set of practices (habitual ways of doing things) that is stereotypically connected with men' (Kiesling 2007: 655). It can therefore be said that masculinity is also a performance which involves voice, language, speech and physical acts. In the scene with the drivers, Nebahat's linguistic practice is understood as masculine because s/he imitates the stereotypical male way of talking as part of the hegemonic masculinity of the era, and in doing so reconstructs masculinity as a social institution. In this scene (figure 4.8 and 4.9), Nebahat not only uses traditional slang words but also produces new ones a lot. By producing slang words, Nebahat does two things: first, s/he finds new words for old meanings, which makes her/him an active agency of language, and second, she gains dominance in the conversation. After hearing her/him using slang, one of the driver friends says, 'Well done, you have to speak like this in order to earn the respect of other drivers which makes you more equal in the competitive world of drivers' (*İşte böyle erkek gibi öteceksin. Şoför tayfası erkekliğe hoşaflanır. Böyle öt ki yerin olsun aralarında*). From this dialogue, we

Fracturing language, voice and speech 123

Figures 4.8 Nebahat with the other drivers.

Figures 4.9 Nebahat is leaving with her new clothes in *Şoför Nebahat*.

can easily understand that language is also a place where masculinities compete. In the crises of masculinity which are produced by military coups, employing language with the usage of the other provides an opportunity for cross-dressing characters to recover broken masculinities.

At the end of the same film, Nebahat (back as a woman) finds the right man and marries him. Her husband says, 'You will be my own driver from now on; you will use our car not a taxi'. While they driving in their car, another car commits a traffic violation and Nebahat begins to swear like man. Then she realizes that her husband has heard her; her husband says, 'I love you in every aspect of you' (figure 4.10). Nebahat raises her pitch to make her voice more feminine and says, 'I love you too'. In this exchange, we can see that there are different aspects of employing language and voice: the man's aspect and the woman's aspect. From this stereotypical incident we see that men tend to be less polite than women, that a woman's voice should be pitched higher, and that men's utterances involve competition and dominance. Cross-dressing

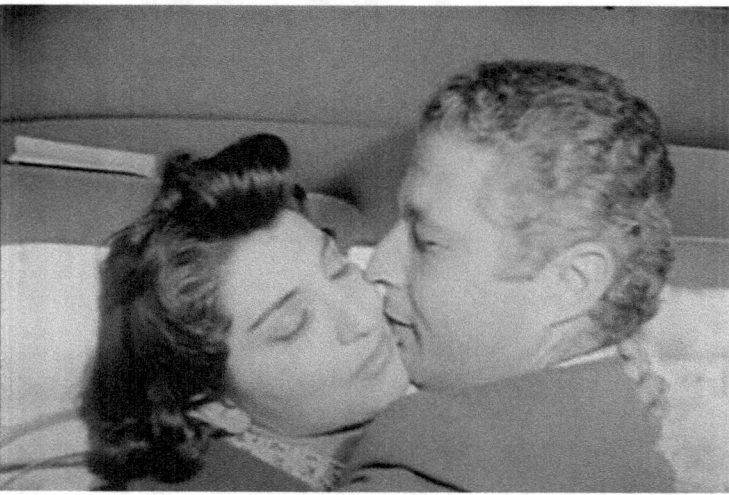

Figure 4.10 Nebahat berates another driver, but her husband loves her for it; two frames from *Şoför Nebahat*.

characters are allowed to use all of these attributes: Nebahat is lovable in any situation (at least, to her husband). Experiencing otherness without being other through the use of the language of the other protects cross-dressing characters against the politics of a military coup which are based on discrimination. It is significant here that, for example, after the 1980 military coup it was announced that all other languages which were used in Turkey, such as Kurdish, were forbidden. The prominent slogan of the coup which was written on the walls of all the prisons was 'Speak Turkish, speak less'. In this political environment, cross-dressing characters can penetrate the language which belongs to the other and can talk as much as they want.

The fracturing of language can be discussed in relation to the effects of experiencing other without being other. In the scenes discussed above, cross-dressing characters are enabled to employ different language formats of different subject positions. They can use the language of the other and gain benefit from this usage without being other In doing so, they make visible the construction strategies of linguistic discourses; they show the performative side of the linguistic act.

Music as sounds of films

The music used in the films is also a way of expressing the tension of the period. In Fistik Gibi Maşallah, traditional songs are played but on western instruments. The film uses western sound and eastern words in order to express a national identity crisis between west and east. Furthermore, the notion of music halls and balls which are key locations in the films was introduced to Turkish citizens as a western form of entertainment imported as part of the Kemalist modernization project. However, traditional songs infiltrate the modern sounds and locations. The film becomes fractured and it admits tradition. In *Şabaniye*, the main song is Kim Bilir? ('Who knows?'), a popular arabesque song of the period. The question 'who knows?' overlaps the emotional geography of the period. The 1980 military coup was the most brutal and effective coup and created a sense of unpredictability because the Kemalist ideology, which had been followed until the 1980s, began to be abandoned after the 1980 coup. The same question, 'Who knows?', which was asked in the 1980s could find its answer in the 2000s with Prime Minister Erdogan and his famous and most repeated sentence, 'We know'. Furthermore, the playback culture and re-productivity of art caused a disembodiment of voice and body in Şabaniye. In *Şeytanin Pabucu*, ezans (calls to prayer) and ilahi (carols) are used as music by the cross-dressing character. The group which moves into Burhan's basement introduce themselves as a band, but the audience does not hear any music. First the sound-track of *Fıstık Gibi Maşallah* is the space where west and east meet; then the sound-track of *Şabaniye* finds its way in the arabesque form which is neither/both western nor/and eastern; and finally, in *Şeytanın Pabucu*, the music disappears and is replaced by ezans (call to prayer) and carols.

Language is not a conveyer by which our ideas and feelings are transmitted. It is a kind of regulation which gives no opportunity for anything to exist outside it. This regulation is the source of ontological security. Therefore, when ontological security has been destroyed by a military coup in Turkey, the fixed and accepted meaning which is structured by language is fractured. This can be seen in cross-dressing films where ontological security is threatened by the cross-dressing performer who is the popular narrative of the era of military coups in Turkey. Many similarities can be found between the cross-dressing character who does not want to lose his/her sound and right to speak and the citizen who want to speak but cannot under military rule. Such scenes can be read as a tension between two sensations: the desire to have unity of body and voice – because this unity creates a subject as a speaking subject in the system of ontological security – and the fear of losing it, which can be accepted as the main tension of the era of a military coup. These scenes can therefore be read as the story of a society metamorphosing between two emotional topographies which are contoured by the need to be heard and the need to speak, in order to regain ontological security.

Even so, language needs voice in order to find one's tongue and requires a listener/reader in order to be interpreted. So when language is fractured, its traces can be followed in voice, in the act of speaking and in listening because all of them work together to create a meaningful truth about the world. Because of this unity, I have discussed in this chapter three different fractures which occur on the linguistic level: voice fracturing, speaking/listening fracturing and gender fracturing, in relation to the three effects of cross-dressing gender performance. In each section, I have discussed how the stable, fixed meanings which are constructed by language can be destroyed by language itself. I have given examples to show how regulations contain a virus, a parasite, which can carry the potential for them to destroy themselves. In order to discuss these issues, I have used the effects of cross-dressing performance on its subject which were discussed in Chapter 2.

The cross-dressing body as a body which is in the process of becoming is a very good example of the potential effects of these parasites or viruses because, as was discussed in the previous chapters, cross-dressing performance in films animates the alternative possibilities of life which seems to us to be meaningful truth by means of language. The cross-dressing body and performance are the beyond categorization and disrupt the rigid hierarchy between categories by means of language which produces meaning.

5

Fracturing space and time: Where is my home? Where is my nation?

Cross-dressing characters are always given an opportunity by their cross-dressing performance to break down the idea of a perception of space and time which is geometrical, unchanged, fixed, linear and a given fact, and this breaking down fractures the linear, progressive way of understanding the world. They start their journey from being to becoming by abandoning their home and changing their memories of the past. After abandoning their home, they settle in liminal spaces. Cross-dressing films usually prefer liminal spaces because they are both/neither public space and/nor private space as locations in films, such as a taxi in *Şoför Nebahat*, a hotel in *Fıstık Gibi Maşallah* and a school dormitory in *Hababam Sınıfı*, in order to gain flexibility in time. In this way, they become liberated from the social control of space and time and they can be in different spaces and times/'nows', if time and space can be accepted as perceptions, not real. These different spaces and times sometimes run parallel but sometimes they cut across one another. These different spaces and times make it possible to discuss the counter-strategies which were used, or were imagined to be used, by subjects who lived under a militaristic hegemony. Furthermore, they not only play with the past and the now but also produce their future with different strategies which can also be accepted as a fantasy of a subject who cannot predict her/his future under the military rule.

In this chapter, I offer a critical reflection on the ways in which cross-dressing characters fracture perceptions of space and time as elements of ontological security. I discuss how space and time lose their control over the subject and how, as products of power relations, they provide opportunities to resist themselves conflicting with themselves by means of the gender confusion created by cross-dressing characters. I discuss these issues in three separate sections. I call the first section *Leaving home and the past*[1]; here I explore the idea of house and home in relation to the past and to memories, and how cross-dressing films use the concept of home. I argue that the idea of home as a space for gaining stable subjectivity is destroyed by cross-dressing characters. Home is discussed as a space where the memories which are the stories of our identities are produced. In this section, the idea of home is also used as a connotation of the nation. I then discuss notion of *Liminal spaces and multiple 'nows'*. Liminal spaces are spaces which can be found in almost all cross-dressing films. I discuss liminal spaces by asking why cross-dressing characters are identified by in-between spaces – what does an 'in-between space' mean? – and how liminal spaces allow cross-dressing characters multiple usage of space and time and how this usage fractures the perception of space and time. Liminal spaces are also discussed as a way of escaping surveillance in this section. Third, I discuss the *Envisaged future* and how cross-dressing characters design their future. I consider these three topics in relation to the three effects of cross-dressing performance and military coups. Before beginning the discussion, however, I want to use this introductory section itself as a 'space' where the idea of space and time in the context of this study is discussed. With this intention, first, I discuss space and time themselves and then I return to discuss cross-dressing gender performances in Turkish cinema and their usage of space and time.

What are space and time?

Cross-dressing performances in Turkish cinema highlight and make visible our fictional relationship with space and time which cannot be discussed without considering power relations. Life and culture are constructed and defined by space and time. It can be claimed that no life can exist unless it has been labelled by space and time. Space and time help people to gain their essential identity and maintain the stability and continuity of this identity. The concept of space-time therefore helps people to maintain their ontological security. Cross-dressing characters break down the continuity and linearity of space and time which are required for *being* but which are the enemy of *becoming* and thus disrupt ontological security. Furthermore, destroying the space and time perception breaks down control of power over the subject. By means of destroying the space and time perception, the subject gains flexibility. In short, cross-dressing disrupts the dominant value of the present: the here and now. In order to discuss how cross-dressing achieves this, I shall first discuss space and time.

As stated above, space and time are important elements of ontological security. Here again, according to Giddens (1990: 92) ontological security refers to 'the confidence that most human beings have in the *continuity of their self-identity* and in the constancy of the surrounding *social and material environments* of action'. To be ontologically secure, the individual must be more or less able to rely on the spaces where people, objects and meanings are placed and oriented. A crucial element, which protects individuals from uncertainty, is habitualization. This is the source of routine forms of behaviour and knowledge which are spatially organized (Berger & Luckmann 1991: 70–85). Furthermore, in order to be ontologically secure, a person should know where s/he belongs. Ontological security requires the sense of where someone belongs in the world, from home to nation. In this sense, not only personal space but also national space as a land is the source of ontological security.

In order to achieve being ontologically secure, people need a continuity which is structured by routine. Routines regulate everyday social life and sustain the continuity of identities. Our daily life is structured in routines by time. It is obvious to us when we should wake up, when we should go to work or school and when we should stay at home. In parallel with our everyday life, our whole life is governed by time. People know when they have to vote, when they got married, when they had children. It can therefore be said that routines which are the main determinants of ontological security can be organized by time.

Space and time are not only elements of ontological security but also the places where ontological security is constructed because, without space and time, routine, memory, belonging and identity, and confidence in them and their continuity, cannot be organized. A question arises here about why and how space and time organize all these things. In order to answer this question, I shall first discuss the idea of space then time.

Academic discussions around the concept of space have a long history. Almost all disciplines have discussed space, but I shall begin with Martin Heidegger, who was one of the most influential philosophers on the idea of post-modernist space perception. For Heidegger (1978: 250) 'a space is something that has been made room for, something that has been freed, namely, within a boundary (horizon) … not that at which something stops but, as the Greeks recognized, … that from which something begins its essential unfolding'. The meaning of space according to Heidegger's point of view is based on it being constructed, cultivated or designated by human action. The space in which we exist is established by human movement through space and human organization in space. Maurice Merleau-Ponty (1962) developed this idea further by putting forward 'the view that place is that part of physical space which we construct in our own minds by investing it with symbolic significance' (cited in Lucas 2014: 198).

Sara Pink (2012: 24) commented that the relationship between space and place has been debated by philosophers (e.g. Gerard Casey 1996), geographers (e.g. Doreen Massey 2005) and anthropologists (e.g. Tim Ingold 2008) who have all agreed that what characterizes places is the bringing together of both material and socio-cultural phenomena. Casey (1996) agreed with Heidegger that our perception of space 'is based on the representation of the "gatherings" which are in place'. Heidegger's view was that it is only possible to comprehend space from within our experience of the things and relations which form the boundaries of places. Massey (2005) suggested that space and time are mutually dependent and that neither dominates the other, a view which does draw on Heidegger's original proposition but seems to have moved closer to Merleau-Ponty's view of places as 'spatio-temporal events' (Massey 2005: 130), and that they comprise collections of spatial 'stories' compiled by the human agents who are involved in constructing them. Pink (2012) observed that Massey's (2005) view suggests that there is 'a distinction between space as an individually perceived phenomenon and place as a collectively co-constructed one'. Ingold (2008) stressed the importance of movement for the way that we perceive space and added that the process of meaning-making in our spatial environment seems to suggest that we fabricate places not as bounded zones, as Heidegger had claimed, but from the effects of motion and perceptual fluidity (Lucas 2014: 198). From these discussions, we arrive at the idea that space is relational and can therefore be understood from the movement between the boundaries of this relation and involves the action of gathering them. Therefore, it cannot be a stable, fixed and unchanging entity, even though it is organized and represented as if it is by power relations. Cross-dressing performance makes these the mobile, unfixed changeable face of space/time with its effects.

At this point, Henri Lefebvre comes to mind. According to Lefebvre (1974), space is a social product which involves not only relations of production but also of re-production. However, saying that 'space is relational, a social product and fluid' is not enough. Space is not only a social product but also a producer of the social relations which are its foundation. Lefebvre, among others, insisted on the importance of considering not only what might be called 'the geometry' of space but also its lived practices and the symbolic meaning and significance of particular spaces and spatializations. According to Massey (1992: 79), 'interrelations between objects occur in space and time;

it is these relationships themselves which create/define space and time'. This created and defined space and time then creates and defines the interrelations between subjects. In this circle, space becomes a tool which is used for naming, classifying and categorizing things and relations. It can therefore be said that space is not a place where objects and subjects simply move, meet, gather and are oriented according to each other, but where they also gain name, category and label. These names, categories and labels in turn also determine the space reciprocally. Because of these reciprocal relations, according to Ernesto Laclau (1990), spatializations are a kind of hegemonization. He suggested that space and time can be used in order to understand social systems. In *New Reflections on the Revolution of Our Time* (1990: 41–69), Laclau argued that 'any repetition that is governed by a structural law of successions is space' and that 'spatiality means coexistence within a structure that establishes the positive nature of all its terms'. That is why, when cross-dressing characters in the films disrupt the unity of space and the structure of space at the same time, they destroy this hegemonization as well. In doing so they can escape the naming, classifying and categorizing of space.

At this point, it is apposite to discuss military coups, national traumas and space relations in Turkey. As discussed above, space is the place where the routine, memory, belonging, identity and confidence about these issues take place. Space is therefore not only the place where traumas which are based on the destruction of routine, belonging, identity and confidence take place but also an element which determines the nature of the trauma. There are two different arguments in these sentences: that the meaning and nature of trauma are determined by space, and that the meaning and nature of trauma change the meaning and nature of space. I prefer to use a different context to discuss these points. Bombing attacks can be given as an example. The same actions gain different meanings according to their place; for instance, bombing France is not the same as bombing Syria because space is determined not only by the relationship between the subjects and objects in it, but also by other spaces. One place as a location can be a space because of the relationship and distinction or differences between places. In order to be space, the important thing is what this particular place does not mean as much as what it does mean, such as local *versus* global, private *versus* public space, west *versus* east and so on. Therefore, not only do space and subject determine each other's position in power relations, but also the relationship between spaces determines the position of the subject and the meaning of space. In other words, these relationships and differences between spaces are a way of mapping subjectivity which can be regarded as a tool of control over subjects. The borders which are called liminal space between different spaces and which determine each other's meaning can help us to discuss the way in which cross-dressing characters use space. This point will be discussed later in this chapter. On the other hand, traumatic events change the meaning of space as well; for example, the twin towers became a symbol of terror rather than being a trade centre. During a military coup, these two reciprocal transformations between spaces and trauma can be observed in Turkey. Military coups have a special meaning for Turkish political life. Military coups have changed the meanings and structures of spaces in Turkey. For example, schools and sports stadiums were transformed into police stations and detention centres not only physically but also relationally; the use of streets was changed and the whole nation became a prison. Cross-dressing films, which are accepted as trauma narratives in this study, disrupt and re-organize spaces as elements and conveyers of ontological security on many levels and these levels can be read in relation to the military coup because the usage of space by the cross-dressing character is based on destroying the control over the subject by using space when the whole country has been transformed into a prison. As well as space, the perception of time has also been disrupted and re-organized both by military coups and by cross-dressing characters: both by the state and by the individual.

The routines of ontological security can be possible only in terms of the organization and the collectivization of time not only for individuals but also for societies. According to Emile Durkheim (1947), everybody in a particular society has the same temporal consciousness and time is a product of the society as a social category. Time consciousness is designed by rhythmic social and economic events. The 'Calendar expresses the rhythm of collective activities, while at the same time its function is to assure regularity' (Durkheim 1947: 10). According to Durkheim, time is the 'subject of collective representation' (in Hassard 1990: 3). Most societies have some kind of time organization but these time organizations are set up for the purpose of serving the society. For example, the days of week can be different according to different market activities: 'The eight-day week of the Khasi is based on their system of trade whereby they hold a market every eighth day' (Hassard 1990: 7). Community cannot be constructed without everywhere being in synchrony with everywhere else. This constructed synchronicity can be seen in the huge clock towers in every modern city of Turkey. In the process of modernization not only have laws, practices and the alphabet been taken from the west, but also time perception, organizations and practice have been taken from the western world. The Turkish calendar and clock time were adjusted to match the western example: previously, the Islamic calendar had been in use, but it was abandoned as part of Atatürk's reforms and replaced by the Georgian calendar in 1925 under the 'Law on the change of the Calendar' (*Takvimde Tarih Mebdeinin Değiştirilmesi Hakkında Kanun*). At the same time in 1925, the old Turkish way of calculating the time of day was replaced by the international clock under the 'Law on the Division of the Day into Twenty-four Hours' (*Günün Yirmidört Saate Taksimi Hakkında Kanun*). Before this law, the rising and setting of the sun were used to calculate the time, but because Turkey is so big that the sun rises and sets at different times across the country, this system was confusing and defied attempts to synchronize communities across Turkey. For the first time, national timetables were organized. Time had to be synchronized according to the western method for the citizens of modern Turkey who had been separated by being in the east. The intention behind building the clock towers at the beginning of the modernization process was to create collective, organized, institutionalized time for all Turkish citizens. Time became a commodity which brought a community together as a nation. In short, routines which are created by the organization and collectivization of time not only protect individuals from chaos in their daily life but also the notion of nation requires synchronized routines.

The routines of ontological security which protect identity from the uncertainty and chaos of life by organizing and collectivizing time are also used as a tool for social control in many cases. If the everyday practices of human beings are organized and controlled, at the same time their way of thinking can be controlled and organized. That is why Giddens (1984: 145) commented that 'discipline can proceed only via the manipulation of time'. Time is controlled, organized, institutionalized and collectivized by routines which shape our daily practices. Our controlled, organized, institutionalized and collectivized daily practices are a means of social control over subjects. If this is done, it can be said that time can work as an institution which is used for surveillance and control.

Military coups threaten the organized and collectivized routines of nations and citizens by enhancing the surveillance system. On the other hand, cross-dressing characters in Turkish films destroy these routines in order to escape the surveillance system. Both military coups and cross-dressing characters use time in order to destroy then re-organize the routines of ontological security because the source of the routines is time. The usage and organization of time are re-structured by both military power and cross-dressing characters. In times of a military coup, the manipulation of time becomes more visible. For example, a curfew is imposed at night and people are only permitted to undertake specific actions at specific times. The daily life routines of citizens are re-organized by the military in order to avoid the formation of large groups. In this way, time as well as space is used to avoid the flux and indeterminacy of un-controlled everyday practices. Time organization under military rule as a surveillance tool fractures the routine of ontological security. It re-categorizes time and then the usual activities and practices acquire new meanings which are different from ordinary times. Time is therefore used as a surveillance tool openly by the military more than at any other times. All these practices and applications which are the consequence of military coups make power relations around time visible. Because the usual temporal ordering of time in routines is a way of hiding that, these imposed activities have to be ordered. These practices of military coups over time allow us to understand how timing activities and ordering time is the re-production of social life in a hierarchical way. When the usual everyday organization of time is threatened by military power, feelings about continuity, coherence and confidence are interrupted. That is why a military coup fractures time in terms of ontological security.

What the cross-dressing character does in films, which I call fracturing space and time, is 'the crisis of spatiality'. The process of becoming of a cross-dressing character which, is the deterritorialization of the subject, can be accepted as a dislocation which is caused by a crisis in space and time. I shall now discuss this crisis under the three different headings.

Leaving home and playing with the past

Cross-dressing films can be read as a story of leaving home, abandoning permanent settlement and deterritorialization. In almost all cross-dressing films, a cross-dressing character departs from his/her settlement and settles in a liminal space. I discuss the idea of leaving home and the question mark about space and time which hangs over the idea of leaving home in relation to ideas of becoming and of the nation as home in this section. However, as usual, first I shall discuss the idea of home and its location in the formation of subjectivity and identity, and then I shall make a connection between the idea of home, cross-dressing and military coup.

It is impossible to think of the body without space/time and of space/time without the body. Power relations work on the body by placing it in a particular space and time. 'Home' has a special meaning compared with other spaces in this sense because, as Gaston Bachelard (1964: 4) put it, 'For our house is our corner of the world, as has often been said it is our first universe, a real cosmos in every sense of the word'. Not only do we live in a home, but also the home lives inside us, and not only do we construct a home, the home also constructs us. Michel De Certeau (1984: 148) stated that 'Our successive living spaces never disappear completely; we leave them without leaving them because they live in turn, invisible and present, in our memories and in our dreams. They journey within us.' 'The house, in particular the childhood home, is therefore understood as an anchoring in a time and place that can be accessed in other times and places. The childhood home remembers and is remembered as a virtual place, constantly called upon for idealistic understandings of security and imaginative possibilities' (Davidson 2009: 339). The idea of the home is therefore the safe-guard system of our stable identity because, according to Bachelard (1964: 17), a 'House constitutes a body of image that gives mankind proofs or illusions of stability'. In other words, the home is one of the main sources of our stable identity and of the continuity of this identity. So a home is a very important space for ontological security. Discussing how a home can do this can help us to understand why cross-dressing characters abandon their house/home.

First, the home is the space where subjects gain knowledge about themselves and about the rest of the world. In other words, a home produces knowledge by organizing everyday life and building memories. The home teaches us limitations by organizing life – what inside/outside means, what self/other means, the value of our activities and the hierarchy between these activities by placing and timing them: where/when we should eat, where/when we should sleep and so on. By means of the home, we know who we were, who we are and who we shall be, because as explained above, a home is a kind of anchor which is in time and space and this anchor establishes a relation with other times, past, present and future, and other spaces. It can do this because the home is the space where memory, which is the source of both identity and knowledge, is structured, where the present is experienced and where the future is imagined. Dallas Roger (2013: 262) spoke about 'inhabiting the home and the role that remembrance, memory and the imagination might play in producing knowledge about the world'. The home can produce knowledge in two ways by using memories. Tonya Davidson (2009: 332) suggested that 'Houses remember and haunt as they animate the memories of previous inhabitants, memories that become embodied by the houses and the current dwellers. Houses also embody histories of design, reflective of broader social attitudes toward intimate places'. The house is not only the centre of our personal history but also a meeting point for our personal history, social history and the histories of previous inhabitants. This is one way in which a house produces knowledge as a source of a stable identity and its continuity.

The second discussion about how the house protects our stable identities can be that our home can enable us to build repetitive behaviour. Bachelard (1964: 14) said that behaviour such as always anticipating the extra-high step before a landing or pushing back doors and expecting specific creaks are memories imbued from early houses. He went on, 'But over and beyond our memories, the house we were born in is physically inscribed in us. It is a group of organic habits' Bachelard (1964: 16). By the witnessing of the rhythms of the everyday, houses become imbued with cumulative sets of memories. Laurence J. Kirmayer (1996: 177), in his taxonomy of memory, described 'procedural memory' as the memories commemorated through habits, gestures and thought-implicit memory. The house as a home is only possible through these repetitive acts as movements through time. In other words, the house is the place where routines are constructed. These routines protect identities against chaos and maintain the security of ontology. Our homes are the main stages where our identities are performed, and where we gain these identities by repetitive routines as performance.

This repetitive behaviour discussion can be linked with how and where children learn from their family. The house is a safe space for our identities because they are constructed in the home. In order to be a family, which is the one of the ideological state apparatuses, we need a home. Home and family are the re-production system of the ideology. The home therefore also produces knowledge about what is outside it. A house can be thought as a value fabric of the system where a child learns what is acceptable to society and what is not. The home produces and reproduces the dominant culture as exchange values. Ideologies are transmitted through or within the social structures of civil society and are exercised within institutions such as the family and the house which the family inhabits. Houses are places where power is exercised. By means of the home, children not only interiorize power but also take their place in the matrix of power relations. Self-disciplined, self-motivated, normalized and standardized children who are created by family education and home organization are transformed into citizens who are willing to be a part of a disciplined society. The concept of home therefore always involves a hierarchy which is produced by the father and mother. Hence, the home is the space where we learn to be a part of society and is therefore the source of our stable identities.

Becoming familiar with our home makes our home an extension of our body and our houses are assimilated in our bodies. The houses with which we are familiar and know well give us access to material objects which work as part of our bodies. Our houses, like our bodies, are seen and enable seeing. Our houses become modes of being just like our bodies. On the other hand, 'who knows because the body knows. You are a body and your body is the potential of a certain world' (Merleau-Ponty 1962: 98). For this reason, the body is a political tool: 'There is no law that is not inscribed on bodies' (De Certeau 1984: 146). All these arguments about the body can be adopted for the idea of the house which is our second body. The home produces knowledge about us and the rest of the world, allows repetitive behaviours which create routines, re-produces and transmits ideologies, and works as our second body. All these establish our identities and maintain the stability and continuity of these identities. Home is therefore the place of the ontological security of *beings*. As already discussed, cross-dressing produces new knowledge about this certain world by using the body. If the body changes its practice which is used for constructing a relationship with the certain world, its information which is gained from this relationship will change. This is the reason why the cross-dressing body has to abandon his/her house/home. But how does abandoning home work in cross-dressing Turkish films?

When we look at the cross-dressing films, we can easily see that abandoning our house/home is compulsory in one way or another. Except for *Şeytanın Pabucu*, all of the case films begin with a leaving home. In *Fıstık Gibi Mşallah*, Fikri and Naci lose their money gambling, they cannot pay their rent and become homeless. Rent is also very important for Şoför Nebahat. After the loss of her father and her divorce, she cannot pay the rent so she has to begin work as a taxi driver and then her taxi identifies her. In *Şabaniye*, Şaban and his mother have to leave their home town because of the blood feud: his father killed the son of the man who then killed his father. This is what starts the blood feud. Şaban and his mother abandon not only their home but also their home town and move to Istanbul. In *Hababam Sınıfı Merhaba*, Arzu leaves her home and moves into a dormitory in order to observe her boyfriend's life. After our discussion of the meaning of house/home, their act of abandoning home gains meaning. As discussed above, home is the source of stable identity because it is the source of the knowledge which we gain about others and about ourselves. The house can do this because it is the place where our memories are located, where ideology is transmitted from one generation to the next, where repetitive acts suffuse the body as performance and which works like our second body. In order to escape our stable identities, we first have to abandon our homes. In order to use the body in a different way, to use our knowledge with different aspects, to reconstruct memories about ourselves, our house and home have to stay behind us. Leaving the house means leaving a stable identity, a system of knowledge.

The home is the place for *being*, not for *becoming*; it has to be abandoned because it is the place where system is structured within the subject. The house is the connection point between subjects and sets of values, ideology, system and power. Leaving home is therefore the first step to *becoming* because it forces the subject to have experiences beyond the previous limits and boundaries. It is the hierarchy of the ontology of the subject because it organizes the memories which are the stories of identity. On the other hand, becoming requires mobility which destroys ontological security. The cross-dressing character as a subject who is in the process of *becoming* has to leave home. Furthermore, as discussed above, the house becomes our second body which enables us to do what the body can do. So no body transformation can happen in our second body. The new body of the cross-dressing subject in films needs new places which are not labelled by power as easily as the home is.

In order to make a connection between the idea of home and the military coups, it can be argued more broadly that home also implies nation. Jale Parla (1990) read the idea of home into her study of the Tanzimat (period in the Ottoman Empire 1839–76) novel *Babalar Ve Oğullar* ('Fathers and Sons'). She claimed that the houses which are abandoned, left, rented out or collapsed are the main spaces of the Tanzimat novel. These houses are a symbol of the Ottoman Empire which was in the process of collapsing. Furthermore, Aksu Bora (2005) claimed that the whole modernization history of the Turkish Republic can be read as abandoning or leaving home, which implies the Ottoman Empire. These ideas can be used for the cross-dressing films in Turkey which were produced during the times of military coups. Leaving home in cross-dressing films can be a symbol of the desire to leave the nation. Military coups turn the nation/home into an uncomfortable place for the subject. Nation and home lose their value systems, stability, routine and confidence. The house/nation is both a shelter which protects us from the outside by giving us an identity and at the same time it is also our border, our obstacle to being free. During the times of military coups in Turkey, the nation/home lost its feature of being a shelter and only its coerciveness remained. After the 1980 military coup, thirty thousand people abandoned their homeland and took refuge in European countries such as France, Germany, Holland and Belgium as political refugees (Karaca 2001).

That is why we do not see the house in these films. In these cross-dressing films, houses are an imaginary formation which we do not see, where the characters do not live. These houses are mentioned but not seen. That is why we can say that the house is not a real space for these films, it is a symbol: a large-scale symbol from body to nation. That is why it has to be abandoned for two reasons: for the body of *becoming* by cross-dressing and for the prison-like nation created by a military coup. So what is the position of home as *space* in *time*? And how can home be used to discuss time fracturing?

A home is kind of anchor which is in time and which establishes a relationship with other times, past, present and future. In other words, home fixes us in time. When cross-dressing characters abandon their home, they become liberated from their fixed past as well because they set free their fixed identity. They therefore have an opportunity to play with the past. Identity is the story about ourselves which we tell others, and memory is the main element of this story. Cross-dressing characters in films have to find their own way to create new narratives of their new gendered identities so therefore, in cross-dressing films, there are several scenes about how the cross-dressing characters create new memories for their new gendered identities. These new memories can then be accepted as sources of new identities.

Memory is the performance of identity. We perform our identities on the stage of memory. Our identities are the embodied form of our memories. Philosophers have long regarded memory as the key to explaining personal identity over time, for reasons of brevity, personal choice or simply as identity according to the context. John Locke (1731) regarded memory as the receptacle of personal identity whereas Joseph Butler (1906) and Thomas Reid (1785) both saw memory as evidence of identity. Autobiographies as accounts of personal identity which are based on memory have always been popular and they envelop the past in what is probably the dominant contemporary view. Memory is the form of the past which spills over into the present. It can be thought of as a warehouse which can be re-structured according to the needs, desires and fears of the present. This is why memory cannot be fixed; it is socially and culturally mediated in at least two ways. First, memory emerges from social interactions which focus on the telling and retelling of significant life events (Nelson & Fivush 2004), and second, it is modulated by the sociocultural models available for organizing and understanding human life, including narrative genres and life scripts (Berntsen & Rubin 2004; Thorne & McLean 2003). However, each re-telling activity of significant life events of human life involves the question of who is doing the telling, when it is being told, what is being told and what is not being told. Memory therefore includes the politics of storytelling which is about remembering and forgetting. That is why, in order to reconstruct today, in the context of films, then, cross-dressing characters have to use memories of the self differently for their new identities. They can change the past according to the needs and desires of the present. In other words, they are active agents who can travel between distinct time periods and re-shape these time periods which are usually accepted as closed, fixed and unchangeable. In doing this, they transform the past into a place of becoming rather than of being. They can play with the past. I am interested in the way that cross-dressing characters create memory because it can be claimed that the strategies which they use to do it include knowledge about the perception of the social order, social interactions and the value system. Creating memory transforms cross-dressing characters into active agents in discourse, which is why these strategies give us a significant opportunity to discuss the system of knowledge of a specific period.

In cross-dressing films, remembering the past and using made-up memories to reconstruct an identity are a common narrative strategy. For example, in *Fıstık Gibi Maşallah,* Fikriye, as a cross-dressed character, makes up memories for her new identity as a condition of her identity. In one scene, she tells a story about how hot she is and how hot her lovers are to the other girls playing in the band by saying 'as a modern, urbanite young girl, of course I have some lovers'. While she is telling stories about her un-experienced memories, at the same time she is abusing the women around her by touching them and kissing them (*see* Figure 5.1). In these made-up memories of Fikriye, we can find a larger historical narrative about love, women and men. Fikriye can abuse women by using these narratives. This scene shows us how the discourse around love at a particular time can be abusive. The love stories of the time turn into a male fantasy controlled by men. As discussed in the previous chapters, this film carries the tension between modernity and tradition and shows how the modernization process has forced women to be seen in the public sphere as a symbol of the modern state. At the same time, modernism and urbanism enable women to experience love, but these love stories are now used as vehicles for abusing women. The made-up memories are based on the fear of modern women who are starting to appear outside the home.

In one scene in *Şabaniye,* Şabaniye explains to enemy family's son Şehmuz why she does not like her brother Şaban by recounting a made-up childhood memory. Şabaniye tells a story about how Şaban always bullied her in the past because he was the only son of the family and sons are always more important

Figure 5.1 A screenshot from *Fıstık Gibi Maşallah*: Fikriye touches and kisses women while telling a love story.

than daughters. In this scene, the cross-dressed character whose identity is in the process of becoming becomes an active agent who can use public forms of memory. Memories of self are constructed by both private consciousness and public knowledge. In other words, our memories, for example childhood memories, come to the present in different forms which are framed by the knowledges which we have of the current period. When we recall the memories, even more so the personal ones, they are framed by knowledge about how the particular time and space were when they were formed. Our memories cannot be separated from the knowledge which we have been gaining over time. In other words, memories do not belong to us entirely. You can never decide whether the things which are remembered actually happened in the way that they are remembered. The cross-dressing characters in films such as *Şabaniye* make up stories about the past by using contemporary discussion (figure 5.2). As I discussed in the previous chapters, this particular film was produced in the period when second-wave feminism was emerging in Turkey. Şabaniye makes up the story by using the feminist discussions of that period.

Figure 5.2 A screenshot from *Şabaniye*: Şabaniye tells a story about Şaban.

In *Şeytanın Pabucu*, Burhan is a cross-dressing character who makes up stories about herself and also about himself. While he is his older sister, he tidies up Burhan's past. In this film, the past is re-organized for the character to be absolved. S/he always re-tells stories of his past in order to create a wonderful future. As his sister, she makes up stories about how Burhan is a brave, honest and even religious man even though he seems to be an alcoholic swindler. This film was produced in the period of the rise of Islamic conservatism in Turkey. The cross-dressing character plays with the past in order to create a brand new identity for himself which is more acceptable for the period. In this film, memories as a temporal ordering device shape the movements and orientation of his body as well. By using these brand new memories, he can come closer to his sexy neighbour. His body gains a new place in which to move by means of the re-structured past. The link between the perception and the memory of identity becomes visible.

In cross-dressing films, the cross-dressing characters use the past and memories as a narrative of the past as the foundation of not only the present but also their new identities. By means of their actions, the past becomes timeless and abstract. They can do these actions because their bodies are the body of becoming. This becoming provides them with mobility between the different discourses of different periods. As has been stated many times in the previous chapters, these films are the films of times of military coup when the actions of remembering and/or forgetting the past are controlled by the military. They were times when memories of nation were under control and were not free. In Turkey's experiences of military coups, history, as the synchronized perception of the past, creates a national identity which has been changed quickly according to the needs of present. For example, the 1960 military coup glorified the Kemalist past whereas with the 1980 coup, Kemalism began to lose its power as a neo-liberal state replaced the national state. After the 2007 ultimatum, the Islamic past of the Ottoman Empire was reconstructed according to the needs of Islamic conservatism (*see* for example Figure 5.3). Each change which has been done to the past fractures the coherence of national identity and the basic trust system of the citizens. When the 'truth' of history changes, new social groups and identities arise and existing groups and identities are excluded by the new truths. New forms of power relations develop between them. It can therefore be said that each military coup resulted in insecurity of the ontology of citizens by changing the 'truths' of the story of national identity. National history, in this sense, is the place where national identity is structured. The idea of nation is based not only on synchronized routines produced by collectivized time but also on the memories of citizens which have been synchronized by what can be called national history. Military coups change the dominant ideas of history which affect the concepts of national identity because each military coup leads to an attempt to re-organize the power relations of the nation and to control the present. The process of making up memories seen in each cross-dressing film involves the tension of the period. Whereas the truths about the past are changed under military rule, cross-dressing characters can pick up any memory from the past which is more acceptable for the new period.

The cross-dressing characters in the films gain flexibility because of their becoming to re-organize and reconstruct the past. They reconstruct the past just as a military coup does, and maybe it can be said just as all people do, but they do it very openly, without rationale, shamelessly. The most important thing is that they are doing it by challenging the narrative and the narration style of the film. Other characters are not able to reconstruct the past; they are prisoners of linear, progressive and measurable time. In *Şabaniye*, Şehmuz and Nazlı are stuck in their past, they are desperately seeking their father's killer. In *Fıstık Gibi Maşallah*, when the leader of the group band finds a cigar, he accuses Gülten because Gülten is known to have had a rebellious past. In *Hababam Sınıfı*

Figure 5.3 The front page of the *Posta* newspaper (11 February 2018): it tells how Recep Tayyip Erdoğan invited living but exiled members of the Ottoman dynasty to Turkey. It is an example of how the perception of the past can be re-organized according to the political needs of the present.

Merhaba, Yakışklı (boyfriend of cross-dressing character) pays the price for his womanizing past. Although the past is not changeable for them, for the cross-dressed characters there is no past, no memory, no personal history because past, memory and personal history make us ourselves and give us identity; they make the world stable. In Deleuze's words, 'becoming has no history'. Cross-dressing characters have no history: they are free to reconstruct their past.

The cross-dressing character fractures the linear, fixed, unchanging past and the past, which is the guarantee of identity, becomes a playground of the cross-dressing character. It is no longer a closed, fixed and stable entity in the present. The past and the memories of cross-dressing characters destroy the perception of linear, measurable, progressive time which is the foundation block of power relations. They can do this because they are in the process of becoming. Their identities are reterritorialized and the symbol of this deterritorialization starts with leaving home in the narrative.

Liminal spaces and multiple 'nows'

Cross-dressing characters usually move into liminal space after leaving home. For example, in *Fıstık Gibi Maşallah*, Fikri and Naci begin to live in a hotel (figure 5.5); in *Hababam Sınıfı Merhaba*, Arzu moves into a dormitory (figure 5.4); in *Şoför Nebahat*, a taxi becomes the main space of Nebahat; and in *Şabaniye*, a music hall can be accepted as a main space of the film. Hotel, dormitory, taxi and music hall are regarded as liminal spaces in the context of this current study. I shall therefore examine the kinds of opportunity which these liminal spaces provide to the characters and how the characters use these opportunities to fracture space and time.

In order to discuss the politics of liminal space, its meaning should be discussed first. The idea of liminality is taken from the Latin word *limen* which means a 'threshold', and this in-betweenness was the subject of anthropological studies by Arnold van Gannep (1960) and Victor Turner (1969). They advanced the idea of liminality 'in which people are betwixt and between all the recognized fixed points in space-time of structural classification' (Turner 1969: 97). Liminality can be used to refer to space 'where the people [are] positioned on a boundary or threshold' (Weller 2006: 102). Turner (1982) emphasized how liminal spaces act to create the contexts where the norms and values of everyday society can be and are suspended. Liminal spaces can generate unsettling, disturbing and dangerous experiences

Figure 5.4 Arzu in the male dormitory in *Hababam Sınıfı Merhaba*.

(Tempest *et al.* 2007) but they can also be sites of togetherness, creativity and self-fulfilment (Simpson *et al.* 2010; Sturdy *et al.* 2006).

After establishing the core of the term 'liminal', its features can now be discussed, I will now discuss its features as represented in film. De Certeau (1984) suggested that in order to analyse a space, the first question which should be asked is who is the owner of the space? The house belongs to women, the street belongs to men and liminal space belongs to either or neither no-one or everyone. A liminal space is a space for nomads who are on a journey. So if the meaning of space is constructed by the relations which take place within it, the meaning of a liminal space takes on great variety and becomes multifarious. The meaning and structure of a space depend on who inhabits the same place. It can be said that liminal spaces are for collective identities, not for individuals. For example, a dormitory is for students, a hotel is for visitors, a taxi is for travellers and so on.

Liminal space is in between binary poles. Liminal spaces are usually both/neither private and/nor pubic, outside and/nor inside, formal and/nor informal, for self and/nor other. In order to describe one place as a liminal space, we need a binary opposition. However, like cross-dressing gender performance, liminal spaces work like the deconstruction effects of these binaries and create ambiguity about space perception. Liminal spaces are for those who want both to escape and to settle, who want to be both nomads and localized. Liminal spaces therefore involve two actions: coming and going, but not staying. The something which happens in between these two actions is transformation.

Figure 5.5 Naciye, Fikriye and Gülten in the hotel in *Fıstık Gibi Maşallah*.

Liminal spaces are the space for transformation. They are often the contexts where identities are challenged or changed, where previous subject positions are no longer sustainable and where actors adopt new identities which may be permanent or remain temporary. Wendelin Küpers (2011: 46) stated that 'liminal spaces and places have always been basic conditions for all transitions of human beings, things and occasions'. 'He argues that the process of transition is intrinsically linked to movement through open, liminal spaces, which are inherently ambiguous, and hold the potential for subversion and transformation' (in Lucas 2014: 199). It can be said that liminal spaces have ambiguous potential and allow the subject to achieve transition. Turner (1969) described 'the transitional or liminal phase as a limbo between a past state and a coming one, a period of personal ambiguity, of non-status and of unanchored identity'. In short, in a liminal space, you cannot stay in the same position: it is the place where you transform into something different. It can therefore be said that liminal spaces are places of uncertainty because you know what the beginning point is but you cannot know what the end point

Figure 5.6 A screenshot from *Şeytanın Pabucu*: Burhan in Kaaba.

will be. Liminal spaces are full of possibilities, hence full of mobility, and they are dynamic spaces. It is therefore not a surprise that cross-dressing gender transformation takes place in liminal spaces. *Şeytanın Pabucu* provides a very good example of this transformation of identities. In the film, Burhan and his sister go to Kaaba to help Burhan to find a way of being a good Muslim because he is an alcoholic and a swindler (see figure 5.6). In Kaaba, Burhan's sister gets lost and Burhan masquerades as her in order to escape his enemies. Kaaba can be accepted as a liminal space; it belongs to no-one but to everyone, it is both private and public. Burhan's transformation takes place in this liminal space, and for this transformation the dominant structure of a given society and the obvious acceptance of roles have to be changed. Being a pilgrim involves the deconstruction of the former life. Burhan deconstructs his former life but in different way compared with a pilgrim.

In view of the above, it is possible to claim that liminal space is uncontrollable. Power loses its control system over liminal spaces. In liminal space, the thread which binds subject and system breaks. Bronwyn Wood (2012: 345) commented that 'liminal space provides a powerful starting point for developing new understanding. Liminal space is flux, unfolding, constantly changing rather than a finished product'.

After discussing liminal space and its features, we can now turn to cross-dressing films and the liminal places which are chosen by cross-dressing characters. As has already been explained, liminal spaces are usually the principal locations of cross-dressing characters after leaving home. Home, as discussed above, provides the core of the stable identity of the self and represents routine, consistency, continuity and security: it is the place of ontological security. As I have argued throughout this book, when ontological security has been threatened by a military coup, the security, routine and continuity of places have been threatened. A home not only represents itself, it also represents nation, homeland and country. During a military coup, the system is changed, and this can be accepted as a transformation of society. So leaving home and settling in liminal spaces cannot be a coincidence in cross-dressing films which are accepted as popular narratives during times of military coup.

Furthermore, as discussed above, the control of power decreases in liminal space, which means that the panoptic social mechanism loses its ability in liminal space. This makes liminal space more useful for any kind of identity transformation. In other words, liminal spaces are more useful spaces than houses for the process of becoming. In this sense, liminal spaces can be considered as connection points on the rhizome for *becomings*. When identity begins its journey in the process of becoming, this journey affects the preference for space where the identity is located. Becoming requires a space where it can be and liminal space as a space of transformation provides this space for the process of becoming. Arzu is no more a woman in a dormitory, Naci and Fikri are no more men in hotels and so on. Moreover, they need this liminal space for the process of becoming. As already discussed, cross-dressing is a way of challenging the gender binary; now we can see that liminal space is a way of challenging the space binary. It is not therefore surprising that liminal spaces are the spaces of cross-dressing performance.

Liminal space can be accepted as a meeting point for subjects who are in the process of becoming in the rhizome, as discussed in Chapter 2. In cross-dressing films, liminal space provides two opportunities for cross-dressing characters. First, it is the place of transformation where stability, routine and continuity collapse and therefore is a place of ontological insecurity. The second opportunity is pertinent for the case of Turkey: liminal spaces are the places where power loses its control over the space. They are therefore the place where collective identities can escape the panoptic mechanism of a military coup.

Liminal space allows cross-dressing characters to be in different spaces at the same time because of this lack of control. These different spaces run parallel to each other at the same time. This situation and the benefits which it gives to cross-dressing characters allow us to ask some important questions about the spatial organization of power relations.

As explained above, cross-dressing characters can be in different spaces and times if space and time are accepted as perceptions and not real. For example, Naci in *Fıstık Gibi Maşallah* can be in three different spaces at the same time: Naci-ye is in the hotel room with the girls in the band, Kemal is on the beach with Gülten and Naci is in Istanbul with the killers. All three versions of Naci have their own time and space and their own stories which are written in their own time and space. The other girls think that Naciye is resting in the hotel room and they want to visit her. However, Naci as Kemal is on the beach with Gülten. So Naci-ye alternates between being on the beach with Gülten and being in the hotel room. At the same time, Naci makes up stories and spreads them as gossip to convince the killers that he is in Istanbul. So he is not in one place, he is everywhere but at the same time nowhere. Three different spaces produce three different representations and knowledge for one character at the same time. Although the narrative space is the beach, the character's spaces are the beach, the hotel and Istanbul. This multiple usage of space can be accepted as a source of the comedy and irony in the film. In *Hababam Sınıfı Merhaba*, Arzu is in her home for her mother but in the dormitory as a man. Her mother is a teacher at the all-male boarding school and is with her daughter every day in the school, but she cannot recognize that the cross-dressed he is her daughter. This place – an all-male boarding school and dormitory – produces different knowledge for the mother; for her Arzu is one of the male students. In *Şabaniye*, Şaban is in Lebanon for the enemy family, Şaban-iye is in the music hall for Şehmuz and Bayram is in the park with his lover Nazlı all at the same time. Between the park, Lebanon and the music hall, Şaban is intangible, mobile. Power has lost its control over Şaban; he can do whatever he wants. It can therefore be said that we can encounter at least three different spaces for one body in cross-dressing films in terms of the other characters. This crisis of spatiality can happen because subjects cannot be controlled in liminal space; they can escape the surveillance which is produced by other characters by using space because they are intangible in space. They cannot be fixed, placed and oriented in a given space by narrative; they are mobile in envisaged places. Cross-dressing characters can therefore fracture the perception of fixed, unchanging, stable and linear space in narrative.

Being in different spaces at the same time creates different nows for cross-dressing characters and these parallel nows destroy routines and make cross-dressing characters more free in linear time. This freedom is lived by cross-dressing characters because it does not take place in the narration; film narration follows linear conventional time. The most important thing here is that this freedom is available only to cross-dressing characters and no other characters can play with the past in the same way. The films follow the conventional and classical narrative and narration style for the other characters and for the audience, but not for the cross-dressing characters because only cross-dressing characters are the bodies of becoming. Cross-dressing characters can use different nows because of their ability to break down the connections between time and space. These fractures highlight and make visible our fictional relationship with time and space, which cannot be discussed without reference to power relations. Cross-dressing characters can be in different nows because of their mobility. But for what purposes do cross-dressing characters use these different nows?

By breaking down routines, different presents are used as means of escaping the surveillance of a specific time, which is the very opposite of the aim of a military coup. The use of the present by cross-dressing characters creates different nows and these different nows help them to escape the surveillance of the present. The multiple usage of now makes cross-dressing characters intangible. The reason why the killers in *Fıstık Gibi Maşallah*, the creditors in *Şeytanın Pabucu* and the enemy family in *Şabaniye* cannot find the characters whom they are seeking is because in the same time phase they can be everywhere and nowhere. As discussed throughout Chapter 2, they are visible but not recognizable because they have fractured the connection points between time and space. For the purposes of this discussion, it can be said that they fracture the relationship between time and space which are structured by power relations and therefore cannot be labelled by any time/space relationship. So they can escape surveillance by using space and time.

By this multiple usage of the present, cross-dressing characters also fracture the perception of the present. The present is no longer a measurable part of space because of this multiple usage, which is why the actions of cross-dressing characters in the present create confusion and cause the collapse of the fabric of everyday experiences for other characters. In this sense, cross-dressing characters in films fracture the trust in ontological security by fracturing the way of operating time as an institution of power because cross-dressing characters create randomness, unpredictability and facelessness in the presents. By means of this action, unquestioning commitment to the established routines which stabilize our identities is fractured. When the established routines are fractured, the ideology which these routines provide is undermined, and this is why, when the actor's ontological security is fractured, the whole system which creates subjects as self and other is fractured.

The multiple usages of the present made by cross-dressing characters and the liminal space in the films work in three different ways. First, the characters can escape the surveillance system of the present(s) because they are de-centred becomings of the present. They are visible but not recognizable; they are here and now but intangible in time and space. Second, cross-dressing characters fracture the operation of time and space as the regulatory systems of ontological security which fabricate everyday routines. And third, ultimately they undermine the discourses which are provided by using time and space. All of these things can gain a lot of new meaning if we regard them as the popular narratives of a culture which organizes the rule of a military coup.

As Giddens observed, routines which are controlled and synchronized by and in time and space allow the continuity of self-identity. Time and space not only provide continuity for identities but are also the main sources of identity. Identity requires continuity and being in time and space. Identity as a narrative of self needs chronological ordering to be told. Identity is a story which is a bridge between past, present and future and through which we perform our stories in time. Time and space give boundaries to the stories and also bind our stories with those of others. The concept of linear and fixed time and space helps people to protect the ontological security of their identity. Therefore, when time and space are fractured, the ontological security of identity is fractured and when ontological security is fractured, the perception of time and space is also fractured.

An envisaged future

The future is the aim of ontological security. Routines, basic trust system, time and space organization and even language have been organized to protect identities from the unpredictability and potential chaos of the future. This is why the fundamental questions of ontological security are 'Will I be the same person in the future as I am today?' and 'Will the life by which I am surrounded remain the same as it is today?' Ontological security protects us from the chaos of the future by using the past and the present. In other words, ontological security is our guarantee of the future. Paul Ricoeur (1984) stated that the future is a form which involves the proposal, anxiety and assumption of now.

Anxieties are always about the future, not the present. Ontological security relieves us from anxieties of self because it works towards to the future. This is why, when a military coup destroys the ontological security of both state and citizen, the main concern becomes the stability and validity of the self in the future, rather than in the present.

In almost all of the selected cross-dressing films there is a formulaic scene in which the cross-dressing character re-organizes the future. The common way of doing this is by telling fortunes. In *Şabaniye*, Şaban tells Nazlı's fortune using a Turkish coffee cup (as seen in Figure 5.7). As his cross-dressed character, Şabaniye predicts how Nazlı will meet her true love: (s)he tells Nazlı that she will be attacked by some bad men but that, luckily for her, there will be a young, handsome, brave man whose name begins with B who will rescue her from them. This young, handsome, brave man whose name begins with B will be Nazlı's true love. Şaban then organizes this attack by paying some men to threaten her and then he rescues her and introduces himself as Bayram. Of course, Nazlı thinks that Bayram is going to be her true love. Then they fall in love. By using a coffee cup, Şaban captures the future and re-organizes it. It is a kind of time travel in words. In similar ways, each character and the various identities which are

Figure 5.7 In *Şabaniye*, Şaban tells Nazlı's fortune using a Turkish coffee cup.

Figure 5.8 In *Fıstık Gibi Maşallah*, Naciye tells Gülten's fortune by reading her hand.

provided by cross-dressing performance re-organize the narrative for each other by manipulating time.

In *Fıstık Gibi Maşallah*, Naciye tells Gülten's fortune by reading her hand (as seen Figure 5.8). He advises her to be on the beach at a specific time and tells her that at that particular time and that place she will meet a man; Naciye describes the man in great detail. Naciye works out what kind of man Gülten is looking for from the questions which she asks. Naci as Naci turns up at the predicted time, meets Gülten and they fall in love. He manipulates the future by making up a story about it. He provides himself with open-ended linkages between the present and the future. Cross-dressing gives mobility to its subject not only between gendered identities but also between past, present and future precisely because of the characters' unrecognizable, uncontrolled and unlabelled performativity.

In *Şeytanın Pabucu*, Burhan tells the fortune of his attractive neighbour when he wants to guide her in his direction. The men who use fortune-telling in this way might normally have escaped the attention of their chosen women. But because of the fortune-telling, the women are prepared to wait for the predicted men and the predicted circumstances in which they will meet them. The cross-dressing characters thus create an expectation about the future which is entirely false but which becomes entirely true. They use their mobility in order to create an expectation about the future and the mobility of their becoming transforms the relationship between the present and the future in the narrative. It can be said that the cross-dressing characters in the films are located between the present and the future; they are time travellers. For them, the future is not predictable, it is knowable. The future is a play-ground for their desires and their wills. Cross-dressing characters in films actually produce the future.

Closure

Space and time are tools of power which are used to produce knowledge to show the correctness, naturalness and genuineness of power relations. Furthermore, space and time produce and are produced by these power relations. These power relations not only enable the subject to acquire identity but also maintain the stability and continuity of this identity. Space and time are therefore elements of ontological security. When cross-dressing characters in films disrupt and then re-organize ontological security, they also disrupt the perception of linear, fixed and stable space and time and re-organize space and time according to their needs and desires. In order to do that, they first abandon the home where the stable identities and knowledge about the world are produced and where ideologies are transmitted from one generation to the next. I suggest that the home also represents the nation, which is transformed into a huge prison by a military coup. Abandoning the home gives a cross-dressing character the opportunity to play with the past because the home produces knowledge about self and other both inside and outside by using memories which construct identities. Then the cross-dressing characters move into liminal spaces which belong to everyone and to no-one and are in-between public and private. Power loses its control over the subject in liminal spaces. The cross-dressing characters therefore become intangible; they cannot be fixed or oriented in spaces. They can be in different spaces at the same time and can thus escape surveillance and the panoptic organization of space, unlike the citizens who live under military rule following a coup. This cross-dressing mobility, visibility but not recognizability also gives the characters an opportunity to design their own future. In order to achieve this, they use the three effects of cross-dressing performance on the body. By means of the use of space made by cross-dressing characters, the idea of space and time is fractured. Military coups disrupt ontological security and the perception of space and time just as cross-dressing films do. Space and time change their meaning and their routine usage under military rule. Diametrically opposite to the restricted usage of space and time for citizens after military coups, cross-dressing characters in films are free to use space and time according to their own needs and desires.

In this current study, time has been regarded as a condition of power which is used to re-organize and re-shape the practices and performances of not only individuals but also the state. Time which is conventionally regarded as linear, measurable, irreversible and progressive is part of a control system over individuals. It is used for giving shape to ways of being, acting and feeling. Time itself is therefore a tool of surveillance. Furthermore, time is accepted as one of the principal foundations of identity. Identities, which are the narrative forms of self, are constructed through the lens of time. Time gives coherence and utterance to the self.

Time is also one of the key elements of ontological security. The routines and the basic trust system of ontological security can be created by means of the perception of time as linear, measurable, irreversible and progressive. The ontological security of the self can only be possible by the acceptance of the journey of the self from past to future through the present. On the other hand, national traumas such as military coups which destroy ontological security also destroy the sense of being secure in time because they re-structure the past, re-organize the present everyday routines and present the chaos of the future.

Cross-dressing characters in the films which are the popular narratives of the times of military coups in Turkey use the notion of time in many different ways. Because of their multiple usages of time they are located not in the present but in an inter-temporal space. They can be simultaneously in the past, present and future. They use the body as a space of becoming rather like a time-travel machine. They use the past as a warehouse of their new identities. They can make up stories about their imaginary past and in this making-up process they use invented memories which involve the dominant discourses of the period. In their remembering and forgetting while they are building up the past, their political intentions can be read. Furthermore, they can use the present very differently. They can be in different spaces at the same time, which destroys the link between time and space, and in this way they can escape the surveillance system which is provided by the past. When the link between time and space is fractured, their bodies become invisible in current space and then they have the opportunity to re-configure the future. By using strategies such as fortune-telling, they can save their self from the chaos of the future.

Cross-dressing characters in films can play with time which is conventionally accepted as linear, measurable and progressive, and which is perceived as related to age and gender, because of the effects of cross-dressing performance on the performer's body. Because they are the body of becoming, cross-dressing performers are mobile between power relations because their bodies are visible but un-recognizable and because their bodies experience otherness without being other. By means of these effects, they fracture the perception of time which provides ontological security.

6

Fracturing masculinity and femininity: Why boys like that, girls like this?

In this chapter, the crises of femininity and masculinity and how they can be read as responses to the tensions of the periods as well as the perception of authority and freedom according to a film's historical position will be discussed. According to Bell-Metereau (1985: 3), 'Almost all cross-dressing films involve the relationship between authority and freedom – the extent to which the male is free to explore his female nature and the extent to which female characters are capable of establishing their own authority.' Although Bell-Metereau's approach is interested in fluidity in the gender binary, the idea of authority and freedom can be seen in many other aspects of cross-dressing films according to their historical locations. However, there is something more important than the visibility of authority and freedom of particular periods. Cross-dressing films can be accepted as a journey from authority to freedom, and back to authority again. 'Journey' is the key word here, and this journey is an open space where authority and freedom are liberated from their meanings as a stable binary and show that they are different faces of the same discourse. Moreover, this journey as an open space gives an opportunity for the subject to be mobile on the map of power relations and to become a critical agency[1] for a while.

In order to perform the act of crossing as a journey, at least one binary opposition is necessary: man/woman, upper class/working class, white/Black, traditional/modern or human/non-human: to put it in simple terms, the self and the other. There is a need for at least two stable and fixed notions. Therefore, the features of the two terms of binary opposition must be seen during the act of crossing. In short, it can be argued that crossing is relational: it includes a relationship between two binary terms. For this reason, first the idea of masculinity and femininity in films will be discussed according to their means of production and the historical contexts within which they were produced. The difference in cross-dressing films is based on their ability to make performance visible. Other films of the period can be discussed under the idea of how gender is represented. However, cross-dressing films show how gender representations are represented. The representation of gender fractures the idea of masculinity and femininity. In this chapter, I shall discuss crises of masculinity and femininity in relation to the idea of authority and freedom of the period, to how the effects of cross-dressing performance help the cross-dressing character to overcome these crises, and to how this overcoming fractures the ontological security. In order to reach this aim, I shall use critical discourse analysis as explained in the introduction.

Fracturing masculinity

Cross-dressing is not a process of being but of becoming, which implies mobility between different poles of a binary. In this mobility, first the current position has to be left behind. This means that the first 'original' gender experiences a crisis for transforming cross-dressing. The five selected cross-dressing films therefore begin by showing hegemonic[2] masculinity in crisis. Under the effects of cross-dressing, the cross-dressing characters try to overcome these crises. In this section, I shall consider the masculinity crisis in the selected cross-dressing films.

It is normally accepted that the military and masculinity have a reciprocal relationship. However, masculinity is also multidimensional and intersectional. The idea of hegemonic masculinity creates a hierarchy between men (Connel 1995). Michael S. Kimmel (2005) stated that the hegemonic man as an ideal manhood creates competition between men. During military coups, a hierarchy forms between military masculinity[3] and civilian masculinity; military coups and the army settle at the top of the hierarchy of masculinities. It can therefore be claimed that military coups change the relationship between masculinities and relocate them. This relocation causes a masculinity crisis. Cross-dressing films begin with the enunciation of this crisis and offer cross-dressing performance as a solution. In *Fıstık Gibi Maşallah,* in order to mark out the masculinity and then disrupt it, in the first thirty minutes the audience only sees one woman. The viewer only sees Naci in the first scene in a car where he is trying to extort money from an old, ugly woman by using his handsome appearance. Living at a woman's expense is one way to disrupt masculinity. In the second scene, the spectator sees a relationship between men: Naci and Fikri try to get money by gambling. Gambling creates a hierarchy between men and in this hierarchy, Naci and Fikri are losers, not winners. They lose not only their money but also their suit jackets. Dress expresses social control of the body according to categories of age, class, gender, religion and race. Dressing, like other power institutions, transforms the imaginary existence of a subject because being a subject is an ongoing process and dress is a way of experiencing the world and a kind of self-construction of identity by using the signification system of dressing. The system of difference which is used to create meaning expresses itself using codes of dress and acts of wearing as ways of expression. The loss of your jacket is related to the abandonment or loss of masculinity. Furthermore, a suit jacket implies not only masculinity, but also symbolized modernity for Turkish culture because of the dress codes and implications of Kemalist modernization. The loss of a man's suit jacket means the loss of his status within the modernization process which was the principal tension of the period. The next scene begins with a man being beaten up in the nightclub where *The Wasps* – the name of Fikri and Naci's group – are performing. Nobody is interested in the performance of the group and some of the audience even jeer at *The Wasps*. Being a *wasp* implies productivity of masculinity in Turkish culture, so their masculinity is being mocked. After losing their money, losing their jackets, losing their body's power, they are now losing their artistic talent in the eyes of the audience. All of these scenes are organized to undermine masculinity and induce in the audience acceptance of the need for the subsequent gender transformation. In this way, the two characters can achieve protection in the eyes of the audience. The audience is convinced the exigency of this transformation without making any judgement. Hence, cross-dressing is portrayed as a purely pragmatic act, as a temporary solution. In *Şoför Nebahat*, masculinity and its power domain are expressed by emptiness. Nebahat's father dies suddenly, her husband cheats on her and they divorce. Her cross-dressing is depicted as an entirely pragmatic act, as a temporary solution, because of the emptiness created by the absence of masculinity. This emptiness can be read as an outcome of militaristic masculinity which destroys the hierarchy between masculinities in ordinary civil times. This crisis and emptiness in terms of masculinities disrupt ontological security: not only are identities and their hegemonic domain fractured, but also their continuity is interrupted by military coups. When the stability and continuity of identities are threatened, ontological security is threatened as well. Therefore, masculinities are ontologically insecure in times of military coups. Cross-dressing films can be accepted as a solution to this insecurity.

Very similar scenes can be seen in *Şabaniye*. However, the description of hegemonic masculinity changed between the 1960s and the 1980s, which is why in *Şabaniye* the masculinity crisis is shown differently. In *Şabaniye*, the masculinity crisis becomes visible through the relationship between mother and son. He lives with his mother and he works by means of his mother, because the owner of the music hall owes a debt of gratitude to Şaban's mother. Although Şaban is an unskilful waiter, his mother always has his back. Even so, he consistently does the wrong thing at the wrong time. On the other hand, the enemy family's son Şehmuz is the other masculine figure of the period. His mother is disabled and unable to walk. Her only hope is Şehmuz, whom she uses as a phallic tool of power. However, he is a gambler and a spendthrift. All of the male characters' positions in the film are determined by their relationship with their parents. The post-1980 period can be read as becoming distant from tradition by means of neo-liberal politics. Furthermore, feminism took root in Turkey in the post-1980 period. The position and situation of women in society rapidly changed; they began to work, to demand their rights and to challenge society. Hence, the masculinity crisis of the period was based on a questioning of the position of men in the family. According to Elizabeth Badinter (1994), what causes a crisis of masculinity is not so much changing roles, but a questioning of male authority (cited in Powrie 1997: 10). Furthermore, neo-liberal politics require the nuclear family as a reproduction centre of capitalism. The loss of father, grandfather or mother gave power to man as head of the family and this power domain cannot in reality be filled by men in 1980s. As Yvonne Tasker (1998: 110) pointed out, 'men became more overtly targeted as consumers of lifestyle. The invitation extended to western men to define themselves through consumption brings with it a consequent stress on the fabrication of identity, a denaturalising of the supposed naturalness of male identity' in the 1980s. It can be claimed that this is also true of Turkish men. The changing family structure and the force of consumption which affected the self-perception of identity can be accepted as sources of the masculinity crisis in 1980s Turkey. The idea of filling this power domain remained an impossible desire for men as head of the nuclear family. According to Kimmel (2005), 'It is difficult for any man to embody the characteristics of the ideal man at every given moment and over the course of his life time, the need to prove our masculinity is thus a constant source of anxiety' (cited in Fineman & Thomson 2013: 83). For example, before becoming female, Şaban, as a male, suffers from a lack of voice and reason. Although he wants to, when he is on stage he cannot sing. He wants to talk but nobody understands him and everyone accuses him of being unreasonable. When he becomes Şabaniye, however, as a woman he becomes a singer and a star. This opportunity is given to Şabaniye by the effects of his/her cross-dressing performance. The effects of cross-dressing performance allow Şabaniye to get rid of the masculinity crisis of the period. By means of cross-dressing, he can change his position on the map of power relations and moreover he can design this map according to his needs because he is not a stable and fixed *being* but rather he is *becoming*. This distinction between lack of voice and being a singer is based on the contradictions of the 1980s period. Şaban's journey from man to woman is a journey from repressed to provoked which is also very similar to the arabesque culture of the period.

In *Şeytanın Pabucu*, hegemonic masculinity is contoured by the collapsed and depressed neo-liberal politics. Menderes's slogan in the 1950s was 'We will grow one millionaire for every single quarter', and after him the president in the post-1980 period, Turgut Özal, encouraged citizens to be greedy and to work together with their eyes open. However, instead of millionaires, little mafia groups grew up in every single quarter. The distance between the classes increased. Neo-liberal dreams became a nightmare. That is why *Şeytanın Pabucu* begins with a dream which turns into a nightmare. Burhan has trouble with the mafia group in his neighbourhood. However, in this case the necessity of cross-dressing is neither the heritage of the father and tradition nor the result of an accident. Rather, it is a fault of character. The character is the symbol of the performance of unsuccessful masculinity. In *Şeytanın Pabucu*, all of the male characters are swindlers but some of them use brute force, some religion and some money as the visible face of power. Religion, bullying and violence are the main sources of the 2000s politics of masculinity.

It can be claimed that the cross-dressing character not only wears the opposite sex's clothes, but also wears the tension of period. For example, in *Şabaniye*, Şaban not only becomes a woman but also becomes rich, even though he belongs to the working class, by means of cross-dressing (see figure 6.1). The act of cross-dressing involves 'class crossing' according to the time period of Turkey's attempts at neo-liberalism. For example, when Şabaniye and her mother enter their new house, her mother looks around and says, '*It is like a museum. How did they find these old things?*' The new owner of old treasures is the new and hot money. In other words, in order to gain access into the aristocracy,[4] one does not have to be born as one of them. The new and hot money owner is encouraged not by being elite but by buying the idea of elitism. Consumption is the motto of the period. Only in this film, *Şabaniye* does the audience watch long shopping scenes. Shopping is presented as a condition of being a woman. The body of Şabaniye transforms into a shop window. The

Figure 6.1 A film poster for *Şabaniye* – 1984. Şabaniye shows off her jewellery.

Figure 6.2 A frame from *Şeytanın Pabucu*: Fatih Ürek as a pilgrim.

relationship between the body and its surroundings is ignored in the film. The body becomes a space where the new and hot money is exhibited. In *Şeytanın Pabucu*, Burhan not only becomes his sister but also becomes a pilgrim, even though he is an alcoholic, by means of the act of crossing (figure 6.2). The period in which the film was made was marked by increasing Islamic conservatism in Turkey. The country started to wear religion as well. By cross-dressing, characters can adjust themselves to the criteria of the hegemonic masculinities of the period by means of the mobility of cross-dressing performance in order to overcome the masculinity crises of the periods.

In short, it can be claimed that men's patriarchal power reflects itself in the making and functioning of the state. Cynthia Enloe (1990: 45) observed that 'Nationalism has typically sprung from masculinized memory, masculinized humiliation and masculinized hope'. So when the state has a problem, the patriarchy becomes part of this problem and *vice versa*. It can be claimed that these films also work as a process of reproducing masculinity by helping men to create a surveillance system through which they regain the power of hegemonic masculinity which was taken away by military masculinity. However, in order to reconstruct masculinities, first the hegemonic masculinity crisis has to be organized by narrative. Therefore, all of the selected cross-dressing films begin by fracturing masculinity, as explained above. After that, it is restored by a cross-dressing act. The mobility of cross-dressing which is provided by *becoming* for a cross-dressing character can change the character's position within power relations. The visible but unrecognizable face of a cross-dresser allows the cross-dressed character not only to escape the panoptic social mechanism of military coups but also to create his/her own surveillance system. All this re-organizes ontological security for those characters whose ontology security is threatened by military coups.

Furthermore, the typology of the rich old man who falls in love with a cross-dressed male character is a recognizable connection because this character can be seen in almost all male-to-female cross-dressing films. This character can also be discussed in relation to masculinity. The old man figure can be read as a type of masculinity which has been set free from his sexuality. This character has at least two main functions in films, which will be discussed using Judith Butler's sex and gender argument and Foucault's bio-power[5] argument. First, he makes visible masculinity and sexuality, in other words the relationship between gender and sex. Simone de Beauvoir said that 'one is not born but becomes a woman' (1953: 295). Although this statement is accepted by most feminists, it should be asked who decides and how it can be decided whether a newborn baby will be a woman or not. Can sex and gender be separated? According to Butler, they cannot be separated; there is no sex without gender. Butler (2006: 70) stated that 'both are inevitabilities within a culture where reproduction becomes the central organizing principle for bodies'. Furthermore, according to Foucault (1990), the science of biology and the determined biological sex of the body make gender discourse natural, coherent and essentialist. Second, he showed that moral ethical rules about sexuality are necessary for the people who can procreate, and therefore are the subjects of bio-power, in Foucault's term. Foucault (1990) went on to state that the growth and care of the population are the main concerns of the state in the art of government, which is why sexual discourse, like other discourses, is structured by taking into consideration reproduction. At the end of *Fıstık Gibi Maşallah*, when the old man realizes that the woman with whom he has fallen in love is a man, he says, 'No problem. No-one is perfect'. In *Şabaniye*, in the same circumstance, the old man says, 'I wish we had had a night together before you came out'. It does not matter for him whether it is Şaban or Şabaniye for them to sleep together. By virtue of their age, these old men[6] are liberated from the ethical rules of procreation and their sexuality does not threaten society.[7]

Another issue which it is also important to discuss in the masculinity crisis is that there is always another character who accompanies the cross-dresser. Cross-dressers are not alone in their transformation. I term this accompanying character an 'anchor of identity' who helps the cross-dressing characters not to forget their 'inner self'. There are usually two characters who decide to change their appearances. One of them can be claimed to be an anchor of identity for the other: in *Fıstık Gibi Maşallah*, Naci and Fikri; in *Şabaniye*, Şaban and his mother; in *Şoför Nebahat*, Nebahat and her daughter; in *Hababam Sınıfı Merhaba*, Ercüment (one of the male students) and Arzu. When one of them has gender, identity or belonging problems because of his/her changed performance, the other helps him/her as an anchor of identity because without an anchor of identity, a cross-dressing character can get lost in the world of possibilities in the rhizome. As was discussed above, cross-dressing destroys not only gendered identity but also the idea of a fixed and stable identity. The other is therefore the witness of identity. Identity is a kind of story about ourselves which we tell others, so it requires another who witnesses us, without whom our identity loses its value. The other is the anchor of identity.

In the selected cross-dressing films, a possibility is offered to the cross-dressing characters for reconstructing the very masculinities which are threatened by a military coup. In order to express this offer, the films begin by portraying masculinity in crisis. In this crisis, cross-dressing performance is presented as a solution. Mobility of cross-dressing gives an opportunity to the characters to re-organize power relations. So they can change not only their gendered identities but also other forms of identity such as class, ethnicity and religion. Furthermore, because of the mobility which is provided by cross-dressing, they can use time, space and language according to their particular needs and this usage upgrades their masculinities to the hegemonic masculinity level. The visible but not recognizable face of the cross-dressers not only enables them to escape militaristic panoptic surveillance but also allows them to create their own surveillance system which gives them hegemony over other characters. All these effects help to reconstruct the ontological security of masculinities which is disrupted by military coups. In this reconstruction, the ontological security process of the other character accompanies the cross-dressing character as an anchor of identity to protect the cross-dresser from the world of endless combinations which exist in the rhizome.

Femininity crisis

It can be said that although the films undermine masculinity, they also reconstruct femininity: a masculinity crisis can be overcome by means of the effects of cross-dressing whereas a femininity crisis still remains because they are not normally cross-dressers. Even so, it is important to discuss these crises in order to understand the perception and representation of authority and the extent of freedom in the three selected periods. I shall discuss in this section women characters in the selected films and how they experience the tension of the period, how they are represented and the ways in which they communicate with the cross-dressing characters.

In *Fıstık Gibi Maşallah*, at the thirtieth minute of the film, the audience sees two women for the first time. First, two legs with high-heeled shoes are seen. The camera pans up the screen from the bottom to the top. Naci and Fikri have become two women wearing western-style hats and gloves. No-one wore these in Turkey in everyday life. They represent the image of the new woman of the Kemalist modernization project. Therefore, being a woman becomes an 'imaginary formation'[8] (Wittig 1992: 59) in the eyes of the viewer, like the modernization process of Turkey. As discussed above, the modernization process is regarded by some as an endless process and involves impossible desires. This impossibility of modernization is embodied in the women's bodies of Naci and Fikri as imaginary formations. Furthermore, the audience can see only the 'copy of being woman which is also a copy' (Butler 2006). In this scene, the spectator sees the process of *becoming* a woman in their grotesque bodies. Very high-heeled shoes, exaggerated clothes and body-parts such as breasts and hips, out-of-proportion bodies, and un-realistic makeup show the fictionality of

Figure 6.3 A frame from *Fıstık Gibi Maşallah*: Fikriye and Naciye wearing western-style outfits in a parody of being women.

being women and being women becomes non-functional (see figure 6.3). Their *becoming* shows us that *being* woman is a political concept.

Şoför Nebahat is structured on the tension between a masculine mother and a feminine daughter. The film begins by making the distinction between two types of woman: the mother, who is masculine, is content with what she has, a woman of her word, brave and strong and who ignores her sexual desires, and the daughter who is sexy, desperate to jump class, is spoiled, wants to live out her sexuality and is selfish. The narrative punishes both of them and proposes a third way to the audience: 'be normal as a normal woman'. This tension between them is based on the father figure. After Nebahat learns that her husband has cheated on her, she abandons him. The husband is a lawyer who can open new class doors for the daughter. Therefore, the daughter blames her mother with her masculine behaviour for causing this unsuccessful marriage. These two women struggle with each other in order to gain phallic power over the house. Nebahat tries to do this by using her masculinity; her daughter tries to do it by using her father. She wants to move into her father's home. Both of them are punished for their desire to gain phallic power. The message of the narrative is clear: do not attempt to gain power which is more suited to a man. It can be said that becoming man is harder than becoming women in films.

In both *Fıstık Gibi Maşallah* and *Şoför Nebahat*, women are shown as struggling with modernity. Kemalism has drawn the boundaries for Turkish women as a part of the modernization process but the modernization process can be read as cross-dressing from the traditional to the modern. As a cross-dressing performance, this modernization process creates a sense of in-between. This is why the representations of the women of Turkey are always between modern and traditional. Like cross-dressing, modernization in Turkey is a kind of endless becoming as a process rather than being. In *Fıstık Gibi Maşallah*, the main woman character is Gülten, who wants to find a rich man to marry and to be a housewife. However, in order to achieve this, Gülten has to be taught to survive for herself the dangers of the modern public sphere. Naci-ye as a women friend of Gülten guides her on how she can win a man; Kemal as a yacht owner lover gives Gülten the opportunity to practise what she has learnt from Naci-ye. Both Naci-ye and Kemal re-produce Gülten for Naci as an ideal woman. According to Teresa de Lauretis (1987), there are two representations of women: 'women' as historically specific individuals and 'Woman' as an imaginary cultural representation. She suggested that the feminine gender is both inside and outside the ideology. The tension which develops between Woman, which as an imaginary representation is therefore an object, and women, which as historical beings, are therefore a subject which puts the feminine gender both inside and outside ideology. The film depicts the journey of woman as an individual being to the imaginary Woman embodied in the character of Gülten. In *Şoför Nebahat*, both Nebahat and her daughter are portrayed as 'historically specific individuals' who are stuck between modernity and tradition. The only way to survive in the public sphere is based on finding an imaginary representation. However, the absence of the father is an obstacle for them in this search. There is therefore a need to discuss the relationship between fatherhood and Turkish modernization.

According to Nilüfer Göle (1991), the psychology of Kemalist men was based on them being fathers and raising women who are appropriate for the ideals of modernization. Göle pointed out that it does not matter whether they are biologically the father or not, Kemalist men felt as if they were the fathers of Turkish women who were at the liminal spaces of modernization. In order to advance the discussion, Jale Parla and her observation about the tendencies of *Tanzimat*[9] novels can be used. According to Parla (1990), the tension of the *Tanzimat* novel was based on the relationship between fathers and sons which can be accepted as the tension between the Ottoman emperor and citizens. The absence of a father is the reason for the seduction of sons by blonde, greedy, *femme fatale* women. Parla (1990) suggested that although *Tanzimat* aimed at being modern, there was still a need for the Ottoman emperor as a father. She concluded that fathers and fatherhood have been the accompanists of the

Turkish modernization process since *Tanzimat*. On the other hand, Kemalist modernization sought to create modern women, unlike *Tanzimat*'s modern bureaucratic men. Göle (1991) stated that Atatürk, as the father of the nation and therefore the symbolic father of all Turks, gave this fatherhood mission to the male citizens of the new modern Turkey. The relationship between Kemalist fathers and their modern daughters has inter-penetrated all kinds of gendered identity relations in the new modern Turkey.

Turning to the cross-dressing films of the 1960s, this tension of male/female relationships which is structured within the relationship between Kemalist fathers and their modern daughters can be found in the cross-dressing films of the period. In *Fıstık Gibi Maşallah*, Naci, Naci-ye and Kemal work together as the 'father' of Gülten who teaches, loves, punishes, rewards and enlightens her to find her 'correct' way. On the other hand, the absence of a father or unsuccessful fatherhood in *Şoför Nebahat* can be accepted as a reason for punishing both Nebahat and her daughter at the end of the film. Nebahat's daughter is portrayed as that very blonde, greedy, *femme fatale* who had embodied one side of the modernization anxieties since *Tanzimat*, and Nebahat herself is portrayed as a symbol of the masculinization of femininity (because her father dies and she abandons her husband), the other side of modernization anxieties, both of which are based on an absence of fatherhood. These modernization anxieties can also be read from the women actors' physical appearances.

Gülten is played by Türkan Şoray, who is called 'the sultan' of Turkish cinema. She is the most important and effective woman star in Turkey, so she can be studied herself both as a text (Dryer 1979) and through the ways in which her audience relate to her (McDonald 1995). According to Seçil Büker (2002: 158),

> In the 1960s as the new city-dwellers started to lose their fear just by chance they encountered on the screen someone who did not scare them or ignore them. They felt good, because they found someone on the screen who was affectionate, looked warm and they were operating on the same place. In *Aşk Rüzgarı* (1960), the male protagonist has three lovers and does not favour the dark, rather plump one, but the audience does. The audience cheers for the dark girl.

This dark girl was played by Şoray, and she began her journey from being a star, which is accepted as a western concept, to being a sultan,[10] which is accepted as eastern. Her darkness represented Anatolia, which was largely invisible to and ignored by Kemalist modernization. Before her, the blonde woman was a very important figure of the modernization process. Cahide Sonku, the first female star of Turkish cinema, was blonde but there was always a distance between her and her audience. According to Büker (2002: 153), 'the audience did not feel close to the star, because she was aloof, polite, and blonde. Sonku managed to conquer the hearts of the city-dwellers. This happened because she looked like the western woman that the typical republican intellectual had always positioned as the ideal. Intellectuals chose to call her "The Turkish Greta Garbo". She was the star of republican ideology.'[11] After Sonku, Türkan Şoray became the symbol of the darkness of eastern people (figure 6.5). It has been said that 'stars articulate what it is to be a human being in contemporary society. They articulate both the promise and difficulty' (McDonald 1995: 83). Interestingly, however, Şoray plays Gülten with a blonde wig in *Fıstık Gibi Maşallah*. Therefore, her blondeness involves many possible readings. In short, her blondeness can be read as a symbol

Figure 6.4 Filiz Akın is a European, urbanite and college girl of Turkish Cinema.

Figure 6.5 Türkan Şoray is the 'dark girl'.

of the women of Turkey being stuck between modern/west and traditional/east. It can also be read as a symbol of cross-dressing from traditional to modern, as discussed above. In *Şoför Nebahat*, Nebahat, who represents the east, is a dark woman, and her daughter, who represents the west, is blonde. Furthermore, Filiz Akın, who plays Nebahat's daughter, was the western face of Turkish cinema after Sonku. In her analysis of four women stars of Turkish Cinema, *Dört Yapraklı Yonca* (2004), Bircan Usallı Silan described Akın as a European, an urbanite and a college girl (figure 6.4). So not only the characters but also the stars of these two films from the 1960s show femininity fractured between modernism and tradition, between west and east.

In *Şabaniye*, women are shown as struggling with feminism. The main woman character of the film, Nazlı, is shown as very masculine (figure 6.6). She wears men's clothes and always carries a gun. She rides a horse and practises shooting with the gun. Although she is keen on traditions, at the same time

Fracturing masculinity and femininity 175

Figure 6.6 A frame from *Şabaniye*; Nazlı is wearing a man's suit whereas Şaban is wearing women's clothes.

Figure 6.7 Aysun Kayacı in *Şeytanın Pabucu*.

she wants her freedom. The feminist slogan of the period transforms into the dialogues of Nazlı in the film. The anxiety about the free movement of woman is embodied in the body of Nazlı: in her body, feminism is caricatured. However, she is taught to become an ideal, imaginary Woman by the love of the cross-dressing character. Her femininity is fractured by feminism and patriarchy according to the position of the text in Turkish political cultural history where feminism meets Turkish women.

In *Şeytanın Pabucu*, the main woman character Aysun Kayacı is shown as a sexual object, which is very different from the other films (figure 6.7). She becomes a commodity in the consumption culture of the 2000s. She does not have a coherent representation of identity or body. Her body is shown as fragmented: her breast, her legs, her bottom are shown in close-up shots at the male protagonist's eye level. In this way, her 'body has been reduced to an erotic exchange value' (Baudrillard 1998: 136) between the audience and the male protagonist by means of the camera position. She becomes an object of desire for the male gaze.[12] She is always harassed but she does not have the ability to understand it because she is harassed by the camera as a male gaze which is not supposed to be there. Furthermore, she looks as if she wants to be harassed. The meaning of femininity is structured by the fact that she serves heterosexual male desire. As Irigaray (1985) pointed out, 'Women are objects or commodities that are exchanged between men.'

Conclusion

This study was based on an initial recognition of the relationship between military coups and cross-dressing films in Turkey. Throughout the book, I have sought to explore this relationship between military coups and cross-dressing film in the Turkish context. I have sought to answer these questions: if a subject changes his/her position on the map of power relations by using cross-dressing, how are other forms of identity, forms of oppression and relationships between discourses and power relations affected and then relocated by this change? Furthermore, how can these changes be read in the contexts of both Turkish culture and military coups? The discussion throughout the study has focused on the question of what cross-dressing does in particular narratives – the work that it performs – rather than the question of what cross-dressing is.

These questions led to the main argument of this book which is that both cross-dressing characters in Turkish films and implications of military coups challenge ontological security at different levels. Cross-dressing characters destroy ontological security by the effects of the cross-dressing performance on its subject. When we look at the opportunities which are provided by cross-dressing characters to both the narrative and the characters, three effects can be seen. First, cross-dressing gender performance provides mobility between all kinds of power relations. I have argued that this mobility is a result of the body of becoming. Second, cross-dressing provides the opportunity to be visible but not recognizable. This effect helps the cross-dressing subject to escape panoptical social mechanisms. This effect has been argued by using the concept of the grotesque. The third effect is that the cross-dresser can experience otherness without being other. This effect has been argued by using the concept of the carnivalesque. All three of these effects can be read as ways to handle the traumas which are caused by military coups. I have suggested throughout this book that cross-dressing films are popular in times of national trauma because the effects of cross-dressing performance provide relief for citizens who find themselves living under military rule.

The key finding of this study is that cross-dressing gender performance is not simply about the gender binary or the clothes codes inherent in the binary, it is embedded in the institutions of power – time, space, language, memory and identity – which have been structured according to the historical position of a text. In other words, cross-dressing is not wearing the clothes of the opposite sex but wearing the tensions of a specific period which are embedded in time, space, language and memory in a gendered way. That is why cross-dressing films in Turkish cinema can be read as a way of dealing with national traumas. Trauma studies usually focus on narratives which are about identity, belonging, memory, recovering and similar issues. This study, however, has shown that the narratives which are usually interpreted negatively – in this case cross-dressing films which are usually accepted as escapist, misogynist, low-culture products – can be read as trauma narratives. This study gives a new perspective for trauma studies as well.

This project has of necessity been limited to a relatively small sample of texts, examining in detail only five films. I believe that close analysis of these five films has allowed me to consider the wider issues which I have sought to address because almost all cross-dressing films use same narrative formula. In addition to films as a popular culture product, alternative popular culture products such as stage performances, opera and the music industry could be the next target for further study in this field. Furthermore, this study has focused on Turkish examples and military coups as national trauma, but other cultures and nations can be researched in order to understand whether is there any relation between cross-dressing performance and any national traumas in the chosen nations and cultures.

Notes

Introduction

1. Masculinity studies are quite a new academic area for Turkish academia. The most influential study of masculinity in Turkish cinema was made by Umut Tümay Arslan in her book *Bu Kabuslar Neden Cemil?* ('What are the reasons for these nightmares, Cemil?') (2004) which discussed fatherhood and the representation of masculinity in the *Yeşilçam* ('Greenpine') melodrama. Volkan Yücel discussed crime drama and masculinity in his book *Kahramanın Yolculuğu* ('The Journey of the Hero') (2014). The new Turkish cinema was discussed by Asuman Suner as a 'new masculine melodrama' in her book, *New Turkish Cinema: Belonging, Identity, and Memory* (2010). Pınar Taş discussed Nuri Bilge Ceylan's films and masculinity in her essay 'Independent Turkish Cinema and Masculinity' (2011). In addition to these studies, discussion of masculinity in Turkish cinema has been based on star studies. For example, Z. Koçer's *Yılmaz Güney in Yıldız İmgesindeki Erkeklik Kurulumları* ('The Star Image of Yılmaz Güney and the Structure of Masculinity') (2012) explored the relationship between political persona, star persona and masculinity in relation to Yılmaz Guney.

2. The melodrama traditions in *Yesilcam* ('Greenpine') give a great opportunity to discuss femininity in Turkish cinema. Hasan Akbulut's books *Melodram Kadına Yakışır* ('Female Images in Turkish Melodrama Films') (2008) and *Melodramatic Image* (2012) discussed genre and gender relations in Turkish cinema. The masculine outlook and absence of women in the new Turkish cinema were discussed by Asumen Suner in her book *New Turkish Cinema: Belonging, Identity, and Memory* (2010). Özlem Güçlü studied *Female Voice and the Silent Image of Women in Turkish Cinema* (2013). The relationship between religion and women and the representation of this relationship on screen were discussed by Gönül Dönmez Colin in her book *Women, Islam and Cinema* (2006). Turkish cinema, female stars and the star/audience relationship in terms of star studies were discussed by Agah Özgüç in *Women of Turkish Cinema* (2008) and by Atilla Dorsay in *Women of Yeşilçam* (2005). The relationship between the 1980 military coup, feminism and the representation of women in Turkish cinema was discussed by Eylem Atkakav in her influential book *Women and Turkish Cinema* (2013). Furthermore, women directors and their film language were discussed by Rüken Öztürk in *Women Directors in Turkish Cinema* (2004).

3   The categories of west and east do not refer to geographical reality; rather they imply power relations between western countries and non-western countries which can be called eastern, third world, or Islamic world according to historical and ideological needs. The system of the cultural representation of west and east which is also the source of the binary category west/east cannot be considered without considering these power relations. My intention is not to generalize these terms. For more detail, see Edward Said's (1978) *Orientalism*. For more detail about the dangers which are embedded in this binary, *see* Cemil Aydin (2017) *The Idea of Muslim World: A Global Intellectual History*.

4   According to Metin And (1976), an expert in traditional performance art and rituals in Turkish culture who studied male-to-female cross-dressing traditional dance, the absence of female-to-male cross-dressers is related to the absence of women in the public sphere. Our knowledge of traditional male-to-female cross-dresser dancers is based on the writings of western travellers. However, they were forbidden to enter women's spaces such as the *harem*. Therefore, writings and pictures about male-to-female cross-dressers include more realistic knowledge than that available on female-to-male cross-dressers. The representation of female desire and sexuality was based on the fantasy of western spectators.

5   Michel Foucault (1990) wrote that the contemporary terminology of sex and homosexuality as a category of modern medicine is based on the eighteenth-century understanding. As David M. Halperin (1990) pointed out, the use of modern terms such as homosexuality in order to understand historical identities can be misleading. Moreover, these terms which were produced by the west are not suitable for discussing eastern identities. However, although I am aware of this, it is still good way to express the situation.

6   Some important studies have pointed out the tension between western and eastern understandings of sexuality. Joseph Massad's influential book *Desiring Arabs* (2007) discussed the influence and impact of Orientalism on shaping Arabs' own perceptions of sexuality. Mehmet Kalpaklı and Walter Andrews analysed Ottoman love poets and discussed cross-cultural parallels in the sociology and spirituality of love in Europe – from Istanbul to London – during the long sixteenth century in their book *The Age of Beloved* (2005). The book edited by Kathryn Babayan and Afsaneh Najambadi, *Islamicate Sexualities: Translation across Temporal Geographies of Desire* (2008), was interested in comparative literature studies and queer theory in the Muslim world, including Arabic, Persian, French, Spanish, Christian and Islamic literature. In that book, papers written by Najambadi, Epps, Traub and Rouhi discussed the validity of the western terminology of sexuality as fixed binary oppositions in treating Arab literature which expresses a range of desires which are not fixed. Dror Ze'evi in his influential book *Producing Desire: Changing Sexual Discourse in Ottoman Middle East* (2006) brought into focus the sexual discourses manifest in a wealth of little-studied source material – medical texts, legal

documents, religious literature, dream interpretation manuals, shadow theatres and travelogues – in an analytical exploration of Ottoman sexual thought and practices from the heyday of the Ottoman Empire in the sixteenth century to the beginning of the twentieth. In his influential book, *Osmanlı'da Seks* ('Sex in Ottoman') (2005), Murat Bardakçı claimed that same-sex relations became a hidden desire after Tanzimat 1839 when the first step of westernization was taken. As seen above, discussions of the tension between western and eastern understandings of sexuality are based on an historical approach. Little attention has been paid to carrying the discussion over to current situations.

7   It can be claimed that 'Turkey's democracy reached a turning point with the meteoric rise of the pro-Islamic Justice and Development Party (AKP) in the 2002 election'. After the 2002 election, 'the AKP, which won the most votes and seats in the National Assembly after the 22 July 2007 elections and formed the government, has also been indicted on the grounds of becoming the focal point of activities against secularism. The resuscitation of the debate on the donning of turbans on the university campuses and other public institutions of Turkey has been defended as a religious right of the religious women by the conservative parties of Turkey, and resisted as the promotion of a symbol of political Islam by the secularist parties and political forces of the country' (Kalaycıoglu 2008: 2).

8   In the 2000s, Turkey encountered trans-national cinema through the work of Fatih Akın, a member of the third generation of immigrant workers in Germany, and his international success. After him, the international successes of Ferzan Özpetek, Kutluğ Ataman, Ayşe Polat, Thomas Arslan and Buket Alakuş attracted academic discussion on trans-national cinema. For more detailed information, see Nejat Ulusay (2008), *Melez İmgeler: Sinema ve Ulusötesi Oluşumlar* ('Hybrid Image: Cinema and Transnationalism'); Özgür Yaren (2008), *Avrupa Göçmen Sineması* ('European Migration Cinema'); Asuman Suner (2006), *Hayalet Ev: Yeni Türk Sinemasında, Aidiyet, Kimlik ve Bellek* ('Ghost House'); Hamid Naficy (2001), *An Accented Cinema: Exilic and Diasporic Film Making;* and Rob Wilson and Wimal Dissayanake (eds) (1996), *Global/Local: Cultural Production and the Transnational Imaginary*.

9   It should be remembered that dress and wearing are subject to surveillance in Turkish politics and culture.

10 Although I am aware that the notions of real and realistic involve many questions, I am using this term in a Zizekian sense. According to Slavoj Zizek (1991), 'real' is an understanding of power relations which affect us. It is not a spiritual or metaphysical idea about a set of universal truths. The narrative of 'realistic' transgender movies in Turkey is based on discrimination against transgender sex workers, such as *Dönersen Islık Çal* (1992, directed by Orhan Oğuz), *Gece, Melek ve Bizim Çocuklar* (1993, directed by Atıf Yılmaz) and *Robert'in Filmi* (1992, directed by Canan Gerede).

Chapter 1

1. It is not the aim of this study to generalize non-western modernization. There are many differences and similarities between them. For example, Indian modernization can be accepted as a 'modernisation without westernization' (Wagner et al. 1999: 511) when its social structure and economic action are taken into consideration. Its modernization sought to protect its heritage. According to Atreyee Gupta (2013), promise of Indian modernization as a post-colonial modernization was based on equality, progress and protecting its citizens from poverty. Turning to African countries' development and Saharan Africa modernization, non-western modernization examples such as Ghana, Kenya, Nigeria, Senegal, Uganda, Zambia and Zimbabwe were shaped according to ethnic traits (Michologolous & Popionnou 2011: 32). Turkish modernization – unlike Indian modernization – was based on rejecting the Ottoman heritage and – unlike African countries – rejecting ethnicity and creating a new identity positioned beyond ethnicities and heritages. Briefly, being a Turk as a national identity is a state project. On the other hand, the way in which modernization went is not an issue: it is always a way of expressing the distinction between west and east because modernization forces countries to reach a level where the western has already reached. Turkey is the best example of this situation.
2. 'The 'Young Ottomans', a group of modern-educated officers and bureaucrats, organized a constitutional revolution to modernize and strengthen state and society on the basis of a positivist and increasingly nationalist set of ideas (Zürcher 2003: 3). Most of them were educated in France and were affected by French literature and art. A French ethos therefore influenced Turkish modern art. For example, speaking French was accepted as a way of being modern. The character of the French babysitter and teacher who worked in *Yali* (the houses of the rich Ottoman aristocratic class) became an important figure for *Tanzimat* literature (*see* Parla 1990).
3. According to Savaş Arslan (2011:18), 'Turkification is not only as a translation and transformation of the west through *Yesilcam*'s own terms and terminology but also as a practice of nationalization'. Turkification may be thought of as a process of coexistence between the west and the east, with various failures, novelties and aggression.
4. In Turkish, male names can be transformed into female names by using a suffix. For example 'Naci' and 'Fikri' are the male names whereas 'Naciye' and 'Fikriye' are female names.
5. Under the military regime, more than 650,000 people were detained; police files were opened on about 1,680,000 people; there were 210,000 political trials in which 7,000 people faced the death penalty; 50 of 517 death penalties were carried out; 300 people died in prisons for allegedly unspecified reasons; 171 people died from

torture, 388,000 people were deprived of their right to a passport; 30,000 people were fired from the civil service, 14,000 people lost their citizenship; 39 tonnes of published material were destroyed and 23,677 associations were closed down (Öngider 2005; Mavioğlu 2004).

6   Bulent Ersoy has a very significant place in Turkish cultural and political life. She is one of those who were victims of the 1980 military coup. In 1980, after the military coup, in a concert at the Izmir International Fair, she showed her new breast to the audience and this resulted in her being arrested. Being transgender in an oppressive military regime was very hard for her. She had to undergo a very difficult legal case and physical examinations in order to be recognized as a woman. Her defence in the court is very important for understanding her political position. She claimed that she was a loyal citizen not an anarchist and that she had no intention to contravene the heterosexual order. During the military regime, she had to work in Germany because her performances were banned by the military regime. Nevertheless, she built up her identity as Muslim, upper class and nationalist. And she never supported any LGBT movement.

7   For example, Mustafa Akyol (2007), *Turkey's Veiled Democracy*, Ali Carkoğlu (2009), *Women's Choice of Head Cover in Turkey*, Metin Toprak (2009), *The Headscarf Controversy in Turkey*, Ömer Caha (2011), *The Islamic Women's Movement*, Bayram Salih (2009), *Reporting the Hijab in Turkey: Shifts in the Pro- and Anti-ban Discourse*, and Banu Gökariksel (2010), *Between Fashion and Market*.

Chapter 3

1   Jennifer Mitzen, 'Ontological Security in World Politics'; Jennifer Mitzen, 'Anchoring Europe's Civilizing Identity: Habits, Capabilities and Ontological Security', *Journal of European Public Policy* (2006) 13, 2: 270–85; Jef Huysmans, 'Security! What Do You Mean? From Concept to Thick Signifier', *European Journal of International Relations* (1998), 4, 2: 226–55; Catarina Kinnvall, 'Globalization and Religious Nationalism: Self, Identity, and the Search for Ontological Security', *Political Psychology* (2004), 25, 5: 741–67; Eli Zaretsky, 'Trauma and Dereification: September 11 and the Problem of Ontological Security' *Constellations* (2002), 9, 1: 93–105; Brent Steele, 'Ontological Security and the Power of Self-Identity: British Neutrality and the American Civil War', *Review of International Studies* (2005), 31, 3: 519–40.

Chapter 4

1   For example, the uncanny voice of which the source is not known is a useful strategy for creating anxiety in horror films. In cross-dressing films, however, the

source of the voice is known. The reason for anxiety in cross-dressing films is not an unknown source of voice but a contradiction between source and voice.

2   We can use the idea of the 'acousmatic voice' proposed by Michel Chion. What we would hear is what Chion in his ground-breaking book on sound in film, *The Voice in Cinema*, calls an acousmatic voice, 'a sound that is heard without its cause being seen' (1999: 18). This acousmatic voice materializes a split between the visual and the sound. 'If the talking cinema has shown anything by restoring voices to bodies, it's precisely that it doesn't hang together; it's decidedly not a seamless match' (Chion 1999: 126). Furthermore, Chion described the subject's attempts to suture the visual and the sonic as 'a complex structural operation (related to the structuring of the subject in language) of grafting the non-localized voice onto a particular body to the voice as its source. This operation leaves a scar' (1999: 126). Chion's reflections on the fragmentation of the subject are helpful for reinterpreting the different dimensions of the cross-dressing scene. The more interesting thing is that the voice of the cross-dressed character is acousmatic for other characters, not for the audience.

3   *Maşallah* is an Arabıc world which is used by Muslims. It means *May Allah preserve him/her*. In street language, it is also used for abusing women.

Chapter 5

1   I shall examine the films by using the perception of past, present and future, although I am aware that this separation is supported by the linear time perception. Time is like a painting; just as a painting cannot be separated colour by colour, shape by shape, time cannot be separated into past, present and future. All three together are in same phase and all three together create one single reality about time. None of past, present, and future has a single meaning; they only acquire a meaning when they are together. Cross-dressing characters in film locate in between past, present and future. That is why I call the cross-dressing performer's use of time in films the inter-temporal asymmetric use of linear time. In order to highlight this inter-temporal usage, I decided to divide the discussion into past, present and future.

Chapter 6

1   At this point, the question should be asked regarding what is being critical. 'Critique is only the experience of the limits of the discourse which might offer the possibility of our becoming critical of transforming ourselves and current

society' (Butler 2002). In this sense, the limit of discourse is the limit of who we are, because subjectivity is the effect of one's belonging to a particular discourse (Foucault 1984). On the other hand, critique cannot go beyond the discourse. However, cross-dressing gives an opportunity to experience the limits.

2   'Hegemonic Masculinity' is the definition of manhood which is dominant in a given cultural context (Connel & Messerschimdt 2005).
3   'The concept of "military masculinities" refers to a particular set of gendered attributes typically found within the institution of the armed forces' (Connel 1995: 57). 'These traits – both performance and ideology – cluster around violence, aggression, rationality, and a sense of invulnerability, and they share in common certain aspects of civilian-based masculinities such as coolness under pressure' (Higate 2003: 29).
4   Many historians such as Ilber Ortayli (2000) and Oliver Bouguet (2011) accepted that there was not an aristocracy as a social class in Ottoman times, so therefore there is not in the Turkish Republic either. I have chosen to use this term because 'hereditary aristocracy' implies a unique social class into which no-one lowborn can climb.
5   Foucault analysed several types of power, such as disciplinary power and sovereign power, and bio-power was one of them. In *The History of Sexuality*, Foucault described bio-power as a power which takes hold of human life: 'Bio power is the power over bios or life, and lives may be managed on both an individual and a group basis' (Taylor 2011: 44) Bio-power is the way of regulating 'the problems of birth, role, longevity, public health, housing and migration' (Foucault 1990: 140).
6   Although Foucault (1990) wrote that non-productive sexual acts were considered sinful and had come to be seen as a threat to society, this situation was only valid for individuals who could actually procreate.
7   However, this is not common in female cross-dressing films.
8   Monique Witting used 'imaginary formation' when she wrote about feminine writings in her essay 'The Point of View: Universal or Particular' in 1980. According to her, the subject is a man and masculine is not a gender, rather it implies being in general. There is only one gender which is feminine. The feminine gender is an artificial mark which is used to create women as a natural group and a political concept. Therefore, according to her, 'woman is an imaginary formation and not a concrete reality' (59).
9   The first modernization movement which took place in the late Ottoman era.
10 The sultan is the wife or mother of the Ottoman *padisah* (emperor). The idea of the star was introduced to Turkish society by Hollywood.
11 On the other hand, the image of the blonde woman was also the symbol of the Young Ottomans' modernization movement called *Tanzimat*. 'The most influential books of Tanzimat involved blonde women protagonists as desirable, beautiful women. The male protagonist Bihruz Bey in the most famous novel which was

written by Recaizade Mahmut Ekrem, *Araba Sevdasi* (1899), falls in love with Perivies Hanim when he sees her blonde hair and green eyes' (Buker 2002).

12 Here it is worth mentioning Laura Mulvey and her ground-breaking article. According to Mulvey (1989: 19), 'Narrative cinema incorporates permutations of the look into its very structure, predetermining how the woman is to be looked at and thus placing all spectators in the "masculinized" position of looking at her'.

References

Abisel, N. (1995). *Türk Sineması Üzerine Yazılar*. Ankara: İmge Yayıncılık.

Acar, F. (2002). 'Turgut Özal: Pious Agent of Liberal Transformation', in Metin Heper and Sabri Sayarı (eds), *Political Leaders and Democracy in Turkey*, pp.163-80. Lanham: Lexington Books.

Ackroyd, P. (1979). *Dressing Up: Transvestism and Drag: History of an Obsession*. New York: Thames and Hudson

Ahmad, F. (1969). *The Young Turks. The Committee of Union and Progress in Turkish Politics, 1908-1914*. Oxford: The Clarendon Press.

Ahmad, F. (1977). *The Turkish Experiment in Democracy 1950-1975*. London: C. Hurst and Co.

Akbal Süalp, Z.T. (2010). 'Taşrada Saklı Zaman-Geri Dönülemeyen', in Z.T. Akbal Süalp & A. Güneş (eds), *Taşrada Var Bir Zaman*, pp.87-116. İstanbul: Çitlembik.

Aksin, S. (2004). *Ana Çizgileri ile Türkiye Yakın Tarihi*. Ankara: İmaj Yayınları.

Aksoyak, İ.H. (2009). For Seventeen Centuries a Registered Köçek: Behzad. *Millî Folklor* 21(84): 127-9.

Aktar, C. (1993). *Türkiye'nin Batılılaştırılması*. Istanbul: Ayrıntı Yayınları.

Althusser, L. (1970). *Lenin and Philosophy and Other Essays*. New York and London: Monthly Review Press.

Althusser, L. (2008). *On Ideology, Radical Thinkers*. London: Verso.

And, M. (1976). Osmanlı Tiyatrosu. *Tiyatro Araştırmaları Dergisi*, Ankara Üniversitesi, Dil ve Tarih-Coğrafya Fakültesi, Tıyatro Bölümü No. 83.

Anderson, B. (1983). *Imagined Communities: Reflections on the Origin and Spread of Nationalism*. London: Verso.

Arat, Y. (1997). 'The Project of Modernity and Women in Turkey', in S. Bozdoğan & R. Kasaba (eds), *Rethinking Modernity and Notional Identity in Turkey*, pp.95-112. University of Washington Press.

Arat, Y. (2000). From Emancipation to Liberation: The Changing Role of Women in Turkey's Public Realm. *Journal of International Affairs* 54(1): 107-23.

Arat, Z. (1994). 'Turkish Women and Republican Reconstruction of Tradition', in Müge Göçek & Shiva Balaghi (eds), *Reconstruction of Gender in the Middle East*, pp.57-78. New York: Colombia University Press.

Arat, Z. (1999). *Deconstructing the Image of Turkish Women*. London and New York: Palgrave Macmillan.

Arcayürek, C. (1986). *Müdahalenin Ayak Sesler 1978-1979*. Ankara: Bilgi Yayınevi.

Aries, P. (1962). *Centuries of Childhood*. New York: Vintage.

Arslan, S. (2009). The New Cinema of Turkey. *New Cinemas: Journal of Contemporary Film* 7(1): 83–97.
Arslan, S. (2011). *Cinema in Turkey*. New York: Oxford University Press.
Atakav, E. (2013). *Women in Turkish Cinema*. London: Routledge.
Atam, Z. (2011). *Yakın Plan Yeni Türkiye Sineması*. Istanbul: Cadde Yayınları.
Austin, J.L. (1962). *How to Do Things with Words*. Cambridge, MA: Harvard University Press.
Avcıoğlu, D. (1996). *Türkiye'nin Düzeni, Dün-Bugün-Yarın*. Istanbul: Tekin Yayınevi.
Ayça, E. (2001). 'Propoganda da da Değiştirmedi Çizgisini, Değiştiremezdi', in Karasu Gürses (ed.), *Kemal Sunal: Film Başka, Yaşam Başka*, pp.15–24. İstanbul: Istanbul Sel Yayıncılık.
Aydemir, Ş.S. (1995). *Tek adam Mustafa Kemal (1922-1938), Cilt III* (12. basım). İstanbul: Remzi Kitabevi.
Aydin, C. (2017). *The Idea Oof Muslim World: A Global Intellectual History*. Cambridge: Harvard university press.
Aydınlı, E. (2009). A Paradigmatic Shift for the Turkish Generals and End to the Coup Era in Turkey. *Middle East Journal* 63(4, Autumn): 581–96.
Aydınlı, E. (2011). Ergenekon, New Pacts and the Decline of the Turkish 'İnner State'. *Turkish Studies* 12(2): 227–39.
Bachelard, G. (1964). *Poetics of Space*. New York: Orion.
Bakhtin, M. (1984). *Rabelais and His Words*. Bloomington: Indiana University Press.
Bakhtin, M. (1986). *Speech Genres and Other Late Essays*. Edited by C. Emerson & M. Holquist, translated by W. McGee. Austin, TX: University of Texas Press.
Balcı, S. (2007). Kronik: XI. Cumhurbaşkanının Seçimi (Chronic: The Election of the 11th President). *Ankara Üniversitesi SBF Dergisi* 62: 237–42.
Batinder, E. (1994). *XY, on Masculine Identity*. New York: Columbia University Press.
Baudelaire (1964). *The Painter of Modern Life and Other Essays*. Translated and edited by Jonathan Mayne. London: Phaidon Press.
Baudrillard, J. (1998). *The Consumer Society: Myths and Structures*. London: Sage.
Bayrak, T. (2014). Karakter Oyuncusu Olarak Sadri Alışık. *TOJDAC* 4(2): 105–12
Bazzano, M. (2014). On Becoming No One: Phenomenological and Empiricist Contributions to the Person-Centered Approach. *Person-Centered & Experiential Psychotherapies* 13(3): 250–8.
Beech, N. (2011). Liminality and the Practices of Identity Reconstruction. *Human Relations* 64(2): 285–302.
Bell, E., Hass, L. & Sells, L. (1995). *From Mouse to Mermaid: The Politics of Film, Gender and Culture*. Bloomington: Indiana University Press.
Bell-Metereau, R. (1985). *Hollywood Androgyny*. New York: Columbia University Press.
Benshoof, M.H. & Griffin, S. (2004). *America on Film: Representing Race, Class, Gender and Sexuality at the Movie*. Malden: Blackwell Publishing.
Berger, P.L. & Luckmann, T. (1991). *The Social Construction of Reality: A Treatise on the Sociology of Knowledge*. London: Penguin.

Berktay, F. (1990). 'Türkiye Solu'nun Kadına Bakışı', in Şirin Tekeli (ed.), *1980'ler Türkiye'sinde Kadın Bakış Açısından Kadınlar, Istanbul: İletişim Yayınları*, pp.7-37. Istanbul: iletişim yayınları.

Berntsen, D., & Rubin, D. C. (2004). Cultural life Scripts Structure Recall from Autobiographical Memory. *Memory & Cognition, 32*(3): 427-42.

Bing, J. & Bergvall, V. (1996). 'The Question of Questions: Beyond Binary Thinking', in V. Bergvall, J. Bing & A. Freed (eds), *Rethinking Language and Gender Research: Theory and Practice*, pp.1-30. New York: Longman.

Biryildiz, E. (1993). Şoför Nebahat mi Olalım, Küçük Hanfendi mi? Istanbul *Marmara iletisim Dergisi* 4: 1-14.

Bora, A. (2005). *Kadınların Sınıfı*. Istanbul: İletişim Yayınları.

Boratav, K. (2000). *Yeni Dünya Düzeni Nereye*. Ankara: Imge Kitabevi.

Bouguet, O. (2011). Old Elites in a New Republic: The Reconversion of Ottoman Bureaucratic Families in Turkey (1909-1939). *Comparative Studies of South Asia, Africa and the Middle East 31*(3): 588-600.

Bourdieu, P. (1977). *Outline of a Theory of Practice*. Cambridge: Cambridge University Press.

Bourdieu, P. (2001). *Masculine Domination*. Cambridge: Polity Press.

Bozdoğan, S. & Kasaba, R. (1998). *Türkiye'de Modernleşme ve Ulusal Kimlik*. Istanbul: Tarih Vakfı- Yurt Yayınları.

Büker, S. (2002). 'Film Does Not Ended with an Ecstatic Kiss', in Deniz Kandiyoti & Ayşe Saktenber (eds), *Fragments of Culture*, pp.147-71. London: I.B. Tauris.

Bull, M. (ed.) (2013). *Sound Studies: Critical Concept in Media and Cultural Studies*. London: Routledge.

Bullough, V.L. & Bullough, B. (1993). *Cross Dressing, Sex, and Gender*. Philadelphia: University of Pennsylvania Press.

Butler, J. (1906). *The Analogy of Religion, Natural & Revealed*. London: J. M. Dent & Company.

Butler, J. (1997). *The Psychic Life of Power: Theories of Subjection*. Stanford: Stanford University Press.

Butler J. (2002). 'What Is Critique? An Essay on Foucault's Virtue', in ingram D. (ed.), *The Political: Readings in Continental Philosophy*, pp.212-26. London: Basil Blackwell.

Butler, J. (2006). *Gender Trouble*. New York: Routledge.

Burak, B. (2011). The Role of the Military in Turkish Politics: To Guard Whom and from What? *European Journal of Economic and Political Studies* 4(1): 1-20.

Cak, S.E. (2009). Köçek ve Çengilerin Toplumsal Cinsiyeti. *Akademik Araştırmalar Dergisi* 43: 49-71.

Caluya, G. (2010). The Post-Panoptic Society? Reassessing Foucault in Surveillance Studies. *Social Identities* 16(5): 621-33.

Can, B.B. (1998). (Az)gelişme efsanesi ve Eurosentrist-modern standardizasyon. *Özgür Üniversite Forumu* 1(4), 186-222.

Carlton, E. (1997). *The State against the State: The Theory and Practice of the Coup d'Etat*. Hants, UK: Scholar Press.
Carol, L. (1865). *Alice's Adventures in Wonderland*. London: Macmillan.
Casey, E. (1996). 'How to Get from Space to Place in a Fairly Short Stretch of Time', in S. Feld & K. Basso (eds), *Senses of Place*, pp.13–52. Santa Fe, NM: School of American Research Press.
Castle, T. (1986). *Masquerade and Civilisation: The Carnivalesque in Eighteenth-Century English Culture and Fiction*. London: Methuen.
Cavarero, A. (2005). *For More Than One Voice: Toward a Philosophy of Vocal Expression*. Stanford: Stanford University Press.
Chion, M. (1999). *The Voice in Cinema*. New York: Columbia University Press.
Cindoglu D. & Esim, S. (1999). Women's Organizations in 1990s Turkey. *Middle Eastern Studies* 35(1): 178–88.
Cixous, H. (1976). *Le livre de Prométhéa*. Paris: Gallimard.
Cixous, H. (1986). *The Newly Born Woman*. Minneapolis: University of Minnesota Press.
Cixous, H. (2007). *Insister of Jacques Derrida*. translated by Peggy Kamuf. Edinburg: Edinburgh University Press.
Coleman, R. (2008). The Becoming of Bodies: Girls Media Effect and Body Image. *Feminist Media Studies* 8(2): 163–79.
Collins, J. & Mayblin, B. (2011). *Introducing Derrida*. Cambridge: Icon Books.
Connel, R.W. (1995). *Masculinities*. Berkeley, CA: University of California Press.
Connel, R.W. & Messerschimdt, J.W. (2005). Hegemonic Masculinities: Rethinking the Concepts. *Gender and Society* 19(6): 829–59.
Constantin, V., Boundas, C.V. & Olkowski, D. (1994). *Gilles Deleuze and the Theater of Philosophy*. New York and London: Routledge.
Çaha, O. (2011). The Kurdish Women's Movement: A Third-Wave Feminism within the Turkish Context. *Turkish Studies* 12(3): 435–49.
Çakırlar, C. (2011). Queer Art of Parallaxed Document: The Visual Discourse of Docudrag in Kutlug Atman's Never My Soul! *Screen* 52(3): 358–75.
Çakırlar, C. (2012). 'Ruhumu Asla: Kutluğ Ataman, Queer Belgesel ve Küreselleşen Sanat', in Cüneyt Çakırlar & Serkan Delice (eds), *Cinsellik Muamması*, pp.11–34. Istanbul: Metis.
Çakırlar, C. & Delice, S. (2012). *Cinsellik Muamması: Türkiye'de Queer Kültür ve Muhalafet*. Istanbul: Metis.
Çınar, M. (2011). The Electoral Success of the AKP: Cause for Hope and Despair. *Insight Turkey* 13(4): 107–28.
Daldal, A. (2005). *1960 Darbesi ve Türk Sineması'nda Toplumsal Gerçekçilik*. Istanbul: Homer Kitapevi.
Davidson, T. (2009). The Role of Domestic Architecture in the Structuring of Memory. *Space and Culture* 12(3): 332–42.
de Beauvoir, S. (1953). *The Second Sex*. London: Penguin Books.

De Certeau, M. (1984). *The Practice of Everyday Life*. Berkeley, CA: University of California Press.

de Lauretis, T. (1987). *The Technology of Gender: Essays on Theory, Film, and Fiction*. Bloomington: Indiana University Press.

Dekker, J.J.H. & Lechner, D.M. (1999). Discipline and Pedagogics in History: Foucault, Ariès and the History of Panoptical Education. *The European Legacy* 4: 37–49.

Delehanty, W.K. & Steele, B.J. (2009). Engaging the Narrative in Ontological (in)security Theory: Insights from Feminist IR. *Cambridge Review of International Affairs* 22(3): 523–40.

Deleuze, G. (1986). *Kafka: Toward a Minor Literature*. Translated by Dana Polan. Minneapolis: University of Minneapolis Press.

Deleuze, G. (1986). *Cinema 1: The Movement-Image*. Minneapolis: University of Minnesota Press.

Deleuze, G. (1989). *Cinema 2: The Time-Image*. Minneapolis: University of Minnesota Press.

Deleuze, G. (1992). *Postscript on the Societies of Control*. Cambridge, MA: MIT Press.

Deleuze, G. (2002). *Dialogues*. New York: Columbia University Press.

Deleuze, G. & Guattari, F. (1987). *A Thousand Plateaus: Capitalism and Schizophrenia*. Minneapolis: University of Minnesota Press.

Deleuze, G. & Guattari, F. (1996). *What Is Philosophy?* New York: Columbia University Press.

Demirel, T. (2004). Soldiers and Civilians: The Dilemma of Turkish Democracy. *Middle Eastern Studies* 40: 127–50.

Dentith, S. (1995). *Bakhtinian Thought*. New York and London: Routledge.

Derrida, J. (1967). *On Grammatology*. Baltimore and London: Johns Hopkins University Press.

Derrida, J. (1987). *Positions*. Translated and annotated by Alan Bass. London: Athlone.

Derrida, J. (2004). *A Dialogue*. Stanford: Stanford University Press.

Derrida, J. (2008). *Islam and the West: A Conversation with Jacques Derrida*. Chicago: University of Chicago Press.

Diner, C. & Toktaş, Ş. (2010). Waves of Feminism in Turkey: Kemalist, Islamist and Kurdish Women's Movements in an Era of Globalization. *Journal of Balkan and near Eastern Studies* 12(1) 41–57.

Dodge, M., Kitchin, R. & Perkins, C. (eds) (2009). *Rethinking Maps: New Frontiers in Cartographic Theory*. New York: Routledge.

Dolar, M. (2006). *A Voice and Nothing More*. Cambridge, MA: MIT Press.

Dorsay, A. (1996). *12 Eylül Yılları ve Sinemamız*. Istanbul: Inkılap Kitapevi ve Yayıcılık.

Douglas, M. (1966). *Purity and Danger*. Abingdon: Routledge.

Dönmez-Colin, G. (2004). *Women, Islam and Cinema*. London: Reaktion Books.

Dyer, R. (1986). *Heavenly Bodies: Film Stars and Society*. New York: St. Martin's Press.

Dryer, R. (1979). *Stars*. London: British Film Institute.

Duncan, M. (2004). The Operatic Scandal of the Singing Body: Voice, Presence, Performativity. *Cambridge Opera Journal* 16(3): 283–306.

Durakbaşa, A. (1999). 'Kemalism as Identity Politics in Turkey', in Z. Arat (ed.), *Deconstructing the Image of Turkish Women*, pp.139–56. Hampshire: Macmillan Press.

Durgun, Ş. (1997). Tamamlanmamış bir proje: Modernleşme ya da demokratikleşmenin önündeki engeller. *Yeni Türkiye 17*: 41–8.

Durkheim, E. (1947). *The Division Of Labor In Society*. New York: The Free Press.

Eidsheim, N.S. (2008). *Voice as Technology of Selfhood: Towards an Analysis of Racialized Timbre and Vocal Performance*. PhD thesis, University of California, San Diego.

Ellis, N. & Ybema, S. (2010). Marketing Identities: Shifting Circles of Identification in Inter- Organizational Relationships. *Organization Studies 31*(3): 279–305.

Emerson, C. (1997). *First Hundred Years of Mikhail Bakhtin*. New Jersey: Princeton University Press.

Enloe, C. (1990). *Bananas, Beaches, and Bases: Making Feminist Sense of International Politics*. London: Pandora Press; Harper Collins.

Ercan, F. (1996). *Modernizm, kapitalizm ve azgelişmişlik*. Istanbul: Sorunsal Yayınevi.

Erdoğan, N. (1998). Narratives of Resistance: National Identity and Ambivalence in the Turkish Melodrama between 1965 and 1975. *Screen 39*(3): 259–71.

Erikson, E. (1950). *Childhood and Society*. New York: Norton.

Ertür, B. & Lebow, A. (2012). 'Şöhretin Sonu: Bülent Ersoy'un Kanunla Imtihani', in Cüneyt Çakırlar & Serkan Delice (eds), *Cinsellik Muammasi*, pp.391–426. Istanbul: Metis.

Esen, S. (2000). *80'ler Türkiyesi'nde Sinema* (2 Basım). Istanbul: Beta Basım Yayım.

Felman, S. (2002). *The Scandal of the Speaking Body: Don Juan with J. L. Austin, or Seduction in Two Languages*. Stanford: Stanford University Press.

Fineman, M.A. & Thomson, M. (2013). *Exploring Masculinities: Feminist Legal Theory Reflections*. Farnham, Surrey: Ashgate.

Flanagan, V. (2008). *Into the Closet: Cross-Dressing and the Gendered Body in Children's Literature and Film*. New York: Routledge.

Foucault, M. (1972). *The Archaeology of Knowledge and the Discourse on Language*. New York: Pantheon.

Foucault, M. (1984). 'What Is Enlightenment?', in P. Rainbow (ed.), *The Foucault Reader*, pp.32–50. New York: Pantheon.

Foucault, M. (1990). *History of Sexuality*. New York: Vintage Books.

Foucault, M. (1995). *Discipline and Punish*. New York: Vintage Books.

Garber, M. (1992). *Vested Interests: Cross-Dressing and Cultural Anxiety* London: Routledge.

Gauntlett, D. (2008). *Media, Gender and Identity: An Introduction*. London: Routledge.

Gellner, E. (1964). *Thought and Change*. London: Weidenfeld and Nicolson.

Gellner, E. (2006). *Nations and Nationalism*. Oxford: Blackwell Publishing

Genç, K. (2013). *Turkey's Glorious Hat Revolution*. Los Angeles: Review of Books.

Giddens, A. (1984). *The Nation State and Violence*. Berkeley, CA: University of California Press.

Giddens, A. (1990). *The Consequence of Modernity*. Stanford, CA: Stanford University Press.
Giddens, A. (1991). *Modernity and Self-Identity: Self and Society in the Late Modern Age*. Stanford: Stanford University Press.
Gill, R. (2007). *Gender and the Media*. Oxford: Polity Press.
Göklap, Z. (1968). *Türkçülüğün Esasları*. Istanbul: Varlık Yayınları.
Göle, N. (1991). *Modern Mahrem*. Istanbul: Metis Yayinlari.
Göle, N. (1996). *Forbidden Modern: Civilization and Veiling*. Ann Arbor: University of Michigan Press.
Göle, N. (2014). The Freedom of Seduction. *NPQ 31*(1): 107–13.
Grozs, E. (1994). 'A Thousand Tiny Sexes: Feminism and Rhizomatics', in Constantin V. Boundas & Dorethea Olkowski (eds), *Gilles Deleuze and the Theater of Philosophy*, pp.187–212. New York-London: Routledge.
Gupta, A. (2013). In a Postcolonial Diction: Post-War Abstraction and the Aesthetics of Modernization. *Art Journal 72*(3): 30–47.
Gusfield, J.R. (1967). Tradition and Modern. *American Journal of Sociology 72*: 351–62.
Güçlü, Ö. (2011). 'New Cinema of Turkey: What Is New? Why Is It Not "Turkish"?', *TAGS Review* 18, Autumn: 33–5.
Güçlü, O. (2012). 'Maksadını Aşan Yakınlaşmalar: 2 Genç Kız ve Vicdan'da Kadın Homososyaliğinin Sınırları', in Cüneyt Çakırlar & Serkan Delice (eds), *Cinsellik Muammasi*, pp. 427–48. Istanbul: Metis.
Gülendam, R. (2001). The Development of a Feminist Discourse and Feminist Writing in Turkey: 1970–1990. *Kadin/Woman 2*: 93.
Gürbilek, N. (1992). *Vitrinde Yaşamak*. Istanbul: Metis Yayınları.
Gürbilek, N. (2001). *Kötü Çocuk Türk*. Istanbul: Metis Yayınları.
Halberstam, J. (2011). *The Queer Art of Failure*. Durham: Duke University Press.
Halperin, D.M. (1989). Is There a History of Sexuality? *History and Theory 28*(3): 257–74.
Halperin, D.M. (1990). *One Hundred Years of Homosexuality and Other Essays on Greek Love*. New York: Routledge.
Hassard, J. (1990). *The Sociological of Time*. London: Palgrave Macmillan.
Hegel, G.W.F. (1929). *Selections*. Edited by J. Loewenberg. New York: Charles Schribner & Sons.
Heidegger, M. (1972). *On Time and Being*. New York: Harper-Row.
Heidegger, M. (1978). 'Building Dwelling Thinking', in D. Farell Krell (ed.), *Martin Heidegger: Basic Writings*, 178–86. Abingdon: Routledge.
Hendricks, P.R. (1998). Two Opposite Animals? Voice, Text, and Gender on Stage. *Theatre Topics 8*(2): 113–25.
Higate, P.R. (2003). *Military Masculinities*. Westport, CT: Prager.
Humphreys-Jones, Claire. (1986). An Investigation of the Types and Structure of Misunderstandings. PhD Thesis. Newcastle-on-Tyne, UK: Newcastle University.
Huysmans J. (1998). Security! What Do You Mean? From Concept to Thick Signifier. *European Journal of International Relations 4*: 226–55.

Ibrahim, A. (2014). Body without Organs: Notes on Deleuze & Guattari's Critical Race Theory and the Socius of Anti-Racism. *Journal of Multilingual and Multicultural Development* 36(1): 13–26. Routledge.

Ilhan, A. (1985). *Yanlış Kadınlar, Yanlış Erkekler*. Istanbul: Doğuş Yayınları.

Ingold, T. (2008). Bindings against Boundaries: Entanglements of Life in an Open World. *Environment and Planning* 40(8): 1796–810.

Insel, A. (1996). *Düzen ve kalkınma kıskacında Türkiye*. Istanbul: Ayrıntı Yayınları.

Irigaray, J. (1985). *This Sex Which Is Not One*. New York: Cornell University Press.

Izenberg, G. (2011). The Modern Notion of Self Has Reached Its Ultimate Conclusion. *Annals of the New York Academy of Science* 1234, Issue: 'Perspectives on the Self': 124–6.

Jones, C.L. (1986). 'Resolving Misunderstanding', in G. McGregor & R.S. White (eds), *The Art of Listening*, pp.43–55. London; Dover, NH: Croom Helm.

Kalaycıoğlu, E. (2008). Attitudinal Orientation to Party Organizations in Turkey in the 2000s, *Turkish Studies* 9(2): 297–316.

Kandiyoti, D. (1988). Emancipated but Unliberated? Reflections on the Turkish Case. *Feminist Studies* 13: 317–38.

Kaplan, N. (2004). *Aile Sinemasi Yılları 1960'lar*. Istanbul: Es Yayınları.

Karaca, E. (2001). *12 Eylül'ün Arka Bahçesinde: Avrupada'ki Mültecilerle Konuşmalar*. Istanbul: Gendas Kültür.

Kasaba, R. (1999). 'Eski ile Yeni Arasında Kemalizm ve Modernizm', in Sibel Bozdoğan and Resat Kasaba (eds), Türkiye'de Modernleşme ve Ulusal Kimlik. İstanbul: Tarih Vakfı Yurt Yayinlari.

Kayser, W. (1857). *Grotesque in Arts and Literature*. Translated by Ulrich Weisstein, 1963. Bloomington: Indiana University Press.

Kemani, H.H. (2012). *Recep Tayyip Erdoğan Ne Diyor?* İstanbul: Kim Ne Diyor Yay.

Keyder, C. (1987). *State and Class in Turkey: A Study in Capitalist Development*. London: Verso.

Keyman, F. & İçduygu, A. (1998). 'Türk modernleşmesi ve ulusal kimlik sorunu: Anayasal vatandaşlık ve demokratik açılım olasılığı', in A. Ünsal (ed.), *75. yılda tebaa'dan yurttaş'a doğru içinde*, pp.169–80. İstanbul: Tarih Vakfı Yayınları.

Kiesling, S. (2007). Men, Masculinities, and Language. *Language and Linguistics Compass* 1(6): 653–73.

Kılıçbay, B. (2006). Impossible Crossings: Gender Melancholy in Lola + Bilidikid and Auslandstournee. *New Cinemas: Journal of Contemporary Film* 4(2): 105–15.

Kimmel, M.S. (2005). *The Gender of Desire: Essay on Man Sexuality*. Binghamton: SUNY Press.

Kinnvall, C. (2004). Globalization and Religious Nationalism: Self, Identity and the Search for Ontological Security. *Political Psychology* 25(5): 741–67.

Kirmayer, L.J. (1996). 'Landscapes of Memory: Trauma, Narrative and Dissociation'. In P. Antze & M. Lambek (eds), *Tense Past: Cultural Essays on Memory and Trauma*, pp.173–98. London: Routledge.

Kongar, E. (2000). *21.Yüzyılda Türkiye*. Istanbul: Remzi Kitabevi.
Kristeva, J. (1980). *Desire in Language: A Semiotic Approach to Literature and Art*. New York: Colombia University Press.
Krolikowski, A. (2008). State Personhood in Ontological Security Theories of International Relations and Chinese Nationalism: A Sceptical View. *Chinese Journal of International Politics 2*: 109-33.
Kuhn, A. (1985). *The Power of the Image*. New York: Routledge.
Küpers, W. (2011). Dancing on the Limen – Embodied and Creative Inter-Places as Thresholds of Be(com)ing: Phenomenological Perspectives on Liminality and Transitional Spaces in Organisation and Leadership. *Tamara Journal for Critical Organization Inquiry* (Special Issue on Liminality) 9(3-4): 45-59.
LaCapra, D. (1998). *History and Memory after Auschwitz*. Ithaca and London: Cornell University Press.
Laclau, E. (1990). *New Reflections on the Revolution of Our Time*. London: Verso.
Lakoff, R. (1975). *Language and Woman's Place*. New York: Harper Row.
Laing, R.D. (1973). *The Divided Self*. London: Penguin.
Landstreicher, W. (2009). *Willful Disobedience*. San Francisco: Ardent Press.
Lanigan, R.L. (1977). *Speech Act Phenomenology*. The Hague: Martinus Nijhoff.
Lauzen, M.M. & Dozier, D.M. (2005). Maintaining the Double Standard: Portrayals of Age and Gender in Popular Film. *Sex Roles 52*: 437-46.
Lawlor, L. (2008). Following the Rats: Becoming-Animal in Deleuze and Guattari. *SubStance* 117(37-3): 169-87. University of Wisconsin Press.
Lefebvre, H. (1974). *Production of Space*. Oxford: Blackwell.
Lerner, D. & Robinson, R. (1960). Swords and Ploughshares: The Turkish Army as a Modernizing Force. *World Politics 13*: 19-44.
Lewis, B. (1962). *The Emergence of Modern Turkey*. London: Oxford University Press.
Locke, J. (1731). An Essay Concerning Human Understanding', in *Four Books*. London: Edward Symon.
Lucas, M. (2014). Nomadic Organisation and the Experience of Journeying: Through Liminal Spaces and Organising Places. *Culture and Organisation* 20(3): 196-201.
Luttwak, E. (1968). *Coup d'état: A Practical Handbook*. London: Allen Lane/Penguin Press.
Lyotard, J.F. (1979). *The Postmodern Condition: A Report on Knowledge*. Manchester and New York: Manchester University Press.
Massey, D. (1992). *Space, Place and Gender*. Minneapolis: University of Minneosata.
Massey, D. (2005). *For Space*. London: Sage.
Mardin, Ş. (2000). *Türk modernleşmesi -makaleler 4*-Edited by M. Turkone & T. Onder, (8. baskı). İstanbul: İletişim Yayınları.
Mavioğlu, E. (2004). *Asılmayıp Beslenenler Bir 12 Eylul Hesaplaşması*. Istanbul: Babil Yayinlari.
May, T. (2003). When is a Deleuzian Becoming? *Continental Philosophy Review 36*: 139-53.

McDonald, P. (1995). 'Star Studies', in Joanne Hollows and Mark Jankovich (eds), *Approaches to Popular Film*, pp.59-97. Manchester and New York: Manchester University Press.

Merleau-Ponty, M. (1962). *The Phenomenology of Perception*. Abingdon: Routledge.

Metz, H.C. (1996). *Turkey: A Country Study*. Washington, DC: Federal Research Division of the Library of Congress.

Michologolus, S. & Popionnou, E. (2011). 'Divide and Rule or the Rule of the Divided? Evidence from Africa', NBER Working Paper 17184.

Mitzen, J. (2006). Ontological Security in World Politics: State Identity and the Security Dilemma. *European Journal of International Relations* 12(3): 341-70.

Morris, P. (1996). 'Folk Humor and Carnival Laughter', in Pam Morris (ed.), *The Bahktin Reader: Selected + Writing of Bakhtin, Medvedev and Voloshinov*, pp.50-61. New York: St Martin's.

Morris, P. (ed.) (1996). *The Bahktin Reader: Selected Writing of Bakhtin, Medvedev and Voloshinov*. New York: St Martin's.

Mulvey, L. (1989). *Visual and Other Pleasures*. London: Palgrave Macmillan.

Mumford, L. (1938). *The Culture of Cities*. London: Secker & Warburg.

Nelson, K. & Fivush, R. (2004). Culture and Language in the Emergence of Autobiographical Memory. *Psychological Science* 15(9): 573-7.

Nişancı, E. (2001). *Geleneksel patrimonyalizmden modern neo-patrimonyalizme bir modernleşme denemesi*. İstanbul: Haliç Üniversitesi.

Norris, C. (1987). *Derrida*. London: Fontana.

Öğün, S.S. (1995). *Modernleşme, milliyetçilik ve Türkiye*. İstanbul: Bağlam Yayınları.

Öngider, S. (2005). *Son Klasik Darbe 12 Eylül Söyleşileri*. Istanbul: Aykırı Yayıncılık.

Ortayli, I. (2000). *Osmanlı Toplumunda Aile*. Istanbul: Timas Yayinlari.

Özbek, M. (2012). *Popüler Kültür ve Orhan Gencebay Arabeski*. Istanbul: Iletişim Yayınları.

Özbudun, E. Ve Hale, W. (2010). *Türkiye'de İslamcılık, Demokrasi ve Liberalizm: AKP Olayı*. Istanbul: Doğan Kitap.

Özdemir, H. (2002). 'Siyasal Tarih', in Sina Ak (ed.), *Türkiye Tarihi, Çağdas Türkiye 1908-1980*, 191-264. Istanbul: Cem Yayınevi.

Özgüç, A. (2006). *Turk Sinemasinda Cinselliğin Tarihi*. Istanbul: Arti 1 Kitap.

Özsoy, S. (2009). Turkish Modernization, Democracy and Education: An Analysis from Dewey's Perspective. *Educational Sciences: Theory and Practice (1925-1931)*.

Parla, J. (1990). *Tanzimat Romaninin Epistemolojik Temellleri*. Istanbul: Iletişim Yayınları.

Pateman, C. (1998). 'The Fraternal Social Contract', in J. Keane (ed.), *Civil Society and the State*, pp.33-57. London: Verso.

Pateman, C. (1988). *The Sexual Contract*. Cambridge: Polity Press.

Peters, J.D. (2004). 'The Voice and Modern Media', in Doris Kolesch & Jenny Schrödl (eds), *Kunst-Stimmen*, pp.85-101. Berlin: Theater der Zeit.

Pink, S. (2012). *Situating Everyday Life: Practices and Places*. London: Sage.
Powers, S., Rothman, D. & Rothman, S. (1993). Transformation Gender Roles in Hollywood Movies between 1946 and 1990. *Political Communication* 10(3): 259–83.
Powrie, P. (1997). *French Cinema in the 1980s: Nostalgia and the Crisis of Masculinity*. Oxford: Clarendon Press.
Refiğ, H. (1971). *Ulusal Sinema Kavgası*. Istanbul: Hareket Yayınları.
Reid, T. (1785). *Essays on the Intellectual Powers of Man*. Cambridge: Cambridge University Press.
Ricoeur, P. (1984). *Time and Narrative*. Chicago: University of Chicago Press.
Rogers, D. (2013). The Poetics of Cartography and Habitation: Home as a Repository of Memories. *Housing, Theory and Society* 30(3): 262–80.
Rossdale, C. (2015). Enclosing Critique: The Limits of Ontological Security. *International Political Sociology* 9: 369–86.
Ruskin, J. (1904). 'The Stones of Venice', in J.G.Links (1960) (ed.), *Grotesque Renaissance*. Cambridge: Da Capo Press.
Russo, M. (1994). *The Female Grotesque: Risk, Excess and Modernity*. New York and London: Routledge.
Said, Edward W. (1978). *Orientalism*. New York: Pantheon Books.
Sarıbay, A.Y. (1982). 'Kemalist ideolojide modernleşmenin anlamı: Sosyo-ekonomik bir çözümleme denemesi' in *Cahit Orhan Tütengil'e armağan*, pp.141-62. İstanbul: İstanbul Üniversitesi İktisat Fakültesi Yayınları.
Schechner, R. (1985). *Between Theatre and Anthropology*. Philadelphia: University of Pennsylvania Press.
Schechner, R. (2002). *Performance Studies: An Introduction*. London and New York: Routledge.
Schouten, J.W. (1991). Personal Rites of Passage and the Reconstruction of the Self. *Advances in Consumer Research* 18(1): 49–51.
Sedgwick, E. (1990). *Epistemology of the Closet*. Berkeley, CA: University of California Press.
Şeker, B. (2013). *Başkaldıran Bedenler: Türkiye'de Transgender, Aktivizim ve Altkültürel Pratikler*. Istanbul: Metis.
Selen, E. (2012). The Stage: A Space for Queer Subjectification in Contemporary Turkey. *Gender, Place and Culture: A Journal of Feminist Geography* 19(6): 730–49.
Senelick, L. (1992). *Gender in Performance: The Presentation of Difference in the Performing Arts*. Hanover, NH: University Press of New England.
Schiller, H. (1976). *Communication and Cultural Domination, M.E.* New York: Sharpe Press
Silverman K. (1988). *Lost Object and Mistaken Subject*. Bloomington: Indiana University Press.
Silverstone, R. (1993). Television, Ontological Security and the Transitional Object. *Media, Culture and Society* 15: 573–98.

Simpson, R., Sturges, J. & Weight, P. (2010). Transient, Unsettling and Creative Space: Experiences of Liminality through the Accounts of Chinese Students on a UK-based MBA. *Management Learning* 41(1): 53–70.

Sotirin, P. (2005). 'Becoming Woman', in Charles J. Stivale (ed.), *Gilles Deleuze Key Concepts*, pp.98–109. Chesham: Acumen.

Stallybrass, P. & White, A. (1986). *The Politics and Poetics of Transgression*. Ithaca, NY: Cornell University Press.

Sterne, J. (2003). *The Audible Past: Cultural Origins of Sound Reproduction*. Durham, NC: Duke University Press.

Sterne, J. (2012). *The Sound Studies Reader*. London: Routledge.

Stivale, C.J. (2005). *Gilles Deleuze Key Concepts*. London: Acumen.

Sturdy, A., Schwarz, M., & Spicer, A. (2006). Guess who's coming to dinner? Structures and uses of liminality in strategic management consultancy. *HumanRelations*, 59(7), 929–60. https://doi.org/10.1177/0018726706067597

Süalp, Z.T.A. (2004). *Zamanmekan: Kuram ve Sinema*. Istanbul: Bağlam.

Süalp, Z.T.A. & Şenova, B. (2008). 'Violence: Muted Women in Scenes of Glorified Lumpen Men', in M. Grzinic & R. Reitsamer (eds), *New Feminism: Worlds of Feminism, Queer and Networking Conditions*, pp.91–6. Vienna: Löcker.

Suner, A. (2004). Horror of a Different Kind: Dissonant Voices of the New Turkish Cinema. *Screen* 45(4): 305–23.

Suner, A. (2005). *Hayalet Ev: Yeni Turk Sinemasinda Aidiyet, Kimlik, Bellek*. Istanbul: Metis Yayinlari.

Suner, A. (2010). *New Turkish Cinema: Belonging, Identity and Memory*. London: I.B. Tauris.

Suner, A. (2011). A Lonely and Beautiful Country: Reflecting upon the State of Oblivion in Turkey. *Inter-Asia Cultural Studies* 12(1): 13–27.

Sutton, D. & Martin-Jones, D. (2008). *Deleuze Reframed: A Guide for the Arts Student*. New York: I.B. Tauris.

Tasker, Y. (1998). *Working Girls: Gender and Sexuality in Popular Cinema*. London: Routledge.

Tasker, Y. & Negra, D. (2007). *Interrogating Post-Feminism*. Durham: Duke University Press.

Taylor, D. (ed.) (2011). *Foucault Key Concepts*. London: Acumen.

Tekeli, Ş. (1982). *Kadınlar ve Siyasi Toplumsal Hayat*. Istanbul:Birikim Yayınları.

Tekeli, Ş. (1986). 'The Emergence of the Feminist Movement in Turkey', in Drude Dahlerup (ed.), *The New Women Movements: Feminism and Political Power in Europe*, pp.179–99. London: Sage.

Tekeli, Ş. (1988). *Türkiye'de Feminist Hareketin Anlamı Ve Sınırları Üzerine*. Istanbul: Alan Yayınları.

Tekeli, Ş. (1990). *1980'ler Türkiye'sinde Kadınlar*. Istanbul: Iletişim Yayınları.

Tempest, S., Starkey, K. & Ennew, C. (2007). In the Death Zone: A Study of Limits in the 1996 Mount Everest Disaster. *Human Relations* 60(7): 1039–64.

Thomassen, B. (2009). The Uses and Meanings of Liminality. *International Political Anthropology* 2(5): 5–27.

Thomson, P. (1972). *The Grotesque*. London: Methuen.

Thorne, A. & McLean, K C. (2003). Late Adolescents' Self-Defining Memories about Relationships. *Developmental Psychology* 39(4): 635–45.

Topçu, A.D. (2006). *Kahkaha ve Hüzün: Sadri Alışık*. Istanbul: Dost Kitabevi Yayınları.

Tsutsui, K. (2009). The Trajectory of Perpetrators' Trauma: Mnemonic Politics around the Asia-Pacific War in Japan. *Social Forces* 87(3): 1389–422.

Turner, V.W. (1969). *The Ritual Process: Structure and Anti-Structure*. Chicago: Aldine.

Turner, V.W. (1982). *From Ritual to Theater: The Human Seriousness of Play*. New York: Performing Arts Journal Publications.

Ulusay, N. (2004). Günümüz Türk Sinemasında Erkek Filmleri. *Toplum ve Bilim 101*: 144–69.

Van Gennep, A. (1960). *The Rites of Passage*. Translated by Monika B. Vizedom and Gabrielle L. Caffee. Chicago: University of Chicago Press.

Wagner, Wolfgang, Duveen, Gerard, Themel, Matthias & Verma, Jyoti. (1999). The Modernization of Tradition: Thinking about Madness in Patna, India. *Culture & Psychology* 5: 413–45, p. 415.

Warhola, J. & Bezci, E. (2010). Religion and State in Contemporary Turkey: Recent Developments in Laiklik. *Journal of Church and State* 1: 1–27.

Weller, S. (2006). Situating (young) Teenagers in Geographies of Children and Youth. *Children's Geographies*, 4(1): 97–108.

White, J. (2003). State Feminism, Modernization, and Turkish Republican Woman. *NWSA Journal* 15(3): 145–59.

White, R.S. (1986). 'Shakespeare and Listening', in Graham McGregor and R.S. White (eds), *The Art of Listening*, pp.124–52. London; Dover, NH: Croom Helm.

Winnicott, D.W. (1971). *Playing and Reality*. London: Tavistock Publications.

Winnicott, D.W. (1974). Fear of Breakdown. *International Review of Psycho-Analysis* 1: 103–7.

Witting, M. (1981). One Is Not Born a Woman. *Feminist Issues* 1(2): 47–54.

Wittig, M. (1992). *Straight Mind and Other Essays*. New York: Harvester Wheatsheaf.

Wolley, J. (2007). Is Ontological Security Possible? *British Journal of Undergraduate Philosophy* 2(2): 176–84.

Wood, B.E. (2012). Crafted within Liminal Spaces: Young Peoples Everyday Politics. *Political Geography 31*: 337–46.

Yalur, T. (2013). 'Osmanlı'da Bir Cinsel Kimlik Olarak Köçek', in *Baskaldıran Bedenler* (ed.), *Berfu Şeker*, pp.67–81. Istanbul: Metis.

Yuval Davis, N. (1997). *Gender and Nation*. London: Sage.

Zizek, S. (1991). *Looking Awry: An Introduction to Lacan through Popular Culture*. Cambridge, MA: MIT Press.

Zürcher, E. (2003). *Turkey: A Modern History* (3rd edn). London and New York: I.B. Tauris.

Filmography

Fosforlu Cevriye (1959, Director: Aydın Arakon)
Aşk Rüzgarı (1960, Director: Nevzat Pesen)
Aslan Yavrusu (1960, Director: Hulki Saner)
Gece Kuşu (1960, Director: Hulki Saner)
Şoför Nebahat (1960, Director: Süreyya Duru)
Belalı Torun (1962, Director: Memduh Ün)
Fıstık Gibi Maşallah (1964, Director: Hulki Saner)
Babasına Bak, Oğlunu Al (1965, Director Türker Inanoğlu)
Yalancının Mumu (1965, Director: Semih Evin)
Asker Anası (1966, Director: Asaf Tengiz)
Efkarlıyım Arkadaş (1966, Director: Türker Inanoğlu)
Kibar Haydut (1966, Director: Yılmaz Atadeniz)
Avanta Kemal (1968, Director: Ugur Duru)
Beş Ateşli Kadin (1968, Director: Seyfettin Tiryaki)
Deliler Almanya'da (1980, Director: Yunus Bülbül)
Beddua (1980, director: Melih Gülgen)
Şabaniye (1984, Director: Kartal Tibet)
Dönersen Islık Çal (1992, Director: Orhan Oğuz)
Komiser Şekspir (2001, Director: Sinan Çetin)
Ruhumu Asla! (2001, Director: Kutluğ Ataman)
Hababam Sınıfı Merhaba (2007, Director: Kartal Tibet)
Plajda (2008, Director: Murat Şeker)
Şeytanın Pabucu (2008, Director: Turgut Yasalar)
Zenne (2011, Directors: M. Caner Alper, Mehmet Binay)

Index

Abisel, Nilgün 28
Ackroyd, Peter 7, 85
acousmatic voice 184 n.2
Akgül, Hakan 1
Akın, Filiz 35, 38, 52, 53, 173, 174, 181 n.8
AKP. *see* Justice and Development Party (AKP)
Akşın, Sina 27
Alışık, Sadri 35-8
Alobora, Mehmet Ali 58
And, Metin 180 n.4
anxiety 4, 11, 20, 28, 44, 91-2, 94, 95, 99, 101, 104, 106, 107, 154, 155, 154, 172, 175, 183-4 n.1
Arakon, Aydın 29
Arat, Yeşim 20, 44
Arslan, Savaş 49, 182 n.3
Art of Listening, The (White) 117
Asena, Duygu 44
Aşk Rüzgarı (1960) 172
Aslan Yavrusu (1960) 8, 12, 32, 33
Atakav, Eylem 42-3
Ataman, Kutluğ 4, 53, 181 n.8
Atatürk, Mustafa Kemal 20-2, 26, 53, 80, 135, 172
Auslandstournee (1999) 5
authority 80, 84, 100, 161, 162, 164, 169
Avant Kemal (1968) 36
Ayça, Engin 49
'Ayy Maşallah' 118, 120

Babalar Ve Oğullar ('Fathers and Sons') (Parla) 140
Bachelard, Gaston 136-8
Badinter, Elizabeth 164
Bakhtin, M. 14, 71, 72, 74, 76, 83-5
Bakkaloğlu, Hilal 55
Bardakçı, Murat 181 n.6
Baudelaire, Charles 24
Bayar, Celal 26
becoming (Deleuze) 65-9
  and mobility 62-4

Beddua (1980) 8-9, 47-8
behaviour, repetitive 138-9
Belalı Torun (1962) 8, 32-4
Bell-Metereau, R. 161
Berktay, Fatmagül 44
Beş Ateşli Kadın (1968) 8, 12, 36
Billingsgate language 84
Black feminism 51
Blue Butterflies *(Mavi Kelebekler)* 38
body fracturing 105-12
Bora, Aksu 140
Bouguet, Oliver 185 n.4
Bourdieu, Pierre 32
Büker, Seçil 172, 173
Bülbül, Yunus 8, 45
Burak, Begüm 50
Burhan (Fatih Ürek) 55, 56, 58, 62, 68, 72, 78, 80, 81, 113-15, 118, 119, 126, 144, 150, 155, 165, 166
Butler, Judith 5, 15, 73-4, 105, 141, 167

Çakırlar, Cüneyt 5
Carlton, Eric 98
carnival 7, 83-5, 87-9, 95, 96
carnivalesque 9, 14, 62, 81, 83-5, 95, 100, 177
Casey, Gerard 132
Castle, T. 84
Cavarero, Adriana 105-6
Çetin, Sinan 9, 53
characters 5, 6, 7, 8, 12, 13, 16, 32, 34, 35, 38, 43, 45, 49, 50, 53, 54, 59, 61, 62, 68-70, 76, 78-81, 85, 87, 88, 91, 95, 96, 101, 103-5, 109, 112-17, 120-5, 129, 130, 133-5, 137, 141-5, 147, 151-4, 156-9, 161-5, 167-9, 174, 177, 184 n.1
Chion, Michel 184 n.2
choreographing theory 14-15, 19, 59
  becoming 65-9
  carnivalesque 83-9
  character 69-71

grotesque 71–82
mobility 62–4
otherness 83
power relations 61–2
civilian masculinity 162
Cixous, Helene 122
class cross-dressing 32, 35
class identity 62, 68, 93
conservatism 3, 39, 54, 81, 120, 144, 145, 166
    Islamic 50–4
consumption 39, 41, 164, 165, 176
critical discourse analysis (CDA) 11

Daldal, A. 28
Davidson, Tonya 137
de Beauvoir, S. 167
De Certeau, Michel 137, 148
de Lauretis, T. 171
Deleuze, G. 14, 62, 65–9, 147
Deliler Almanya'da (1980) 8, 45, 46
Demirel, Süleyman 39
Democrat Party (DP) 26
Dentith, Simon 84
depoliticizing effect 39, 42–4
Derrida, Jacques 77, 78
Derviş, Suat 29
deterritorialization 6, 65–8, 77, 93, 111, 136, 147
Dialogues (Deleuze) 65, 67
discontinuity 14, 41
Dolar, Mladen 105
Dört Yapraklı Yonca (2004) 174
Doruk, Belgin 31
dress 3, 4, 22, 24, 35, 38, 78, 122, 163
Duncan, Michelle 106
Durkheim, Emile 134
Duru, Sürreya 38
Dyer, Richard 53

Efkarlıyım Arkadaş (1966) 8, 12, 35, 36
Eğilmez, Ertem 54
Eidsheim, Nina 108
e-memorandum 51
Emerson, Carl 84
Enlightenment 3, 25
Enloe, Cynthia 167
Envisaged future 130, 154–7
Erdoğan Ne Diyor? ('What is Erdoğan saying?') (2012) 58
Erdoğan, Nehir 57, 58

Erikson, Erik 91, 93
Erksan, Metin 8, 28
Ersoy, Bülent 4–5, 47–8, 183 n.6
Ertuğrul, Muhsin 8
Ertür, Başak 4–5
Evren, Kenan 39
exaggeration 74–6

femininity 2, 13, 16, 17, 104, 161, 162, 179 n.2
    crisis 169–76
feminism 9, 21, 23, 29, 43, 44, 51, 52, 121, 143, 164, 174–6, 179 n.2
Feminist 43
femme fatale 171, 172
fes 3–4
Fethullah Gülen Movement 1
Figenli, Yavuz 45
Fıstık Gibi Maşallah (1964) 8, 12, 13, 36–8, 54, 76, 78, 80–2, 85–7, 95, 109, 125, 126, 129, 139, 142, 143, 145, 147, 149, 152, 153, 156, 162, 168–73
flexibility 69, 129, 130, 145
Fosforlu Cevriye (1959) 8, 12, 29–32, 35, 62
Foucault, M. 11, 41, 167–8, 180 n.5, 185 n.5, 185 n.6
fracturing 10, 15–16, 61, 64, 96–7, 100, 101, 103–5, 136, 153
    by feminism 174–6
    gender 162
    language 103–6, 112, 120–7
    masculinity 162–9
    modern and tradition 23
    power relations 8, 88
    speaking and listening 112–20
    voice and body 105–12
freedom 11, 32, 41, 83, 87, 99, 104, 153, 161, 162, 169, 175

gambling 139, 162
Garber, Marjorie 35
Gece Kuşu (1960) 30–2, 35, 62
Genç, Kaya 21–2
gender 32, 35
    binary 3, 5, 93, 118, 151, 161, 178
    cinema and 2
    discourse 17, 19, 51, 118, 167
    feminine 171, 185 n.8
    fractures 126, 162
    identity 5–6, 29, 43, 44, 51, 61–2, 66–9, 72, 74, 77, 88, 93, 141, 156, 168

issues 44, 48
performance 5, 10, 49, 54, 61, 70, 73-4, 91, 94, 95, 97, 100, 108, 126, 130, 148, 177, 178
politics and 5
and sex 167
voice and 105, 109
Gender Trouble (Butler) 105
Giddens, A. 9, 10, 15, 91-2, 95, 130-1, 135, 154
Girik, Fatma 32, 34
Global Positioning System (GPS) 68
Gökalp, Ziya 23-4
Göle, Nilüfer 171-2
grotesque 6-7, 9, 14, 62, 70-83, 85, 38, 94-6, 100, 169, 177
Guattari, F. 66-8
Gülendam, Ramazan 44
Gülgen, Melih 9, 47
Gülten 38, 95, 109, 110, 145, 149, 152, 156, 171-3
Günay, İzzet 37, 38
Günşıray, Orhan 32
Gupta, Atreyee 182 n.1
Gürbilek, Nurdan 41, 42
Gürpınar, Ayşe Gelgeç 44
Gusfield, Joseph R. 23

Hababam Sınıfı Merhaba (2007) 12, 13, 54, 57, 58, 62, 78-82, 106, 107, 129, 139, 145-8, 152, 168
hacı (pilgrim) 68, 81
Halberstam, Jack 97
Halperin, David M. 180 n.5
Hat Law and Dress Revolution 21-2
headscarf 4
hegemonic masculinity 122, 162, 163, 165, 167, 169, 185 n.2
hegemonization 133
Heidegger, Martin 131, 132
Hendricks, Pamela 109
History of Sexuality, The (Foucault) 185 n.5
home 136-47
homosexuality 42, 180 n.5
Humphreys-Jones, Claire 114
Hürriyet 63, 64, 79, 80

identity 1-3, 69, 141
anchor of 168
class 62, 68, 93

gender 5-6, 29, 43, 44, 51, 61-2, 66-9, 72, 74, 77, 38, 93, 141, 156, 168
group 43, 98
memory and 141-4
national 10, 20, 23-5, 27, 28, 42, 54, 125, 145, 132 n.1
personal 141
politics 52
religious 93
self-identity 10, 92, 93, 131, 154
stable 10, 16, 65, 67, 68, 91-3, 137-40, 151, 157, 168
Ideological State Apparatus (ISA) 53
Ilgaz, Rıfat 54
IMF 41
İnanoğlu, Turker 3, 35
independent art budget commission 27
industrial capitalism 27
Ingold, Tim 132
Inquest Commission 26
Irigaray, Luce 121-2, 176
Islamic conservatism 50-4

journey 6, 22, 25, 38, 52, 53, 58, 65-8, 93, 129, 137, 148, 151, 158, 161, 165, 171, 172
Justice and Development Party (AKP) 1, 4, 50, 51, 53, 181 n.7

Kadınca 44
Kaktüs 43
Kandiyoti, Deniz 43, 44
Kant, Immanuel 24, 25
Kasaba, Reşat 25
Kemalism 26-7, 42, 145, 170
Kemalist modernization 3-4, 20-7, 43, 44, 46, 50-4, 80, 120, 125, 145, 163, 169, 171, 172
Kentmen, Hulusi 32
Keyder, Çağlar 27
Kibar Haydut (1966) 36
Kimmel, Michael S. 162, 164
Kirmayer, Laurence J. 138
Kılıçbay, Barış 5
köçek 3-5
Köksal, Neriman 29
Kolçak, Eşref 31
Komiser Şekspir (2001) 9, 53, 55
Kongar, Emre 27
Kristeva, Julia 121, 122

Küpers, Wendelin 149
Kurdish feminism 45, 51–2, 125
Kurdish Workers' Party (PKK) 51

Laclau, Ernesto 133
Lakoff, Robin 121
language 1–2, 4, 78, 84, 85, 88, 91, 92, 96, 99–101, 154, 169, 178
  Billingsgate 84
  fracturing 103–6, 112, 120–7
  music and 125–7
  text and 12
Language and Woman's Place (Lakoff) 121
Law on the change of the Calendar 135
Law on the Division of the Day into Twenty-four Hours 135
Leblebici Horhor (1923) 8, 29
Lebow, Alisa 4–5
Lefebvre, Henri 29, 132
LGBT movement 9, 29, 51–3
liberating energy 84
Liminal spaces and multiple 'nows' 16, 130, 147–54
linguistic reality 78
listening fracturing 112–20
Locke, John 25, 141
Lola + Bilidikid (1999) 5
Luttwak, Edward 98

macho cinema 52
mapping 15, 19–20, 45, 133
Maşallah 184 n.3
masculinity 2, 13, 16, 17, 38, 54, 104, 117, 118, 122, 123, 161, 162, 169, 170, 179 n.1
  civilian 162
  crisis 169
  fracturing 162–9
  hegemonic 122, 162, 163, 165, 167, 169, 185 n.2
  military 162–3, 167, 185 n.3
Massey, Doreen 132–3
memory 69
  and identity 141–4
  procedural 138
Menderes, Adnan 26, 165
Merleau-Ponty, Maurice 131–2
militarism 98–100
military
  force 50, 51

masculinity 162–3, 167, 185 n.3
memorandum 19, 50–1, 61
regime 63, 79, 83, 88, 117, 182 n.5, 183 n.6
rule 10, 16, 26, 27, 98, 99, 104, 105, 108, 112, 115, 126, 129, 136, 145, 157, 177
ultimatum 12, 51, 145
military coup 1, 2, 8–12, 13, 15–17, 19, 25–9, 35, 36, 38–41, 49, 51, 59, 61–4, 70, 79–81, 88, 89, 91, 96, 103, 105, 108, 111, 117, 118, 123, 125, 126, 130, 133–6, 145, 151, 153–5, 157, 158, 162, 163, 167–9, 177, 178, 183 n.6
  election 39
  home and 140–1
  1960 26–7
  ontological security and 97–101
milli cinema 28
Mitzen, Jennifer 94, 97
mobility 2, 5–6, 8, 11, 29, 32, 36, 45, 56, 58, 62–9, 83, 88, 92, 93, 96, 100, 105, 112, 140, 144, 150, 153, 156, 157, 162, 167, 168, 177
modernization process 1–4, 19–28, 31, 35, 37, 41, 44–6, 49, 50, 52–4, 80, 125, 134, 135, 140, 142, 163, 169–72, 181 n.6, 182 n.1, 185 n.9, 185 n.11
modern/traditional cross-dressing 23, 35
Motherland Party (ANAP) 39
Mulvey, Laura 186 n.12
music 125–7

national cinema 25, 28
national identity 10, 20, 23–5, 27, 28, 42, 54, 125, 145, 182 n.1
National Security Council 39
national trauma 1, 9–11, 15, 17, 19, 59, 133, 158, 177, 178
neo-liberalism 38–45, 49, 52, 58, 80, 145, 164, 165
New Reflections on the Revolution of Our Time (Laclau) 133
non-western modernization 24, 25, 182 n.1

Olanlar Oldu (2017) 1
ontological security 9–11, 15, 16, 35, 59, 61, 62, 89, 91, 103, 105–8, 112, 120, 126, 129–31, 134–7, 139, 140, 151,

153–5, 157–9, 162, 163, 167, 169, 177
  and cross-dressing 91–7
  and military coup 97–101
Ortayli, Ilber 185 n.4
otherness 2–4, 7, 10, 62, 83, 85, 87, 88, 100, 105, 121, 125, 159, 177
Ottoman 3–5, 10, 20–4, 27–9, 52, 80, 140, 145, 171, 180–1 n.6, 182 n.1, 185 n.4, 185 n.11
Özal, Turgut 39, 165
Özbek, Meral 41
Özgüç, Agah 8, 179 n.2
Öz, Gürgen 54
Özpetek, Ferzan 4, 52–3, 181 n.8

panoptic social mechanism 2, 6, 11, 53, 62, 70, 78, 79, 81, 83, 88, 100, 116, 117, 151, 157, 167, 169, 177
Parla, Jale 140, 171
Pateman, Carole 21
performance theory (Schechner) 73–4
performativity theory (Butler) 73, 74, 105
personal identity 141
Peters, John Durham 109
Pink, Sara 132
Plajda (2008) 9, 54, 56
politics 2, 4, 5, 8, 14, 19, 20, 25–7, 29, 32, 39
  ANAP 39
  and cross-dressing films 8–14
  culture and 4, 19, 42
  depoliticizing effect 39, 42–4
  and gender performance 5
  of liminal space 147
  military and 26, 50, 125
  neo-liberal 39, 49, 58, 80, 164, 165
popular cinema 2, 28
power relations 4–8, 11, 13, 33, 49, 59, 61–2, 67–70, 72, 78, 84, 88, 93, 96, 101, 111, 121, 129, 130, 132, 133, 136, 138, 145, 147, 152, 153, 157, 159, 161, 165, 167, 168, 177, 180 n.3, 181 n.10
presentism 24
privatization 41
procedural memory 138
Purple Needle campaign 43

Refiğ, Halit 28
Reid, Thomas 141

relationality 65, 83, 89, 91, 101
religious identity 93
repetitive behaviour 138–9
Repressive State Apparatus (RSA) 53
rhizome 64, 66–9, 85, 93, 151, 168, 169
Ricoeur, Paul 154
Roger, Dallas 137
routine 10, 11, 35, 59, 91, 94–6, 98–100, 107, 131, 133, 136, 140, 151, 157
Russo, M. 71

Şabaniye (1984) 9, 12–13, 45, 48–50, 53, 58, 62, 68, 75–6, 78, 80–1, 93, 107–8, 116–17, 125, 126, 139, 142–5, 147, 152, 153, 155, 163–6, 168, 174–5
Saner, Hulki 8, 30, 32, 38
Schechner, Richard 73, 74
second-wave feminism 43, 44, 51
secularism 4, 20, 50, 51, 181 n.7
Şeker, Murat 9, 54
Selen, Eser 4
self-identity 10, 92, 93, 131, 154
sexuality 1–3, 44, 53, 167, 168, 170, 180 n.6
Şeytanın Pabucu (2008) 9, 12, 13, 54–8, 62, 68, 72, 78, 80, 81, 93, 113–15, 118–20, 125–6, 139, 144, 150, 153, 156–7, 165–7, 175, 176
Sezin, Sezer 37, 38
Silverman, Kaja 122
Smith, Adam 25
Şoför Nebahat (1960) 8, 12, 13, 36–8, 78, 80, 122–5, 129, 139, 147, 163, 168, 170–2, 174
Some Like It Hot (1959) 13, 36, 54
Sonku, Cahide 172–4
Şoray, Türkan 38, 172–4
space
  home 136–47
  and time 10, 11, 16, 29, 32, 34, 59, 62, 63, 68, 69, 96, 98, 117, 118, 120, 129–37, 143, 147, 152–4, 157, 158
  and trauma 133–4
speaking fracturing 112–20
stable identity 10, 16, 65, 67, 68, 91–3, 137–40, 151, 157, 168
Stage, The: A Space for Queer Subjectification in Contemporary Turkey (Selen) 4

Stallybrass, Peter 84
state-feminism 21, 43
Sterne, Jonathan 105, 113
Sunal, Kemal 49
Suner, Asuman 52, 179 n.1, 179 n.2
surveillance 2, 4, 7, 11, 22, 32, 35, 43, 53, 62, 69–71, 78–81, 83, 100, 104, 115–17, 120, 130, 135, 136, 152–4, 157, 158, 167, 169
Swiss Civil Code 21

Tanzimat 27, 31, 140, 171–2, 181 n.6, 182 n.2, 185 n.11
Tasker, Yvonne 164
tavşan 3
Tekeli, Şirin 44
temporary cross-dressing performance 12
Thousand Plateaus, A (Deleuze and Guattari) 66
Tibet, Kartal 9, 49, 58
time
  home and 140–1
  space and 10, 11, 16, 29, 32, 34, 59, 62, 63, 68, 69, 96, 98, 117, 118, 120, 129–37, 143, 147, 152–4, 157, 158
trans-national cinema 4, 181 n.8
trust 9–10, 61, 91–6, 98–101, 107, 112, 145, 153, 154, 158
Turkification 37, 182 n.3
Turner, Victor 34, 147, 149

Uçakan, Mesut 28
undecidability 6, 70, 77–9, 81, 88, 93, 96, 116
Ün, Memduh 8, 28, 32
urbanization process 49
Ürek, Fatih 13, 54, 55, 166

van Gennep, Arnold 147
violence 39, 44, 84, 98, 165
voice fracturing 105–12
Voice in Cinema, The (Chion) 184 n.2
voice performativity 16, 104, 105, 108–9, 116

Wasps *(Eşek Arıları)* 38
Wasps, The 163
westernization process 3, 21, 27, 37, 54, 80, 181 n.6, 182 n.1
White, Allon 84
White, Jenny B. 21
White, R. S. 117
Wittig, M. 121
women 20–1
  feminism 174–6
  films 42–4, 170
  headscarf in 4
  in Islam 52
  language and 121–2
  and love 142
  and men 105, 121
  and modernization process 35, 142, 169–72
  movement 51
  Ottoman 21–2
  representations of 171
Women in the 1980s: Turkey from the Women's Perspective (Tekeli) 44
Women's Circle 43
Wood, Bronwyn 150
World Bank 41

Yalur, Tolga 5
Yasalar, Turgut 9, 55
Yeşilçam cinema 28, 48, 179 n.1, 179 n.2, 182 n.3
YÖK (the Council of Higher Education) 39
Yuval-Davis, Nira 20

zenne 3–4, 12
Zizek, Slavoj 181 n.10
zone of proximity 68

www.ingramcontent.com/pod-product-compliance
Lightning Source LLC
Chambersburg PA
CBHW062228300426
44115CB00012BA/2261